gaze
and
voice
as
love
objects

SIC

A series edited by Slavoj Žižek and Renata Salecl

SIC stands for psychoanalytic interpretation at its most elementary: no discovery of deep, hidden meaning, just the act of drawing attention to the litterality [*sic!*] of what precedes it. A "*sic*" reminds us that what was said, inclusive of its blunders, was effectively said and cannot be undone. The series SIC thus explores different connections of the Freudian field: each volume provides a bundle of Lacanian interventions into a specific domain of ongoing theoretical, cultural, and ideologico-political battles. It is neither "pluralist" nor "socially sensitive": unabashedly avowing its exclusive Lacanian orientation, it disregards any form of correctness but the inherent correctness of theory itself.

gaze and voice as love objects

*Renata Salecl
and
Slavoj Žižek,
editors*

sic **1**

DUKE UNIVERSITY PRESS   Durham and London 1996

© 1996 Duke University Press

All rights reserved

Printed in the United States

of America on acid-free paper ∞

Typeset in Sabon by Tseng

Information Systems, Inc.

Library of Congress Cataloging-in-

Publication Data appear on the

last printed page of this book.

Second printing, 2000

Contents

Introduction 1

PART I GAZE, VOICE

1 Mladen Dolar, *The Object Voice* 7
2 Alenka Zupančič, *Philosophers' Blind Man's Buff* 32
3 Elisabeth Bronfen, *Killing Gazes, Killing in the Gaze: On Michael Powell's* Peeping Tom 59
4 Slavoj Žižek, *"I Hear You with My Eyes"; or, The Invisible Master* 90

PART II LOVE OBJECTS

5 Mladen Dolar, *At First Sight* 129
6 Fredric Jameson, *On the Sexual Production of Western Subjectivity; or, Saint Augustine as a Social Democrat* 154
7 Renata Salecl, *I Can't Love You Unless I Give You Up* 179
8 Slavoj Žižek, *"There Is No Sexual Relationship"* 208

Notes on Contributors 251
Index 253

Renata Salecl/Slavoj Žižek | **Introduction**

In the psychoanalytic community, we often encounter a nostalgic longing for the good old heroic days when patients were naive and ignorant of psychoanalytic theory—this ignorance allegedly enabled them to produce "purer" symptoms, that is, symptoms in which their unconscious was not too much distorted by their rational knowledge. In those days, there were still patients who told their analyst, "Last night, I had a dream about killing a dragon and then advancing through a thick forest to a castle . . . ," whereupon the analyst triumphantly answered, "Elementary, my dear patient! The dragon is your father, and the dream expresses your desire to kill him in order to return to the safe haven of the maternal castle. . . ." Jacques Lacan wagers exactly the opposite: the subject of psychoanalysis (the person analyzed) is the modern subject of science, which means—among other things—that his symptoms are not now and have never been by definition "innocent," they are always addressed to the analyst *qua* subject who is supposed to know (their meaning) and thus as it were imply, point toward, their interpretation. For that reason, one is quite justified in saying that we have symptoms that are Jungian, Kleinian, Lacanian, and so on, that is, whose reality involves implicit reference to some psychoanalytic theory. Today, the "free associations" of a typical educated patient (analysand) consist for the most part of attempts to provide a psychoanalytic explanation of his or her disturbances. . . .

What is effectively at stake in this ongoing battle between the two versions of psychoanalysis is not only the destiny of psychoanalysis but the destiny of modernity as such: are we to persist in reflective knowledge, or are we to return to some kind of intuitive wisdom? This battle, the continuation of the old *bataille des lumières*, is nowhere fought so ferociously as in the terrain of the relationship between the sexes. A good hundred years ago, the sudden emergence of the figure of the hysterical woman (in the works of Richard Wagner, August Strindberg, Otto Weininger, Franz Kafka, Edvard Munch, and others) announced a crisis of sexual relationship in whose shadow we continue to live. From the charmingly naive assertion of harmony in the couple in Mozart's *Magic Flute,* the pendulum swung to the other extreme, bearing witness to a radically *antagonistic* relationship between the sexes: man and woman are in no way complementary, there is no preestablished harmony here, each of the two sexes poses a threat to the other's identity.... There are two ways to approach this crisis. According to the first, obscurantist one, this imbalance results from the fact that modern subject has lost its roots in the organic unity of tradition, which is why a return to some kind of premodern wisdom (in the guise of the new "holistic paradigm" destined to replace the old "mechanistic," "Cartesian" paradigm, for example) will also abolish the antagonism between the sexes and reestablish their lost harmony.

The second approach asserts that the late-nineteenth-century perception of the hysterical woman as a threat to male identity rendered visible a universal feature that was here all the time, only in the mode of "in-itself," that is, it was not yet "posited," not yet "for-itself." So there is no incompatibility between the precise historical context (the great crisis of the relationship between the sexes one hundred years ago, which also gave birth to psychoanalysis) in which "There is no sexual relationship" (Lacan) became a commonplace and Lacan's claim that this statement is universally valid: in a proper dialectical analysis, universality and historicization are strictly correlative. Freudian psychoanalysis is, as the standard judgment goes, a product of the late nineteenth century; however, its insights are "universally valid" not *in spite of* the historical context of their discovery but *because of* it.

Lacan's "There is no sexual relationship" provides a simple answer to the eternal question, Why is there love in the world? Love is a lure, a mirage, whose function is to obfuscate the irreducible, constitutive "out-of-joint" of the relationship between the sexes. The famous Freudian "partial objects"—leftovers of a prephallic *jouissance,* that is, of a *jouis-*

sance not yet "sublated" in, mediated by, the paternal metaphor—give body to the elusive obstacle that prevents the fulfillment of sexual relationship. Lacan added to Freud's list of partial objects (breasts, faeces, phallus) two other objects, voice and gaze. It is therefore by no means accidental that gaze and voice are love objects par excellence—not in the sense that we fall in love with a voice or a gaze, but rather in the sense that they are a medium, a catalyst that sets off love.

Three conclusions are to be drawn from these premises. First, love cannot be reduced to a mere illusion or imaginary phenomenon: beyond its fascination with the image of its object, true love aims at the kernel of the real, at what is in the object more than the object itself, in short, at what Lacan called *l'objet petit a*. Love—as well as hate—is supported by what remains of the object when it is stripped of all its imaginary and symbolic features. Secondly, love is therefore an inherently *historical* phenomenon: its concrete configurations are so many (ultimately failed) attempts to gentrify, tame, symbolize, the "unhistorical" traumatic kernel of *jouissance* that makes the object unbearable. Thirdly, love is never "just love" but always the screen, the field, on which the battles for power and domination are fought. Is voice, as a catalyst of love, not the medium of hypnotic power par excellence, the medium of disarming the other's protective shield, of gaining direct control over him or her and submitting him or her to our will? Is gaze not the medium of control (in the guise of the inspecting gaze) as well as of the fascination that entices the other into submission (in the guise of the subject's gaze bewitched by the spectacle of power)? More than sixty years ago, in the wake of the Fascist threat, Walter Benjamin proposed to counter the Fascist aestheticization of the political with the leftist politicization of the aesthetic. In a homologous way, today, more than ever, one should counter *the sexualization of the political* (from the overtly reactionary New Right "grounding" of the political hierarchy in the "natural" familial hierarchy of the sexes, through the New Age endeavor to reestablish the balance of feminine and masculine cosmic principles, to the pseudo-Freudian reduction of political struggles to an expression of libidinal deadlocks—rebellion as the acting out of an unresolved Oedipal complex, etc.) with *the politicization of sexuality* (by analyzing the political overdetermination of the way sexual difference is perceived in an actual society).

Each of the two parts of the present volume opens up with an elaboration of basic concepts (voice and gaze; love), to which are then attached three concrete historical analyses. Part 1—*Gaze, Voice*—opens up with Mladen Dolar who, unlike the Derridean deconstructers of phonocentrism, works out the consequences of the Lacanian theory of voice and gaze as the two objectal remainders of an excessive presymbolic *jouissance*. The essay that follows Dolar's, by Alenka Zupančič, focuses on the paradoxical role of blindness in the Enlightenment tradition from Descartes to Kant: the paradigmatic case of the subject delivered from false prejudices and deceptive illusions is a blind person. Next, Elisabeth Bronfen's close reading of Michael Powell's cult film, *Peeping Tom*, deploys the Hitchcockian motif of the murderous gaze. Finally, Slavoj Žižek provides the passage to part 2. First, he articulates the difference between gaze and voice as "partial objects"; then, he tackles the way gaze and voice are involved in politico-ideological struggles, by way of focusing on the enigmatic relationship of the racist and/or sexist subject to the object of his hate. What is the *target* of the outbursts of racist or sexist violence? What are we aiming at, what do we endeavor to annihilate when we exterminate Jews or beat up foreigners in our cities? The answer is double: violence aims at the symbolic fiction that sustains the Other's identity and, beyond it, at the phantasmatic "kernel of the real" of the Other's identity. In part 2—"Love Objects"—it is again Mladen Dolar who, via an analysis of the Freudian notion of the Uncanny [*das Unheimliche*], articulates the meanders of *l'objet petit a* as the cause of transferential love. In the first of the three concrete analyses that follow Dolar, Fredric Jameson proposes an alternative to the Foucauldian account of early Christianity: St. Augustine's invention of sexuality as the innermost secret of the human subject enabled him to mitigate the subversive "sting" of Christianity and to qualify it for the role of hegemonic ideology in a class society. Next, Renata Salecl explores the paradoxes of the relationship between love and social institution in bourgeois society apropos of three literary texts (Edith Wharton's *Age of Innocence* and "The Muse's Tragedy," Kazuo Ishiguro's *The Remains of the Day*). In an analysis of Wagner's operas and of two contemporary "Wagnerian" love films (Kieslowski's *A Short Film on Love*, Sautet's *A Heart in Winter*), Slavoj Žižek's concluding essay endeavors to answer the question, Why is it that today, in a time when it seems that the "universal tendency to debasement in the sphere of love" (Freud) has reached its apogee, authentic love is only possible insofar as it avoids its consummation? Why does a love object retain its dignity only as rejected?

PART I | **gaze, voice**

Mladen Dolar

1
The Object Voice

In the beginning there was Saussure, or so the story goes. To be sure, our story begins much earlier—maybe it has indeed "always already" begun—but let us take our provisional starting point in this somewhat dubious *doxa* of our times.

The Saussurean turn has obviously a lot to do with the voice. If we are to take seriously the negative nature of the linguistic sign, its purely differential and oppositive value, then the voice—as the supposedly natural soil of speech, its seemingly positive substance, its firm substratum—has to be put into question. The voice has to be carefully discarded as the source of an imaginary blinding that has hitherto prevented linguistics from discovering the structural determinations that enable the tricky transubstantiation of voice into the linguistic sign. The voice is the impeding element that one has to be rid of in order to initiate a new science of language. Beyond the sounds of language that traditional phonetics has painstakingly described—spending much time over the technology of their production, helplessly ensnared by their physical and physiological properties—there lies a very different entity that the new linguistics has to unearth, the phoneme. Beyond the voice "with flesh and bones" (as Jakobson will say some decades later), there lies the fleshless and boneless entity defined purely by its function—*the silent sound, the soundless voice*. The new object demands a new science: high hopes are now vested in phonology instead of traditional phonetics. The question of how the different sounds are produced is seen as obsolete; what counts are the differential oppositions of phonemes, their purely relational nature, their reduction to distinctive features. They are isolated by their ability to distinguish the units of signification, but in such a way that the specific signifying distinctions are irrelevant, their only importance being *that* they take place, not what they might be. The phonemes lack substance, they are completely reducible to form, according to one of the most famous of Saussure's dictums, and they lack any signification of their own.[1] They are just senseless quasi-algebraic elements in a formal matrix of combinations, and it is ultimately only to them that the Saussurean definition of sign fully applies (such will be Jakobson's criticism of Saussure): they are the only stratum of language which is entirely made of purely negative quantities, their identity is "a pure alterity" (Jakobson 1963, 111, 116). They are the senseless atoms that in their combination "make sense." Phonology, defined in such a way, was ordained to take a preeminent place in structural linguistics. Indeed, it was soon to turn into its showcase, the paramount demonstration of its abilities and explanatory strength. Some decades had to elapse for it to reach its fully developed form in Troubetskoy's *Grundzüge der Phonologie* (1939) and in Jakobson's *Fundamentals of Language* (1956). Some criticism had to be made of the Saussurean presuppositions (Jakobson's critique of Saussure's dogma about the linear nature of the signifier), some respect had to be duly paid to its other predecessors (Baudouin de Courtenay, Henry Sweet, etc.), but its course was secure. All the sounds of a language could be described in a purely logical way; they could be placed into a logical table based just on the presence or absence of some minimal distinctive features, ruled entirely by one elementary key, the binary code. In this way, most of the oppositions of traditional phonetics were reproduced (voiced/voiceless, nasal/oral, compact/diffuse, grave/acute, labial/dental, etc.), but all these were now recreated as functions of logical oppositions, the conceptual deduction of the empirical, not as an empirical description of sounds that one has found. As the ultimate exhibit, one could present the phonological triangle as the simple deductive matrix of all phonemes and their "elementary structures of kinship," the device that will reach some notorious fame in the heyday of structuralism. Having dismantled sounds into mere bundles of differential oppositions, phonology could then also account for the surplus that is necessarily added to purely phonemic distinctive features—prosody, in-

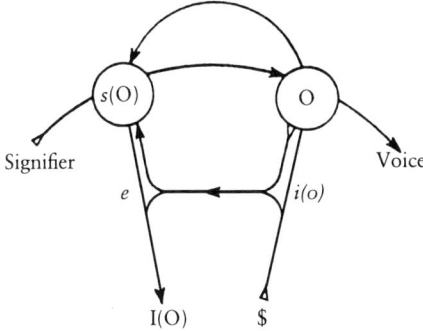

1

tonation, and accent, melody, redundant elements, variations, and so on. The bones, flesh, and blood of the voice were divided without remainder into a web of structural traits, the checklist of presences and absences. The inaugural gesture of phonology was thus the total reduction of the voice as the substance of language. Phonology, true to its apocryphal etymology, was about killing the voice—at its origin, there is the Greek *phonē*, voice, but one can also quite appropriately hear *phonos*, murder.

Let us now make a somewhat abrupt jump to Lacan. In the famous graph of desire (figure 1), one can find, maybe rather surprisingly, a line that runs from the signifier on the left to the voice on the right (Lacan 1989, 306): there is the signifying chain, reduced to its minimal features, which yields, as a result or as a leftover, the voice. A certain reversal has taken place: the voice is not taken as a hypothetical or something of mythical origin that the analysis would have to break down into distinctive traits, not a diffuse substance to be reduced to structure, but rather the opposite—it stands as the outcome of the structural operation. We can put aside, for our particular purpose, the specific nature of the operation that Lacan tries to demonstrate—the retroactive production of meaning, the "quilting point," the nature of the subject involved in it, and so on. So why is there voice as the outcome? Why does the signifier run out into voice as its result? And which voice do we find there— the one that phonology has killed? If it was successfully murdered, why does it recur? Does it not know that it is dead? Maybe we can sum up this curious recurrence in a Lacanian thesis: the reduction of the voice that phonology has attempted—phonology as the paradigmatic showcase of structural analysis—has nevertheless left a remainder: not as any positive feature that couldn't be reduced or entirely dissolved into its binary logical web, not as some seductive imaginary quality that would escape this operation, but precisely as the object in the Lacanian sense. It is only the reduction of the voice—in all of its positivity, lock, stock, and barrel—that produces the voice as the object. This dimension of the voice is difficult to cope with. It cannot be broken down into differential oppositions, since it was this dissolution that produced it in the first place. So there is no meaning that could be assigned to it, since meaning springs only from those oppositions. It is not a function of the signifier, since it presents precisely a nonsignifying remainder, something resistant to the signifying operations, a leftover heterogeneous in relation to the structural logic which includes it.

Furthermore, this remnant has nothing to do with some irreducible individuality of the voice, the personal surplus over the standard mold, the unmistakable individual flavor or timbre that makes each voice instantly recognizable. Nor is it reducible to what Barthes has called "the grain of the voice"—"the materiality of a body speaking its mother-tongue," "the body in the singing voice" (1982, 238, 243). For to attach the voice to the body and to endow it with materiality involves all kinds of obstacles—one is ultimately faced with an unbridgeable gap, since the trouble is that the object never fits the body. And further, it cannot be tackled by introducing the singing voice, the music, as the proper dimension of voice, one that would transcend the narrow framework of speech and would retain the ineffable realm of expression beyond signification. For music, with all its seductive force and irresistible appeal, is rather an attempt to domesticate the object, to turn it into an object of aesthetic pleasure, to put up a screen against what is unbearable in it. "If we make music and listen to it, . . . it is in order to silence what deserves to be called the voice as the object *a*" (Miller 1989, 184). But, one should add (we shall come back to this later at some length), this gesture is always ambiguous: music evokes the voice and conceals it, it fetishizes it, but also opens the gap that cannot be filled.

The remnant, not being differential and not concurring to signification, seems to present a sort of counterweight to differentiality, since the differential logic always refers to absence, while the voice seems to embody the presence, a firm background for differential traits, a positive basis for their inherent negativity. Although its positivity appears to be very elusive—just vibrations of the air, which are gone as soon as they are produced, a pure passing, not something that could be fixed or that one could hold on to, since one can only fix the differences, as phonology has so exhaustively done. In a more specific Lacanian sense, in the context of the graph, one could say that it presents the counterweight, not just to differentiality, but also, and in the first place, to the subject. For the graph was, among other things, constructed to demonstrate that the minimal signifying operation necessarily yields the subject as a purely negative entity that is produced in the retroactive vector, an entity gliding along the chain since it doesn't possess a signifier of its own—the subject is always only represented by a signifier for another signifier, as the famous dictum goes. In itself it is without foundation and without a substance; it is a lack, an empty space necessarily implied by the nature of the signifier—such was for Lacan, as it is well known, the nature of the subject that can be assigned to structure. So the voice seems to endow this empty and negative entity with a counterpart, its "missing half," so to speak, a "supplement" that would enable this negative being to acquire some hold in positivity, a "substance," a relationship to presence.

So is the voice as the residue, the remnant of the phonological operation, to be related to presence? Does it offer a privileged, although admittedly elusive, evocation of the present, thus counteracting the purely negative differential features, the Saussurean determination *in absentia*, which ultimately always gets the upper hand over presence as soon as we use language? Does the object voice, which Lacan has pinpointed as the necessary implication of the structural intervention, run into the notorious "metaphysics of presence" as its most recent and most insidious variation?

Obviously, the entire phonological enterprise was heavily biased, as Derrida has convincingly shown. There was a prejudice at its core—the prejudice that it shared with the bulk of metaphysical tradition from which it has unwittingly inherited it, the prejudice that, maybe, defined that tradition as metaphysical, that is, as "phonocentric." It consisted in the simple and seemingly self-evident assumption that the voice is indeed the basic element of language, its natural embodiment, and is consubstantial with it, whereas writing presents its derivative, auxiliary, and parasitic supplement, at the same time secondary and dangerous. Or so the story goes.

By this account, the remainder is not to be looked for on the side of the voice at all—quite the contrary. If the entire metaphysical tradition "spontaneously" and consistently espoused the priority of the voice, it was because the voice always presented the privileged point of auto-affection, self-transparency, the hold in the presence. The voice offered the illusion that one could get immediate access to an unalloyed presence, an origin not tarnished by externality, a firm rock against the elusive interplay of signs, which are anyway surrogates by their very nature and always point to an absence. So if there is indeed a remainder, it has to be sought on the side of writing, the dead letter that disrupts the living voice, the supplement that usurps its subsidiary place to tarnish presence. And ultimately, it is not the writing in its positive and empirical appearance that is at stake, but more fundamentally the trace, the trace of alterity that has "always already" dislocated the origin. Saussure himself was torn between two opposing tendencies: on the one hand, the tendency that prolonged the traditional stance and made him condemn writing as secondary to voice but as threatening nonetheless to "usurp the leading role" (Saussure 1972, 45), and on the other hand his insight that "the essence of language . . . is alien to the phonic character of the linguistic sign" (21). The subsequent fate of phonology was thus to be caught between the two as well: between, on one hand, its unquestionable prejudice that the voice was the natural matter of language and thus the evident place to start, and, on the other, its operations, which dismantled the living presence of the voice into the lifeless differential matrix—except for the residue that Lacan took to be the paradoxical object voice.

The Derridean turn has thus, by a very different way, made the voice the preeminent object of philosophical inquiry, demonstrating its complicity with the principal metaphysical preoccupations. If metaphysics, in this rather overarching view, is carried by the propensity to disavow the part of alterity, the trace of the other, to hold on to some ultimate signified against the disruptive play of differences, to maintain purity of the origin against supplementarity, it can only do so by clinging to the privilege of the voice as a source of an originary self-presence. The divide between the interior and the exterior, the model of all other metaphysical divides, derives from there:

> The voice is *heard* (understood)—that undoubtedly is what is called conscience—closest to the self as the absolute effacement of the signifier: pure auto-affection that necessarily has the form of time and

which does not borrow from outside of itself, in the world or in "reality," any accessory signifier, any substance of expression foreign to its own spontaneity. It is the unique experience of the signified producing itself spontaneously, from within the self. (Derrida 1976, 20)

This illusion—the illusion par excellence—is thus constitutive of interiority and ultimately of consciousness, the self, and autonomy. *S'entendre parler*—to hear oneself speak—is maybe the minimal definition of consciousness. I will not dwell on the well-known numerous, ramified, and rather spectacular consequences that Derrida has drawn from there.

To hear oneself speak—or just simply to hear oneself—can be seen as an elementary formula of narcissism that is needed to produce a minimal form of a self. Lacan spent much time, in his younger days, meditating over another elementary narcissistic device, the mirror. The mirror was to fulfill the same function—to provide the minimal support needed to produce a self-recognition, the imaginary completion offered to the multiple body, the imaginary blinding that goes along with it, the recognition that is intrinsically a miscognition, the constitution of an "I" as well as the matrix of a relationship to one's equals, the ambiguous source of love and aggression—all the well-known panoply of the notorious mirror phase. Lacan was later to isolate the gaze and the voice as the two paramount embodiments of the object *a*, but his early theory has given an unquestionable privilege to the gaze as the paradigmatic instance of the Imaginary, elevating it into a model. Yet the voice can be seen as in some sense even more striking and more elementary—for isn't the voice the first manifestation of life and, thus, isn't hearing oneself, and recognizing one's voice, an experience that precedes the recognition in the mirror? And isn't the mother's voice the first problematic connection to the Other, the immaterial tie that comes to replace the umbilical cord and shapes much of the fate of the earliest stages of life? Doesn't the recognition of one's voice produce the same jubilatory effects in the infant as those accompanying the recognition in the mirror?

There is a rudimentary form of narcissism attached to the voice that is difficult to delineate since it seemingly lacks any outside support. It is the first "self-referring" or "self-reflective" move, but as pure auto-affection at the closest of oneself—an auto-affection that is not re-flection, since it is seemingly without a screen that would return the voice, a pure immediacy, where one is both sender and receiver in one's pure interiority. In a deceptive self-transparency one coincides in both roles without a gap and without a need for any exterior mediation. One can speak of an acoustic mirror, as it were (cf. Silverman 1988), only there is no mirror. There is no need for recognition in one's external image, and one can see there the kernel of consciousness prior to any reflection. For if there is a surface that returns the voice, the voice acquires an autonomy of its own and enters into the dimension of the Other, it becomes a deferred voice, and the narcissism crumbles. The best witness is, after all, Narcissus himself, whose story, maybe not surprisingly, involves both the gaze and the voice. But his curious "affair" with the nymph Echo, who could only echo his words and couldn't speak by herself, is a story of a failed love and a failed narcissism—the voice returned is not his own voice, and he would rather die than abandon himself to the other (" 'Ante,' ait, 'emoriar, quam sit tibi copia nostri,' " says Ovid). And when the nymph dies, only her voice is left, which still makes echo to our own, the voice without a body, the remainder, the trace of the object.

There is, however, inside that narcissistic and auto-affective dimension of the voice, something that threatens to disrupt it—the voice that affects one at the most intimate level, but which one cannot master and over which one has no power or control. Where the voice presented itself as a problem for psychoanalysis, it was always as the intractable voice of the Other that imposed itself upon the subject. In its most spectacular form, there was the extensive experience of "hearing voices," the vast field of auditory hallucinations that imposed themselves as more real than any other voices. In a more common form, there was the voice of consciousness, telling us to do our duty, in which psychoanalysis was soon to recognize the voice of the superego—not just an internalization of the Law, but something endowed with a surplus that puts the subject into a position of ineradicable guilt: the more one obeys, the more one is guilty. To put it into the somewhat simplified form of a slogan: the surplus of the superego over the Law is precisely the surplus of the voice; the superego has a voice, the Law is stuck with the letter. There was the hypnotic voice that demanded submission, and its mechanism—the repetition of some formula that lost all meaning by being repeated—was precisely an attempt to isolate the object voice from sense.[2] If psychoanalysis was to establish itself by sharply opposing hypnosis and its suggestive powers, it had to take into account and analyze the ominous authority of that strange object. There was aphonia, a frequent hysterical symptom, the loss of control over one's own voice, the sudden inability to use one's voice, the enforced silence—the silence that, all the more, makes the object voice appear, maybe in its pure form, for in its specificity it is, after all, devoid of phonic substance. At the bottom of it, there lay the problem of the mother's voice, the first presentification of a dimension of the Other, endowed with retroactive fantasies of a primary fusion prior to the introduction of a signifier and a lack (cf. e.g., the Kristevian *chora*), and also ambiguously giving rise to paranoic fantasies of "entrapment"; the voice that was both the nest and the cage (cf. Silverman 1988, 72ff., 101ff.).

So, for psychoanalysis, the auto-affective voice of self-presence and self-mastery was constantly opposed by its reverse side, the intractable voice of the Other, the voice that one could not control. But both have to be thought together: one could say that at the very core of narcissism, there lies an alien kernel that the narcissistic satisfaction may well attempt to disguise, but which continually threatens to undermine it from the inside. At the time when Lacan, impelled by his initial insight, wrote his famous pages on the mirror phase, he still didn't possess a theory of the object, and he later had to add several lengthy postscripts to his early sketches—most notably in the seminar on the four fundamental concepts of psychoanalysis (Lacan 1979), where a whole section bears the title "The Schism of the Eye and the Gaze." The gaze as the object, cleft from the eye, is precisely what is dissimulated by the image in which one recognizes oneself, it is not something that could be present in the field of vision, yet haunting it from the inside.[3] If it appears as a part of the image, as it occurs, for example, in the experience of the double, which has filled a whole library of romantic literature, it immediately disrupts the established reality and leads to catastrophe (see my essay "At First Sight" in part 2 of this volume). By analogy, there is a schism between the voice and the ear (cf. Miller 1989, 177–78). The same inner disruption of narcissism has to be introduced here and the same inherent ambiguity of the seemingly self-transparent auto-affection.

As soon as the object, both as the gaze and as the voice, appears as the pivotal point of narcissistic self-apprehension, it introduces a rupture at the core of self-presence. It is something that cannot itself be present, although the whole notion of presence is constructed around it and can be established only by its elision. So the subject, far from being constituted by self-grasp in the clarity of its presence to itself, only emerges in an impossible relation to that part that cannot be presentified. Only insofar as there is a Real (the Lacanian name for that part) as an impossibility of presence, is there a subject. The voice may well be the key to the presence of the present and to an unalloyed interiority, but it detains in its innermost reaches that inaudible and unbearable object voice which makes the presence all but transparent. So if for Derrida the essential of the voice lies in auto-affection and self-transparency, as opposed to the trace, the rest, the alterity, and so on, for Lacan that auto-affection is where the problem starts. Derrida's deconstructive turn deprives the voice of its ineradicable ambiguity by reducing it to the ground of the illusory presence, while the Lacanian account tries to disentangle from its core the object as an interior obstacle to self-presence. For the object embodies the very impossibility of attaining auto-affection, it introduces the scission, the rupture in the middle of the full presence and refers it to a void.

The most convincing feature of Derrida's extensive analyses is his ability to demonstrate how a seemingly marginal theme—that of the primacy of voice over writing, the phonocentric bias—consistently recurs throughout the whole history of metaphysics and how it is inherently and necessarily linked with all major metaphysical preoccupations. This one very limited approach seems to be sufficient to write the history of metaphysics in all its vast ramifications. The sheer extent of it is overwhelming, its coherence compelling.

Yet, the phonocentric bias is maybe not the whole story of the metaphysical treatment of the voice. There exists a different metaphysical history of voice, where the voice, far from being the safeguard of presence, is considered dangerous, threatening, and possibly ruinous. There is a history of the voice receiving a vote of no confidence. Not just writing, but also the voice can appear as a menace to metaphysical consistency and can be seen as disruptive of presence and sense. Lacan didn't have to invent the ambiguity of the voice and its perilous reverse side—metaphysics has been well aware of it all along. The particular place where one can look for this is in philosophical treatments of music—again a rather limited perspective, to be sure, but one that casts long shadows. So let us attempt a very brief survey of some paradigmatic cases.

In one of the oldest (although rather questionable and mythical) texts about music, the Chinese emperor Chun (ca. 2200 B.C.) gives the following simple precept: "Let the music follow the sense of the words. Keep it simple and ingenuous. One must condemn pretentious music which is devoid of sense and effeminate" (quoted by Poizat 1991, 197–98). Despite the simplicity of this piece of advice (and coming from an emperor, it is more than advice; it is, rather, a prescription to be followed, raising intricate issues of the relationship of music to power), the main concerns, which will recur throughout history with astonishing obstinacy, are already there in a nutshell: music, in particular the voice, shouldn't stray away from words, which endow it with sense; as soon as it departs from its textual anchorage, the voice becomes senseless and threatening, all the more so because of its seductive and intoxicating powers. Furthermore, the voice beyond sense is self-evidently equated with femininity, whereas the text, the instance of signification, is in this simple paradigmatic opposition on the side of masculinity. (Some four thousand years later, Wagner will write in a famous letter to Liszt, "Die Musik ist ein Weib," music is a woman.) The voice beyond the words is a senseless play of sensuality, it is a dangerous attractive force, although in itself empty and frivolous. The dichotomy of voice and "logos" is already in place.

A couple of millennia or so later, it is still well in place with Plato:

> A change to a new type of music is something to beware of as a hazard of all our fortunes. For the modes of music are never disturbed without unsettling of the most fundamental political and social conventions. . . . It is here, then, I said, that our guardians must build their guardhouse and post of watch.
>
> It is certain, he said, that this is the kind of lawlessness that easily insinuates itself unobserved.
>
> Yes, said I, because it is supposed to be only a form of play and to work no harm.
>
> Nor does it work any, he said, except that by gradual infiltration it softly overflows upon the characters and pursuits of men and from these issues forth grown greater to attack their business dealings, and from these relations it proceeds against the laws and the constitution with wanton license, Socrates, till finally it overthrows all things public and private. (*Republic* 4, 424c–e)

To say the least, music is no laughing matter. It cannot be taken lightly but has to be treated with the greatest philosophical concern and utmost vigilance. It is a texture so fundamental that any license inevitably produces general decadence; it undermines the social fabric, its laws and mores, and threatens the very ontological order. For one must assign an ontological status to music: it holds the key to a harmony between "nature" and "culture," the natural and the man-made law.[4] Should one interfere with that sphere, everything is put into question, and the foundations are truncated. Decadence starts with musical decadence: in the beginning, in the great times of origin, music was regulated by law and was one with it, but soon the things got out of hand:

> Afterward, in course of time, an unmusical license set in with the appearance of poets who were men of native genius, but ignorant of what is right and legitimate in the realm of the Muses. Possessed by a frantic and unhallowed lust for pleasure, they . . . created a universal confusion of forms. Thus their folly led them unintentionally to slander their profession by the assumption that in music there is no such thing as a right and a wrong, the right standard of judgment being the pleasure given to the hearer, be he high or low. (*Laws* 3, 700d-e)

Once one blasphemously gives way to pleasure as the standard ("It is commonly said that the standard of rightness in music is its pleasure-giving effect. That, however, is an intolerable sentiment; in fact, 'tis a piece of flat blasphemy" *Laws* 2, 655d.), once one has refused to comply with the law in music, there is no end to insidious consequences—impudence, moral disintegration, the collapse of all social bonds.[5]

In order to prevent this truly apocalyptic vision—the end of civilization, a return to chaos initiated by innocuous-looking changes in musical forms—one has to impose a firm regimentation of musical matters. The first rule, the prime antidote for combating the monster, is: "The music and the rhythm must follow the speech" (*Republic* 3, 398d; and again 400d). For the core of the danger is the voice that sets itself loose from the word, the voice beyond logos, the lawless voice.

Other prescriptions follow. One must proscribe the modes that mollify the soul or induce laxity—the "dirgelike" mixed Lydian, the higher Lydian ("for they are useless even to women who are to make the best of themselves, let alone to men," 398e) as well as the Ionian. One must retain those fit for men, both for warriors and for manly modesty and moderation—the Dorian and the Phrygian.[6] Again, the sexual division is seen to run through music (and this will continue to our day with the sexual connotations of major and minor tonalities, *durus* and *mollis*).[7] Consequently, one has to ban polyharmonic instruments that permit free transitions among the modes, "modulations," and in particular the flute, "the most many-stringed of instruments" (399d). There is in fact an additional, simpler, and more compelling reason for that: one cannot speak words while playing the flute.[8] The wind instruments have the vicious property that they emancipate themselves from the text, they are substitutes for the voice as the voice beyond words. No wonder that Dionysus has chosen the flute as his preferred instrument (cf. Pan's pipes), while Apollo has decided on the lyre. "We are not innovating, my friend, in preferring Apollo and the instruments of Apollo to Marsyas and his instruments" (399e).[9] And no wonder that the flute is fit for women: "I also propose that we dispense with the services of the flute girl who has just come in, and let her go and play to herself or to the women inside there, whichever she prefers, while we spend our evening in discussion . . ." (*Symposium* 176e). The flute is played by a girl and her proper audience are women (a quick slide leads from flute to questionable virtue), while men will engage in philosophy—not to mention the mythical connections of flute with Gorgon, and so on.

So there lies in music both the best remedy and the ultimate danger, the cure and the poison. It is curious how Derrida's famous analysis of *pharmakon* (cf. "Plato's Pharmacy" in Derrida 1972), the remedy and the ruin, as applied to writing, can also apply to the voice: "Education in music is most sovereign, because more than anything else rhythm and harmony find their way to the inmost soul and take strongest hold upon it, bringing with them and imparting grace, if one is rightly trained, and otherwise the contrary . . ." (*Republic* 3, 401d–e). So the question is how to strike a balance between its beneficial and dangerous effects, where to draw a line:

> Now when a man abandons himself to music, to play upon him and pour into his soul as it were through the funnel of his ears those sweet, soft, and dirgelike airs . . . and gives his entire time

to the warblings and blandishments of song, the first result is that the principle of high spirit, if he had it, is softened like iron and is made useful instead of useless and brittle. But when he continues the practice without remission and is spellbound, the effect begins to be that he melts and liquefies till he completely dissolves away his spirit, cuts out as it were the very sinews of his soul and makes of himself a "feeble warrior." (*Republic* 3, 411a–b) [10]

So how can one hope to achieve the right measure with this dangerous sort of enjoyment? Up to a point, music is sublime and elevates the spirit; from a certain limit, however, it brings about decay, the decline of all spiritual faculties, their disintegration in enjoyment. Where shall one stop? Can the philosopher set a limit to this unbounded, limitless enjoyment? Can he keep the cure without introducing the fatal poison?

Let us, for the present purpose, leave aside Aristotle, who has curiously devoted most of book 8 of his *Politics* to music as the central part of his theory of education; let us jump another millennium, or almost, and open Augustine's *Confessions*, book 10, 33. There we read the following striking meditation about "sinning by the ear":

> Now, in those melodies [*sonis*] which Thy words breathe soul into, when sung with a sweet and attuned voice, I do a little repose.... But with the words which are their life and whereby they find admission into me, themselves [melodies, *soni*] seek in my affections a place of some estimation, and I can scarcely assign them one suitable. For at one time I seem to myself to give them more honour than is seemly [*decet*], feeling our minds to be more holily and fervently raised unto a flame of devotion, by the holy words themselves when thus sung, than when not; and that the several affections of our spirit, by a sweet variety, have their own proper measures in the voice and singing, by some hidden correspondence wherewith they are stirred up. But this contentment of the flesh, to which the soul must not be given over to be enervated, doth oft beguile me, the sense not so waiting upon reason, as patiently to follow her; but having been admitted merely for her sake, it strives even to run before her, and lead her.

We should not be surprised by now to find the voice again as the paramount source of danger and decay. The remedy, too, is familiar: stick to the Word, the word of God, make sure the word maintains the upper hand, to be rid of the voice beyond the word, the unbounded voice. So Athanasius has acted most wisely when prescribing that the psalms should be sung "with so slight inflection of voice that it was nearer speaking than singing." Shouldn't singing be rather banned to avoid the ambiguity?

> When I remember the tears I shed at the Psalmody of Thy Church, in the beginning of my recovered faith; and how at this time, I am moved, not with the singing, but with the things sung, when they are sung with a clear voice and modulation most suitable [*cum liquida voce et convenientissima modulatione*], I acknowledge the great use of this institution. Thus I fluctuate between peril of pleasure, and approved wholesomeness; . . . by the delight of the ears, the weaker minds may rise to the feeling of devotion. Yet when it befalls me to be more moved with the voice than the words sung, I confess to have sinned penally, and then had rather not hear music.

Again, it is a question of the limit, the impossible good measure, for music is both what elevates the soul to divinity and a sin, *delectatio carnis*. It presents carnality at its most insidious since it seems liberated from materiality, it is the subtlest and the most perfidious form of the flesh.

The oscillation of St. Augustine defines very well the bulk of what was to happen in the next thousand years and more in the troubled and intricate relationship of the Catholic Church to music. The main problem that kept emerging with a strange perseverance was that of regimentation and codification of sacral music, ultimately the confinement of the voice to the holy script, the letter. But whatever the attempted regulations, there was always a crack, a loophole, a rest that kept recurring, a remnant of a highly ambiguous enjoyment. It could take, for example, the form of *iubilus*, the space allotted to "alleluia," where the general principle of one syllable to one note was omitted, the voice taking over in its own jubilation, the melisma without a support. In a very curious development, the notes without words were later underpinned with new words and whole sequences (in the technical sense of the term), thus threatening heretical intrusions into the text. But isn't *iubilus*, although perilous, at the same time also the most appropriate way to praise God? Augustine himself says so: the jubilation expresses what cannot be expressed by words, the singers are so overwhelmed with joy that they abandon words and give way to their heart. "Et quem decet ista iubilatio, nisi ineffabilem deum?" (quoted in O'Donnell's commentary on the *Confessions*, 1992, vol. 3, 218-19). So it is only the pure voice beyond words that matches the ineffability of God. But then again, can we ever be sure that it is really God that we are praising?

One can follow the same predicament with the enormous problems posed by the introduction of polyphony, since when several voices sing at the same time and follow their own melodic lines, the text becomes unintelligible. We see it again in the battle against chromatics, since the semitones threaten to undermine the harmonic structure and introduce mollification of the spirit, the proscribed enjoyment. Each new musical invention had devastating effects and was immediately seen, in a very Platonic manner, as a way to moral ruin. Pope John XXII had to issue a curious decree concerning music, *Docta sanctorum Patrum*, in 1324, trying to put things in order, but to no avail. The Council of Trent, in the sixteenth century, had to toil with the same problem and commended the same antidote of intelligibility versus voice: *in tono intelligibili, intelligibili voce, voce clara, cantu intelligibili* . . . (cf. Poizat 1991, 144-45). All the documents seem to have been written by the same hand and guided by the same single obsession: to pin down the voice to the letter, to limit its disruptive force, to dissipate its inherent ambiguity.

Yet, not everything fitted within this monotonous picture. Some mystical currents proposed an astonishing reversal of this massive paradigm: music is the only appropriate way to God since it is aiming precisely at a God beyond the word. It is a way to a limitless and ineffable being, a quality that Augustine was already aware of. What is at stake is an enjoyment beyond the signifier, something that opens the perspective of the Lacanian problem of feminine *jouissance* (which Lacan himself tackled precisely through the women mystics; cf. Lacan 1975, 70-71). But if God is the musical principle par excellence and the divine word attains its true dimension only in the singing voice, then the radical consequence could follow that the mere word belongs to the devil. This extreme conclusion was indeed drawn by Hildegard of Bingen, the famous twelfth-century abbess, who — beside her philosophical preoccupations and conferring with some of the most illustrious men of her time — largely devoted her time to composing. In *Ordo virtutum*, a musical morality play, we have the story of a soul being tempted by the devil and rescued by the virtues—virtues personified and, of course, singing. In a most curious tour de force, the devil is the only masculine and the only speaking role, being confined just to words, to mere "logos." An inherently nonmusical creature, the devil is the devil because he cannot sing. (One could add: No wonder that his temptations couldn't amount to much.) Of course the church was bound to be doubtful and worried—the synod in Trier, in 1147, almost condemned her as heretic, asking whether her visions were to be assigned to the devil rather than to God. Is the voice that she hears and writes down really the voice of God? Is there a way to tell?— It took the authority of Bernard of Clairvaux to rescue Hildegard.[11]

The question that was raised finally boiled down to this: Does music come from God or from the devil? For what is beyond the word announces both the supreme elevation and the vilest damnation. What raises our souls to God makes God ambiguous; beyond the word one cannot tell God from the devil. Music may well be the element of spiritual elevation beyond worldliness and representation, but it also introduces, for that very reason, the indomitable and senseless *jouissance* beyond the more tractable sensual pleasures. There is no assurance or transparency to be found in the voice, quite the contrary, the voice undermines any certainty and any establishment of a firm sense. The voice is boundless, warrantless, and, no coincidence, on the side of woman. But if it introduces this fatal ambivalence, then the only consistent course would be to ban church music altogether—and indeed, this radical conclusion at the opposite extreme was drawn by the Puritans: for fifteen years, from 1645 to 1660, in the time of Cromwell, music was banned from the Anglican Church, music books and sheets were burned and organs demolished as "the devil's pipes" (cf. Poizat 1991, 44). God was restored to the word, and to silence.

Let me finish this "brief history of metaphysics" with the French Revolution, although many more detours should be taken into account, more details scrutinized and more authors examined. At the height of the victorious Revolution, somebody had the brilliant idea to create, in 1793, the Institut national de la musique, an institution through which the state would take care of music in the best interest of the people.[12] François-Joseph Gossec, who was in charge of the project, has duly written in a programmatic text that its goal should be to promote music "which would support and animate the energy of the defenders of equality and to prohibit music which mollifies the French soul by its effeminate sounds in the salons and in the temples consecrated to imposture" (quoted by Attali 1977, 111). The music has to be drawn into the open, out of the courts, churches, and concert halls, it has to be performed in the open air, accessible to everyone; the melodies should be such that the people can sing along, not the pompous and pretentious artifices that only serve the degenerate. Gossec himself entered music history as the initiator of the mass choir and one of the first composers for brass orchestras. Musicians should become state employees, not dependent on the generosity of the rich, and the whole musical enterprise should be well planned and organized from above.[13]

So the tables could be reversed and the same weapons could be turned against the Church, now seen as the major agent of the voice against the sense. But the defenders of reason were for once unwittingly in perfect accord with their enemies, the senseless and effeminate voice was equally dangerous to both. It is also highly indicative that one of the first decrees of the Revolution was the prohibition of the public singing of castrati, who became the emblematic and monstrous figureheads of the perversity and corruption of the ancien régime—the embodiments of its degenerate *jouissance* epitomized by the voice.[14]

One can draw, from this brief and necessarily schematic survey, the tentative conclusion that the history of "logocentrism" doesn't run quite hand in hand with "phonocentrism," that there is a dimension of the voice that runs counter to self-transparency, sense, and presence: the voice against the logos, the voice as the other of logos, its radical alterity. "Metaphysics" has always been very well aware of that, as we have seen, compulsively clinging to a simple exorcising formula, repeating it over and over again, compelled by the same invisible hand throughout millennia. Maybe what defined it as metaphysics was also the banishment of the voice. The "phonocentric" voice was just one part of the story, its narcissistic fulfillment, the illusory pledge of the presence, reduction of its inherent ambivalence and its part of alterity. Yet, by this simple division we haven't yet reached the proper dimension of the object voice. It is here that the Lacanian problem really starts.

In the simple paradigm I have tried to draw up, the logos—in the largest sense of "what makes sense"—was opposed by the voice as an intrusion of otherness, *jouissance,* and femininity. But there is also another voice: the "voice of the Father," the voice that inherently sticks to logos itself, the voice that commands and binds, the voice of God. If there is to be a covenant, there has to be a voice. This is the problem that Lacan brings up in his seminar on anxiety (May 22, 1963), taking his inspiration in the striking analysis that Theodor Reik has made of the shofar, a primitive horn used in Jewish religious rituals, one of the most ancient wind instruments.

Where does the astounding force of the shofar come from? It is, for example, blown four times, at the close of Yom Kippur, in very long continuous sounds that are reputed to fill the soul with an irresistible profound emotion.[15] There is no melody, just prolonged sounds reminiscent of a bull roaring. Reik sees the key to its secret in the Freudian myth of "totem and taboo":

> The specifically anxious, groaning, blaring, long-sounding tone of the shofar is made understandable as reminiscent of a roaring bull; it obtains its fateful significance by presenting, to the unconscious psychic life of the listener, the anxiety and the ultimate death struggle of the divine father, one could say his "swan's song," if the comparison wasn't so utterly out of place here. . . . When the image of the father was rediscovered in the totemic animal and worshipped as divine, those who recognized it imitated its voice by onomatopoeic sounds. The imitation of the animal's cry signified both the presence of God among the believers and their identification with him. The horn, the most characteristic trait of the totemic god, gave birth in the course of centuries to an instrument that was now used as the means of acoustic imitation. (Reik 1928, 235–36)

So one has to recognize, in the sound of the shofar, the voice of the Father, the cry of the dying primal Father of the primitive horde, the leftover, which comes both to haunt the foundation of his Law and to seal it. By hearing his voice, the community of his believers establishes its covenant, its alliance with God, they assert their submission and obedience to the Law. The Law itself, in its pure form, before commanding anything specific, is epitomized by the voice, the voice that commands total compliance, although senseless in itself. The letter of the Law can acquire its authority by the remnant of the dead Father, that part of him which is not quite dead, what remained after his death and testifies to his presence—his voice—but also to his absence, a *stand-in for an impossible presence*, enveloping a central void. It is the ritual repetition of his sacrifice and the reminder of the impossible origin of the Law, covering up its lack of origin. But this gesture is highly ambiguous, for who has to be reminded? Who is ultimately the addressee of that voice? In Lacan's words, "Is not the one whose memory has to be awoken, whom one has to make remember, is it not the God himself?" For the function of that voice, apart from presentifying God, is also to remind God that he is dead, in case he has forgotten.

The sound of the shofar takes its support from the Bible, and Reik carefully lists all its numerous occurrences. Each of them is remarkable; they all occur at dramatic moments, most often when a covenant has to be established or reasserted, the most significant being the moment of the foundation of the Law when Moses receives the tablets of the Law on Mount Sinai. It was the sound of the shofar that, at that foundational instance, testified to the presence of God for the people, for they could only hear this terrible and commanding sound, and only Moses could speak to God and make out what he said. The shofar, conventionally translated as "trumpet," was the element of the voice in the midst of thunder as the natural "noise":

> On the morning of the third day there were peals of thunder and lightning, and a heavy cloud over the mountain, and a very loud trumpet blast, so that all the people in the camp trembled. (Ex. 19.16)

> When the people witnessed the thunder and lightening, the trumpet blast and the mountain smoking, they all feared and trembled. So they took up a position much farther away and said to Moses, "You speak to us, and we will listen; but let not God speak to us, or we shall die." (Ex. 20.18)

So the shofar is there as the voice without content that sticks to the Law, the support of the Law underpinning its letter. There is, in this inaugural moment, a division between the voice heard by the people, as a terrible commanding presence, and the Law of which only Moses could "make sense." But there is no Law without the voice.[16] It seems that the voice, as a senseless remainder of the letter, is what endows the letter with authority, making it not just a signifier but an act. It is, as Lacan says, "that something which completes the relation of the subject to the signifier in what might be called, in a first approach, its *passage à l'acte*."[17] Those "primordial signifiers" are inherently "acts," "namely, something that happens when the signifier is not just articulated—which supposes only its relation, its coherence with the others in a chain—, but when it is uttered and vocalised." But what is at stake is not really the notion of act or of vocalization but the status of the object that is fundamental to both and which "has to be detached from phonematisation as such." The object voice bears witness to the rest of that presupposed and terrible Father's *jouissance*, which couldn't be absorbed by the Law, that reverse side of the Father that Lacan calls *le-père-la-jouissance*, his ultimate deadly cry that accompanies the instituted law. It is the part that can never be simply present—but is not simply absent, either: the object voice is the pivotal point at the intersection. It discloses the presence and gives ground to its imaginary recognition—recognizing oneself as the addressee of the voice of the Other as well as recognizing one's own voice in a self-presence—but it is at the same time what inherently lacks and disrupts any notion of a full presence; it makes it a truncated presence, which covers the lack.

The metaphysical picture we have drawn is therefore misleading. If the Law, the word, the logos, had to constantly fight the voice as the other, the senseless bearer of *jouissance*, feminine decadence, it could do so only by implicitly relying on that other voice, the voice of the Father accompanying the Law. Ultimately, we don't have the battle of "logos" against the voice, but *the voice against the voice*. Yet, is that inaudible voice pertaining to logos something entirely different from the anathemized voice bringing unbounded *jouissance* and decay? Is the *jouissance* that the Law persecutes as its radical alterity other than the aspect of *jouissance* pertaining to Law itself? Is the voice of the Father an altogether different species from the feminine voice? Does the voice of the persecutor differ from the persecuted voice? The secret is maybe that they are both the same; that there are not two voices, but only one object voice, which cleaves and bars the Other in an ineradicable "extimacy": "And why not interpret one face of the Other, the God face, as supported by feminine *jouissance?* . . . And since it is there too that the function of the father is inscribed in so far as this is the function to which castration refers, one can see that while this may not make for two Gods, nor does it make for one alone" (Lacan 1982, 147).[18] For what endows the Law with authority is also what irretrievably bars it, and the attempts to banish the other voice, the voice beyond logos, are ultimately based in the impossibility of coming to terms with Law's inherent alterity, placed at the point of its inherent lack which voice comes to cover. This structural point is what Lacan, in his algebra, has designated by S($\cancel{A}$), the point of the always missing ultimate signifier, which would totalize the Other, the point of the lacking foundation of the Law, and also the point that has an intrinsic relation with femininity and the nonexistence of Woman.[19] It is at this point of alterity in the Other that the object is situated. Masculine and feminine positions are then two ways of tackling the same impossibility; they arise from the same predicament as two internally linked versions of the same voice, which retains an ineradicable ambiguity.

Notes

All translations have been done by the author, with the exception of those listed in the Works Cited.

1 Saussure's *Cours* has caused some confusion, since it is not in the part that explicitly deals with phonology that his novelty is to be found. We have to look elsewhere: "Moreover, it is impossible that the sound, the material element, belongs by itself to language. It is secondary for it, a matter that it uses. . . . [The linguistic signifier] is by its essence by no means phonic, it is disembodied, constituted not by its material substance, but exclusively by the differences that separate its acoustic image from all others." What defines the phonemes is not "their proper and positive quality, but simply the fact that they do not get confounded among them. The phonemes are above all oppositive, relative and negative entities" (Saussure 1972, 164).

2 The commanding authority of the voice is already inscribed in the very posture of listening. As soon as one listens, one has started to obey. The verb *to obey* stems from French *obéir,* which in turn stems from Latin *oboedire,* to listen. One can find the same etymological connection in German, where *Gehorsam,* obedience, comes from *hören,* to listen, and in a considerable number of other languages. *His Master's Voice* is thus a most appropriate emblem.

3 Among many formulations, one can here single out the less well-known but very clear ones from Lacan's seminar on anxiety (May 22, 1963), the session where the gaze is put into analogy and opposition with the voice: "[U]nder the form of *i(a)* my

image, my presence in the Other, is without a rest. I cannot see what I lose in it. This is the sense of the mirror stage. . . . *a*, what is lacking, is not specular; it cannot be seized in the image."

4 This is also why music is treated in a very different way from painting, which poses interminable problems of imitation, copies, mimesis, etc.

5 "So the next stage of the journey toward liberty will be refusal to submit to the magistrates, and on this will follow emancipation from the authority and correction of parents and elders; then, as the goal of the race is approached, comes the effort to escape obedience to the law, and, when that goal is all but reached, contempt for oaths, for the plighted word, and all religion. The spectacle of the Titanic nature of which our old legends speak is reenacted; man returns to the old condition of a hell of unending misery" (*Laws* 3, 701b-c).

6 For Aristotle's analogous views on the modes, cf. *Politics* 8, 1340b. Yet, a bit further on (1342b) he takes issue with that particular passage in the *Republic* concerning the Phrygian mode.

7 Cf. also: "It will further be necessary to make a rough general distinction between two types of songs, those suited for females and those suited for males, and so we shall have to provide both with their appropriate scales and rhythms; it would be a dreadful thing that the whole tune or rhythm of a composition should be out of place, as it will be if our various songs are inappropriately treated in these respects" (*Laws* 7, 802e).

8 Cf. "There is yet another objection to the flute as a means of education: you cannot sing or recite while you are playing it. Though used by the ancients, it was rightly forbidden to youths and freemen by our more immediate ancestors" (Aristotle, *Politics* 8, 1341a).

9 Cf. "Bacchic frenzy and all such emotions are expressed more adequately by the flute than by any other instrument . . ." (Aristotle, *Politics* 8, 1342b).

10 Aristotle will have to deal with the same problem. The liberal studies, with music in the highest place of honor, are quintessential to education, but to those "a freeman may devote himself only up to a certain point; if he goes too far, hoping to reach perfection, the disastrous consequences will ensue" (*Politics* 8, 1337b).

11 For Hildegard, who has turned into a somewhat fashionable figure lately, cf. Peter Dronke, *Women Writers of the Middle Ages*, 1984 (Cambridge: Cambridge UP); Barbara Newman, *Sister of Wisdom*, 1987 (Berkeley: U of California P); and Sabina Flanagan, *Hildegard of Bingen*, 1989 (London: Routledge). None of these quite do justice to her musical work.

12 The project was presented to the Convent on the eighteenth *brumaire*, year 2 (1792) of the Revolution: another memorable eighteenth *brumaire*, which preceded by seven years its more famous counterpart, Napoleon's seizure of power in 1799. Marx's theory could thus be extended: Napoleon's coup d'état was itself already a repetition, quite in accordance with Plato's view that musical changes prefigure social ones, only that with Plato, they announced decadence, whereas here they were the harbinger of a new dictatorship.

13 François-Joseph Gossec (1734-1829) acquired his musical knowledge and some

glory as a court composer. In 1766 he became *intendant de la musique* of prince Condé and in 1774 *maître de musique* at the Royal Academy, then the founder and the first director of the École royale de chant. After the Revolution he was music inspector and one of the principal holders of musical authority in France for a quarter of a century. In 1816, after the downfall of Napoleon and the restoration of the monarchy, he was summarily fired for his allegiance to revolutionary ideas, so he died in great poverty and entirely forgotten. Among his numerous works one can find, e.g., *Hymne à Jean-Jacques Rousseau, Hymne à l'Être Suprème, Hymne à la liberté, Chant du 14 juillet.*

14 For lack of space, I cannot venture here into the fascinating realm of the history of castrati: their rise within the Catholic Church in the sixteenth century; their quasi-angel-like demeanor, which seemingly dissociates the enjoyment of the voice from sex; their massive presence in the opera; their incredible vogue, which lasted some three centuries; their gradual decline, until they were confined to the Sistine Chapel, which had been their cradle and their sanctuary all along—the core of perversity at the very heart of the church; and finally their banishment, as late as 1903, by Pope Leo XIII. They raise in the most immediate way the question of the relation between voice and castration, the more obvious demonstration of the structural tie between castration and the object in psychoanalysis (cf., e.g., Lacan's graph of desire, where voice and castration are to be found in parallel and analogous places—Lacan 1989, 315). For the history of castrati, the best accounts so far are probably those by Patrick Barbier, *Histoire des castrats,* 1989 (Paris: Grasset) and Hubert Ortkemper, *Engel wider Willen,* 1993 (Berlin: Henschel).

15 The shofar is also used on a number of other ritual occasions, which are carefully scrutinized by Reik. On July 27, 1656, Spinoza heard the sound of a shofar accompany the formal text of excommunication read by a priest.

16 This constellation is by no means limited to Judaism and Christianity. It appears in some version in almost all ancient mythologies where the bond between voice and creation, and specifically between voice and the foundation of a primeval Law, seems to be a commonplace. Cf., e.g.: "Considerable information about the nature of music and its role in the world is provided by the myths of creation. Each time that the genesis of the world is described with some precision, the acoustic element intervenes at the decisive moment of action. Whenever a deity manifests the will to give birth to itself or to another deity, to bring forth the sky and the earth or the man, it emits a sound. . . . The source from where the world emanates is always an acoustic source" (Schneider 1960, 132). Schneider gives many diverse instances taken from a variety of ancient and "primitive" cultures and convincingly demonstrates the necessary link between the voice, religion, and the basic social rituals, the umbilical cord between voice and a rudimentary social bond. An enormous amount of anthropological material is painstakingly analyzed in the excellent book by Gilbert Rouget, *La Musique et le transe,* 1980 (Paris: Gallimard).

17 For Lacan, *passage à l'acte* is a concept sharply opposed to *acting out*. It is difficult to find a good English equivalent. Quotations are taken from the text of a privately printed seminar.

18 The whole section of *Encore* from which this passage is taken actually bears the title "God and the *Jouissance* of T̶h̶e̶ Woman".
19 "The woman relates to S($A̸$), which means that she is already doubled, and is not all. . . ." "[T]he Supreme Being . . . is situated in the place, the opaque place of the *jouissance* of the Other—that Other which, if she existed, the woman might be" (Lacan 1982, 152, 153).

Works Cited

Aristotle. 1973. *"Politics" and "The Athenian Constitution"*. Ed. and trans. J. Warrington. London: Everyman's Library.
Attali, Jacques. 1977. *Bruits*. Paris: Presses Universitaires de France.
Augustine. 1924. *The Confessions*. Trans. E. B. Pusey. London: J. M. Dent.
———. 1992. *Confessions*. 3 vols. Ed. James J. O'Donnell. Oxford: Clarendon Press.
Barthes, Roland. 1982. *L'Obvie et l'obtus*. Paris: Seuil.
Derrida, Jacques. 1972. *La Dissémination*. Paris: Seuil.
———. 1976. *Of Grammatology*. Trans. G. Spivak. Baltimore: Johns Hopkins UP.
Jakobson, Roman. 1963. *Essais de linguistique générale* 1. Paris: Minuit.
Lacan, Jacques. 1962/63. "L'angoisse." Unpublished seminar.
———. 1975. *Encore*. Ed. J.-A. Miller. Paris: Seuil.
———. 1979. *The Four Fundamental Concepts of Psycho-Analysis*. Harmondsworth: Penguin.
———. 1989. *Écrits: A Selection*. Trans. A. Sheridan. London: Tavistock/Routledge.
Lacan, Jacques, and the École freudienne. 1982. *Feminine Sexuality*. Ed. J. Mitchell and J. Rose. London: Macmillan.
Miller, Jacques-Alain. 1989. "Jacques Lacan et la voix." In *La voix: Actes du colloque d'Ivry*, by Ivan Fonagy et al. Paris: La Lysimaque.
Plato. 1978. *The Collected Dialogues*. Ed. Edith Hamilton and Huntington Cairns. Princeton: Princeton UP.
Poizat, Michel. 1991. *La Voix du diable*. Paris: Éditions Métailié.
Reik, Theodor. 1928. *Das Ritual: Psychoanalytische Studien*. Leipzig: Internationaler Psychoanalytischer Verlag (Imago-Bucher).
Saussure, Ferdinand de. 1972. *Cours de linguistique générale*. Paris: Payot.
Schneider, Marius. 1960. "Le Rôle de la musique dans la mythologie et les rites des civilisations non européennes." In *Histoire de la musique* 1, ed. Roland-Manuel. Paris: Gallimard (Bibliothèque de la Pleiade).
Silverman, Kaja. 1988. *The Acoustic Mirror*. Bloomington: Indiana UP.

2

Philosophers' Blind Man's Buff

Alenka Zupančič

It might seem very odd that for two centuries the blind man has been an obsessive and emblematic theme of the Enlightenment. His presence is ubiquitous and overwhelming, so the question arises whether there is a necessary inner connection between the project of the Enlightenment and the figure of the blind man. Is there a secret link between the emergence of a new type of subjectivity, the subject of the Enlightenment, and blindness? If the Enlightenment, as its name implies, tried to impose a new type of vision and insight, why was it so preoccupied at its core with blindness? Could one paradoxically maintain that the subject of the Enlightenment is essentially blind? And more specifically, could one establish an inherent link between that new subjectivity and what Lacan has called the gaze as the object *a*? Let us consider some paradigmatic cases in which blindness and vision have stood at the very center of theoretical concerns.

Res videns

What does Descartes consider the perfect and exhaustive representation of the mechanism of vision?—the body of a *blind man*, extended by two obligatory sticks that he holds crossed in his hands (figure 1). The only way to represent and to *explain* the process of vision is to do it via the figure of a blind man. The first immediate implication is that for Descartes, the "blind man" does not function as the opposite of those who see. As a (blind) *man* he perceives in his own way everything that others do, including color. Color is no more than the response of the brain to a certain kind of sensory stimulus, the differences among colors are comparable to the differences among different movements of the stick and the different kinds of resistance that objects offer to the movement of the stick.[1] However, Descartes's point is not simply that the blind in some way "see" as we do, that there is no important difference—the stakes are much higher. It is not the blind who are compared to "us" (who see), it is "we" who have to be compared to the blind in order to be able to understand what happens when we see. Moreover, it is not the "man" (the blind *man*) who is at stake here: the figure of a "blind man" could be seen as the optical version of *res cogitans,* of the thing that thinks. In the same way that the "pure subject of thought," when taken seriously, loses all marks of subjectivity and becomes a thinking *thing,* the "blind man" that appears in the *Dioptrique* incarnates what we may call a "seeing thing," *res videns.* So, paradoxically, the "blind man" comes to personify the very essence of seeing, "he" is but a walking pair of eyeballs attached to the brain. Not only is the figure of a blind man not opposed to what constitutes the "mechanism" of seeing, but it functions as its *condensation.* Light being understood—as it is in the Cartesian universe—as a "very subtle and fluid matter," the two sticks are simply two "condensed" rays of light, the arms and the upper body of a "blind man" no more than a "corpus" of sensors, nerves, and other "optical devices," and his head simply the brains, where the "picture" is formed out of the different sensory impulses.

At this point, one should ask the obvious question: How is it that, in Descartes, the figure of a "blind man" is so utterly compatible with everything that relates to seeing and to optics in general? The answer is provided by Lacan in his lectures entitled "The Gaze as *objet petit a.*"[2] Lacan proposes a scheme of vision that he first introduces by presenting its two constitutive parts (figure 2). On the left we have the "geometral" aspect of vision; on the right, the aspect related to the function of the gaze (here represented by the "point of light"), and below we see the scheme with the two triangles superimposed, "as in fact they are in the functioning of the scopic register."[3] The figure of the blind man functions so well in Cartesian optics because Cartesian optics *is* fundamentally the "optics of the blind"—it is the optics that Lacan refers to as the "geometral" (as opposed to "perspective") optics of a "flat," "geometral" space that the blind man has no difficulty in conceiving:

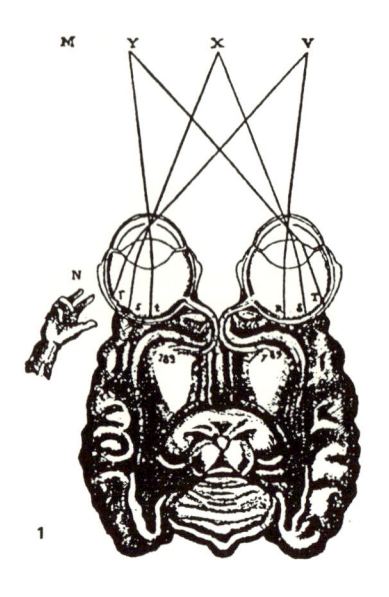

We would get him, for example, to finger an object of a certain height, then follow the stretched thread. We would teach him to distinguish, by the sense of touch in his finger-ends, on a surface, a certain configuration that reproduces the mapping of the images — in the same way that we imagine, in pure optics, the variously proportioned and fundamentally homological relations, the correspondences from one point to another in space, which always, in the end, amounts to situating two points on a single thread.[4]

This configuration implies a point-by-point correspondence of two unities in space, that is to say, the relation of an image, insofar as it is linked to a surface, with the "geometral" point. However, this mode, which Lacan calls "the mode of the image in the field of vision," does not exhaust what the field of vision has to offer. Although it enables us to "imagine" *everything there is to see,* it allows what concerns vision to escape totally; it is — as Lacan puts it — simply the mapping of space, not sight. What is it then that distinguishes sight, besides "everything there is to see"? What is it that the blind man cannot see, if not what there is to see? What a blind man cannot see is precisely what *cannot be seen* and what is introduced into the field of vision by the function of the gaze. A blind man cannot *see* the lack. The field of vision is essentially organized around what cannot be seen and what appears as a "screen" or a "stain," a "spot": the gaze which, in the space of light, always presents

```
Object | image  →  Geometral    Point of  ←  screen | Picture
                    point        light

          The gaze  ⟨═══ image ═══⟩ The subject of
                         screen        representation
```

2

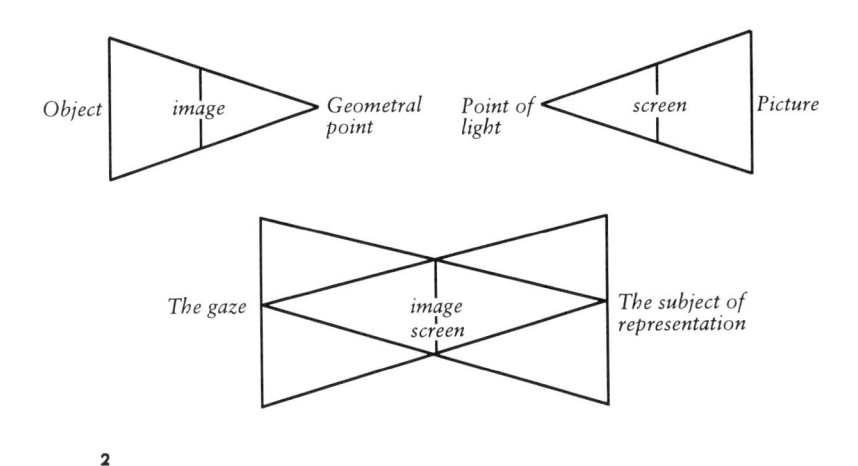

itself as a play of light and opacity. In other words, the main obstacle that prevents the "mode of the image," the geometral dimension, from exhausting the field of vision, consists in the fact that the latter essentially includes the dimension of the lack. It is the gaze that is always "lacking," eluding our grasp: "In our relation to things, in so far as this relation is constituted by the way of vision, and ordered in the figures of representation, something slips, passes, is transmitted, from stage to stage, and is always to some degree eluded—that is what we call the gaze."[5] Thus, on the one hand, there is the "geometral dimension" (of vision), which enables me to constitute myself as a subject of representation, the I/eye of the *cogito*. On the other hand, there is the "dimension of the gaze" where the "I" turns itself into a *picture* under the gaze. It follows from this double frame that "where the subject sees himself... it is not from there that he looks at himself."[6] The dichotomy between looking (at) and seeing, between the gaze and the eye, governs the logic of the scopic field. This is why, according to Lacan, one of the most current illusions of philosophy—the illusion of the consciousness *seeing itself seeing itself*, which turns it into a self-consciousness—necessarily "elides" the gaze.

The Dark Room

The understanding, like the eye, whilst it makes us see and perceive all other things, takes no notice of itself; and it requires art and pains to set it at a distance and make it its own object.—John Locke, *An Essay Concerning Human Understanding*

The strange obsession with the blind in late-seventeenth- and eighteenth-century philosophy deeply marked all the important philosophers of the time. Leibniz, Locke, Berkeley, Diderot, Condillac, and many others, discussed the issue at length and invented various "techniques" that would enable the philosopher to draw as many philosophically interesting consequences as possible from it. The great point of interest was particularly the passage "from dark into the light" that was made possible thanks to the progress in surgical skills—the cataract operation. Before addressing the question of what it was that fascinated philosophers in this phenomenon, one should stress that this curious preoccupation with the blind was not merely a matter of fascination. The introduction of the figure of the blind man into philosophy was in itself a response to a strictly philosophical problem. The philosophy of John Locke is exceptionally instructive in this light.

In his anti-Cartesian orientation, Locke created a kind of "twilight zone" of philosophy on which his younger contemporaries expected to throw some light by making the blind the instrument of "philosophical experiment."

As the principal addressee of Locke's critique, as the Other of the new philosophy that was just taking shape, Descartes played a crucial role in the story that we are about to explore. It is not just his *Dioptrique* that is in question here, but the fundamental principles of his philosophy. To put it simply: if, via the *cogito* argument, the certitude of the thinking subject, *res cogitans*, is established, the passage to the "exterior world" involves a certain jump; it cannot be performed in a purely linear way. We may know with certainty that we think, but nothing guarantees the certainty and the truth of the "content" of our thoughts. In order to institute a science about the external world (and about ourselves as *res extensae*, as bearers of sensitive qualities), it is necessary to assume the existence of a God who is incapable of deception, who created eternal truths and, as Descartes puts it, planted them in our souls as seeds. Thus, "man is the subject of knowledge, and can play the *possessor* of the world, only in so far as he is *depository* of the truths of an Other."[7] In the *Essay*, Locke sets about to establish the following: all these ideas—supposed to be innate, planted by the Other—are *mine*, they belong to me as a human. What was before simply *given* now has to be (proved) *acquired*, without any recourse to an Other, and in a strictly linear way that allows no "jumps." The only way to acquire anything is of course via experience, or, more precisely, via sensations. Understanding is now given a new inaugurating metaphor, which already announces and makes way for the role to be played by the "blind"—the metaphor of the *dark room*.

> I pretend not to teach, but to inquire; and therefore cannot but confess here again,—that external and internal sensations are the only passages I can find of knowledge to the understanding. These alone, as far as I can discover, are the windows by which light is let into this *dark room*. For, methinks, the understanding is not much unlike a closet wholly shut from light, with only some little openings left, to let in external visible resemblances, or ideas of things without.[8]

The first book of the *Essay* is dedicated entirely to arguments demonstrating the nonexistence of "innate ideas." Locke's arguments aim at the assumption that "innate ideas" are something that humans "have" in their consciousness from the very beginning, as already "fully developed." He challenges the existence of innate ideas, referring to "children and idiots" who have not the least apprehension or thought about truths such as "Whatsoever is, is" or "It is impossible for the same thing to be and not to be"—which, of all others, "have the most allowed title to innate."[9] This reference to "children and idiots" also enables Locke to dismiss the most popular argument in favor of "innate truths," the argument of "universal consent."

This change of ground, the replacement of the given with the acquired, introduces a new ordering principle of truths. Truths, principles, or ideas are now ranged according to the degrees of their evidence. They run from those that are *immediately* perceived (and are part of what Locke calls intuitive knowledge) to those where "the mind is at pains of proving or examining them." So, "the discourse of the *Essay* covers step by step, without rupture or jump, the entire field of Cartesian knowledge and joins the other frontier, the one that, facing the divine infinity, limited the field of Cartesian understanding. Everything that was before only borrowed, is now acquired. Everything but the value of the truth of this everything."[10]

This implies a new theory of language—in which, basically, we can understand and properly use a certain word only if, once in our lives, we have "perceived" the object that it stands for—and hence the refusal of the "analogical" mode of representation defended by Descartes. No words, as indicative and plastic as they may be, can make a man, who has never experienced light, understand the word. "And therefore, should Des Cartes's globules strike never so long on the retina of a man who was blind by *gutta serena,* he would thereby never have any idea of light, or anything approaching it, though he understood never so well what little globules were, and what striking on another body was."[11] From what has been said so far, it is clear that the figure of the "blind man" that was to haunt eighteenth-century philosophy is far from being the same as the one found in Descartes's philosophy. Yet, in the light of Lacan's developments concerning the "scopic register," it will appear that there is a certain logic that is shared by the two apparently contradictory approaches.

Suppose a Man Born Blind . . .

Suppose a man *born* blind, and now adult, and taught by his touch to distinguish between a cube and a sphere of the same metal, and nighly of the same bigness, so as to tell, when he felt one and the other, which is the cube, which is the sphere. Suppose then the cube and sphere placed on a table, and the blind man be made to see: *quoere,* whether *by his sight, before he touched them,* he could now distinguish and tell which is the globe, which the cube?

This quotation from Molyneaux's letter to Locke, together with various answers, is to be found, among others, in Locke (*The Essay*), Berkeley (*An Essay towards a New Theory of Vision*), Leibniz (*Nouveaux essais sur l'entendement humain*), Diderot (*Lettre sur les aveugles*), and Condillac (*Traité des sensations*). The question posed by Molyneaux was one of *the* questions of the time.

Let us start with the basic dilemma of Locke's philosophy. Locke succeeded in *acquiring* everything but the value of the truth of this everything. In other words, how are we (as readers) to understand his discourse *as true?* The answer is: By making it our own. "I shall appeal to every one's own observation and experience"—this is the key that Locke offers us in order to accept his theory as true.

Yet, we have all been brought up blindly and are ruled by opinion—where are we to seek experience that could be genuinely "ours"? Where are we to look for ideas that are entirely *acquired,* that is, ideas that consist solely of what we ourselves have experienced (or are able to prove true), with no "stain" of something simply given and accepted—where are we to find "prejudice-free ideas"? This proves to be a very difficult task, especially since belief, opinion, and probability—what Locke calls the "twilight state" of human understanding—are directly in the service of survival: "He that will not eat till he has demonstration that it will nourish him; he that will not stir till he infallibly knows the business he goes about will succeed, will have little else to do but sit still and perish."[12] It is apparent that even to survive, we need some knowledge that is nowhere to be grounded. One could say that the existence of a "subject supposed to know," a supposition of the Other who knows, an ungrounded belief, is required already on the level of mere existence.

The problem that prejudices posed to empiricist philosophy is even more neatly articulated and developed by Berkeley in his *Essay towards a New Theory of Vision*. Berkeley radicalizes Locke's problem by showing how experience or perception is not always pure but can be a major source of "prejudice" and wrong conceptions.

Berkeley seems to proceed in quite a "Lacanian" way, starting with a distinction between two essential components of vision, the "immediate" and the "mediate" objects of sight, even though they are, "as it were, most closely twisted, blended, and incorporated together."[13] "Pure sight" has to be distinguished from what comes from other senses—especially the touch—and coestablishes our "field of vision." What I see with the "visible eye" is only a play of light and opacity, of colors, *in myself,* inside my mind. It is the "tangible eye" that informs me of the space, the extension, the distance, the figure, the motions. . . . The play of light and obscurity is the only object of sight and constitutes a class of ideas that are entirely different from "tangible" ideas and from all others that come from other senses. Their combination and connection is only a matter of judgment.

However, ideas coming from different sources are, as noted before, very "closely twisted" and "incorporated together." The prejudice on account of which we say, for instance, that we *see* an object that is *two foot high,* is "confirmed and riveted in our thoughts by a long tract of time, by the use of language, and want of reflection."[14] We are used to perceiving visible figures as marks of tangible figures, and these marks are "constant and universal, their connection with tangible ideas has been learnt at our first entrance into the world." This is "an universal language of the Author of Nature," whereby we are "instructed how to regulate our actions *in order to attain those things that are necessary to the preservation and well-being* of our bodies, as also to avoid whatever may be hurtful and destructive of them."[15]

Thus, as soon as we open our eyes, they suggest ideas of distance, bodies, and tangible figures. So "swift and sudden and unperceived" is the transition from visible to tangible ideas "that we can scarce forbear thinking them equally the immediate object of vision." The prejudice that is grounded on these, and whatever other causes, "sticks so fast that it is impossible without obstinate striving and labour of the mind to get entirely clear of it."

Even from this sketchy presentation of Berkeley's theory of vision, it is clear where the fundamental problem lies: *the prejudice, the first mirage, is situated already on the level of perception that is taken as a natural fact.*[16] This is the point that Molyneaux's question aims at, and this is the place where the question of the blind becomes so relevant for the very principles of philosophy:

> In order to disentangle our minds from whatever prejudices we may entertain with relation to the subject in hand, nothing seems more apposite than the *taking in our thoughts the case of one born blind,* and afterwards, when grown up, made to see. And though, perhaps, it may not be an easy task to divest ourselves entirely of the experience received from sight, so as to be able to put our thoughts exactly in the posture of such a one's, we must, nevertheless, as far as possible, endeavour to frame true conceptions of what might reasonably be supposed to pass in his mind.[17]

A man born blind and afterward made to see would, on first opening his eyes, make a very different judgment of objects "intromitted by them" from what others do. He would not consider ideas of sight with reference to, or as having any connection with, ideas of touch: his view of them would be entirely defined within themselves, it would be a "pure sight." To a man born blind and later made to see, sight would not give any ideas of distance—he would see the most distant objects, as well as the closest ones, as residing in his eye, or more exactly, in his mind. In other words: he would reach the edge, where he could perceive the *purely visual dimension,* without any "alloys" coming from other senses, without any influence of the habit and prejudice resulting from *experience*. This is one of the most interesting points: the experience that is the "trademark" of empiricist philosophy proves to be in itself one of the major sources of prejudice. It is via our experience that ideas of different origins come to be bound together in an "indistinguishable mass." In this context, a man born blind and made to see is "an instrument . . . intended to *produce*—in the same way as we produce in chemistry some pure substances that exist in nature only in the composed form—a pure sensation, i.e., the reverse side of a simple idea."[18] Given that prejudices abound even on the level of elementary perception, a "blind man made to see" is situated somewhere *beyond* perception, language, habit, and experience, in a place that sensualistic philosophy needs in order to claim its own credibility. It is a place where no being can survive a longer period of time, as is clearly stated by Locke and also pointed out by Berkeley.

What is ultimately at stake here can be described as an effort to disentangle the two (Lacanian) triangles, which, once a field of vision is constituted, are always already superimposed. This disentanglement requires that we step beyond the mirror of representations where we see ourselves as constituted egos. This "transgression" is imperative if we are really to "possess" our knowledge (and be more than mere depositories of unsustained opinions), if we are to take responsibility for our experience from the very outset. In order to accomplish this task, the philosopher has to conduct the mental experiment "inside" his understanding. We do not have to experiment on the blind; what we have to do, as Berkeley puts it, is *to take in our thoughts the case of one born blind*, imagine ourselves in his place, "put ourselves in his shoes," and "frame true conceptions of what might reasonably be supposed to pass in his mind."

The Step into Fiction and the "Birth of the Gaze"

I therefore notify that it is very important to put oneself in the place of the statue that we are about to observe. One has to begin to exist with it, and to have but one sense, when it has but one; to acquire but the ideas it acquires, to contract but the habits it contracts: in a word, one has to be but what the statue is. The statue will only judge things the way we do when it has all our senses and all our experience; and we will only judge the way it does if we suppose ourselves to be deprived of everything the statue lacks. I believe that readers who put themselves exactly in the place of this statue, will have no difficulty understanding this work; others will make numerous objections to me. —Condillac, *Traité des sensations*

The story of the blind man traversing philosophy gets a new significant turn with Condillac:[19] it becomes necessary to fabricate some kind of (fictitious) experimental model of the origins.

The model invented by Condillac is that of a statue; a statue internally "organized" just as we are, but covered on the outside with marble and animated by a spirit that induces no ideas in it. The marble that covers the surface of the statue does not allow it to use any of its senses. Condillac reserves for himself the power and "liberty to open them the way we choose to the different impressions to which they are susceptible."[20] Thus, it is the author who will, bit by bit, scrape the marble off the "body" of the statue in order to clear (in different combinations) the way for different senses and observe "what is going to happen."

The entire genesis of understanding is derived from the sensation as *materia prima*, and regulated by the principle of pleasure and pain. Condillac first provides the statue with the sense of smell. If, immediately after this operation, the statue, thus confined to the sense of smell, is presented with a rose, it will be, in relation to ourselves, a statue feeling the smell of a rose; yet, in relation to itself, the statue will be nothing but the very smell of this flower. So the statue exists (for itself) only as this smell, and smells in general are no more for the statue than its own different "modes of being" (*manières d'être*).[21] In other words, the statue finds itself beyond the "mirror of representation," where there are yet no "ego limits." This inaugural step of consciousness, which recognizes in the other its own *manière d'être*, occurs each time we confine the statue to only one sense. According to Condillac, a statue already "equipped" with all senses but that of touch, is still not able to form any idea of the "exterior," the "ego limits," that is, of something not immediately perceived by the statue as a *part of itself*, as its own "mode of being." The four senses together do not provide the statue with any notion of (external) extension, space, distance—there is nothing that would break the "flatness" of its experience. The only way to introduce these ideas is by the sense of touch to which Condillac dedicates an entire part of his book (part 2). Of course, here too things are happening gradually: touch also needs to "evolve" in order for the soul to arrive at ideas of the "outer world." The first step in this "evolution" is the discovery of the statue's own body. The marble is now transformed into skin and if the statue "runs its hand along its arm and, without interruption, to its chest, its head etc., it will feel, so to speak, under its hand a continuity of the *self*; and in this manner the hand . . . will unite in one continuum the parts that were previously separated."[22] Once the body, under the statue's fingers, is composed into a whole and conceived as the "self" [*le moi*], the statue will discern the things that are not part of this "self" by the "absence of reply."[23] Here one sees clearly that it is touch that constitutes the geometral space (of vision) and institutes the subject of representation.

From this point on, Condillac proceeds by adding each of the other senses gradually to the sense of touch. What especially interests us here is the way touch associates with sight. Since light and colors are the only components of the purely visual dimension, the eye needs touch in order to learn the movements proper to sight, to connect its perceptions with the edges of the rays and thus to judge distances, magnitudes, positions, and figures. Here, Condillac introduces an interesting distinction: "The statue doesn't need to learn how to see, but it has to learn how to look. . . . It seems that we don't know that there is a difference between seeing [*voir*] and looking [*regarder*]."[24] The statue doesn't need to learn to see because it sees what there is to *see*: a colored light array. But it has to learn to *look*. What is at stake here is precisely the function of the gaze, which changes the field of vision considerably. The "purely visible" is a realm "inhabited" by the gaze. A statue confined to the sense of sight, with no experience of the touch, sees only the gaze or, more precisely— and insofar as everything outside it is just its own "mode of being"—it sees its own gaze. In other words, the statue sees no*thing*, because what it sees is a part of itself *qua* thing. Now the touch has to teach it how to look, that is, to make it conceive the consciousness of what it sees as a consciousness of something other than itself, of something which is "exterior," which "is seen" outside. The statue, being at first nothing but a part of a net composed of rays and sparkling colors, now emerges as an eye, as the *organ* of sense. The organ replaces and "expels" the gaze, and this "minimal operation" makes the statue see as we do: from now on the statue, as all the other mortals, *has eyes in order not to see.*

It is possible to relate the Condillac's fictitious model to some suggestions made by Lacan in *The Four Fundamental Concepts*. Condillac's mythical presentation of the origins of sight could be compared to the Platonic myth of hermaphrodites "split" by Zeus into two parts, male and female, each condemned restlessly to seek for the other—a myth designed to explain sexual difference and above all the lack of a harmonious relation between the sexes. So, if Plato's myth accounts for Lacan's dictum that "there is no sexual relationship," Condillac undertakes to account for — to fabricate a story that would account for — some of Lacan's other statements. For instance, that subjectivation coincides with alienation (conceptualized by Lacan in terms that have nothing to do with "humanistic" complaints about alienation), with the loss of some (mythical) part of the subject; that this loss is "incarnated" in a privileged object (*objet petit a*) that embodies the lack as such and evokes it by its essentially elusive character; and that it is precisely the gaze that functions as the *objet petit a*. According to Condillac, there is a fundamental "alienation" and loss at the origin of the sight *stricto sensu*. The subject *literally* has to give up, to renounce a major part of him/herself. When the statue was just seeing, had not yet learnt how to look, everything it saw was part of itself. The statue was "one with the universe." But in order to become a subject, to assume a place from which it could say "I" — the place of the subject of representations in Lacan's scheme of vision — the statue had to "cut" itself off, to split off from the rest of the world. From the "thing that sees," the pure gaze, it had to be transformed into a looking subject, and to accomplish this it had to "expel" the thing that is to become "the most precious object," the gaze.

Condillac considers his theoretical conclusions — developed thanks to the fictitious model of the statue — to be provable and objectively verifiable by an actual experiment. This experiment would be an organized operation of the cataract, and Condillac suggests the following procedure:

> A very reliable way of experimenting, so as to dissipate all doubts, would be to enclose the blind person on whom we are about to operate in a glass box. . . . If, as I presume, this man does not see beyond his box, it follows that the space he will recover with his eyes will be less considerable if his box is smaller: it will be one foot, half a foot, large, or even smaller. In this way, we will be sure that he could not have seen the colors [as being] outside his eyes, had the touch not taught him to see them on the edges of his box.[25]

This is the ideal way to reduce and "neutralize" the influence that touch has on sight; the surrounding objects would be, for a man subjected to that treatment, nothing but painted glass, for he could not reach beyond it with his hand. The more we shrink this glass cage, the closer we come to the ideal circumstances of the experiment which tries to "reestablish the state of the statue that had just been given sight. The glass has the rigidity of stone, yet it is transparent. Immobile, covered by the skin of glass, the subject of Condillac's experiment is reduced to a pure sensitive retina, the place where the petrifying man encounters the statue that we are about to animate."[26]

The next step in this direction (that of searching for the mythological "birth of the gaze," for the Origins) was made by Chevalier de Merian in his seminar on the artificially blind.[27] In this seminar, we will find a point that may seem—given the philosophical background of the problem discussed—arbitrary, just a "side product" of the philosophical preoccupation with the blind, yet it is the sort of "side product" that is highly significant in respect to the ideas of the "mainstream production." It is a point of extreme fascination.

The technique suggested by Merian introduces many novelties, by which he tried to remove a difficulty, a major hindrance, that surfaces in the experiments usually suggested. As contemporary physiologists and surgeons pointed out,

> [A] cataract scarcely produces total blindness, and total blindness is not something one recovers from. It follows that these blind persons who have already combined, even though imperfectly, the dim light which they enjoy with the tangible extension, would no longer be able to have, when their eyes were opened, purely visual perceptions with no alloys. The colors and the light that they see *are already outside them, and spread in space, or they are at least outside their eyes*. So that these men are no longer capable of satisfying our interest in purely visible extension.[28]

So Merian suggests an improvement: we should take, he recommends, children out of the cradle and let them grow up in absolute darkness until they reach "the age of reason" (*l'âge de la raison*). Some of them would just be "left to nature," others would get various levels of education, and some would be given the "most excellent education that their state permits."

Let us now examine the part of Merian's text that is a veritable epic dedicated to the moment of "first sight," the transition from the dark into the light, and which merits longer quotation:

> Even if it was a real loss to be deprived of sight during a certain period—will it not be abundantly compensated for? ... What a torrent of delight will flood them, how carried away will they be when we make them pass from night to day, from darkness to light, and when a new universe, a sparkling world opens out for them as from the midst of chaos. Is there anything comparable to such an instant? And life spent in intoxication with pleasure, does it not offer only a pale image of this instant? For, after all, almost all our pleasures are nothing but repetitions.... I imagine them immobile with astonishment at the first impression of light, this magnificent being that has been so far screened from their sight, and at the variegated play of colors that has light for its inexhaustible source. Once they recover from their surprise and begin to move, how many times will they fall; as sight is joined to touch they will see this light and these colors project themselves into the space and illuminate, paint, decorate the earth and the firmament, when little by little they feel the greenery of the fields, the enamel of the prairies, the cheerful empire of Flora *moving out of them, as if created before their eyes,* and in the distance, they will see the woods, the mountains that restrict their view with their pale shades and terminate the horizon.[29]

The first thing that strikes us in this outpour of enthusiasm is the obviously "mediated" nature of fascination, the fact that the person watching a blind man beginning to see is far more fascinated by this scene than is the concerned subject. This is also clear from reports that have been made on this moment of passing from "darkness to the light." Consider the following account from Diderot, concerning a man who had just a cataract removed. Not only was he not in the least fascinated by what he saw, he "even had to be harshly forced to use the sense that had been restored to him; Daviel beat him repeating, 'Will you look, you clumsy oaf! ...' He walked and worked, but everything we do with our eyes open, he did with his eyes closed."[30] The phantasmatic construction of the "seers," the frame into which the "blind man" was placed, is animated by the desire that operates already in Condillac's reduction of a man to a pure sensitive retina: the desire to find some original, primordial instant of the "statue that has been given sight," to *witness* the moment of the "birth of the gaze," the moment of encounter between the subject and the gaze that always escapes us because it takes place at a time, soon after birth, when we are not yet able to be *aware* of it.

This is why, in these writings, we so frequently come across the expression "the age of reason," the supposed stage at which we turn into "beings endowed with reason," that is, capable of rational consciousness. Although this age is purely imaginary (it is never clearly determined), it is a necessary postulate of all the "technology" involved in this kind of experiment. But if the threshold of the "age of reason" is never strictly fixed, things are different with the moment of the "birth of the gaze." It doesn't coincide, as one may think, with the moment when the bandages are removed from the eyes after an operation (or, in Merian's case, with the moment at which the children are allowed to leave their dark quarters). In this theoretical universe, as we could observe in all the discussed authors, the first period of seeing is understood as the time when the subject of the experiment believes all he sees to be "part of himself," to take place "in his own eyes." The interval that separates the "stage of pure sight" (purely visual perceptions) precedes the moment of the "birth of the gaze," which is described as the moment when the subject feels how the light and the visible objects are "leaving him," are "moving out of him," as Merian puts it, and are constituted outside, in *front* of his eyes, as something *other* than himself.

Despite the appearance to the contrary, we are dealing with an evasion of the function of the gaze. Descartes lost from view the dimension of the gaze by focusing his theory of vision solely upon its "geometric" aspect (Berkeley would say, by focusing upon the "tangible eye"). However, the "new philosophy" paradoxically loses the gaze, so to speak, by focusing exclusively upon it. More precisely, the real of the dimension of the gaze is avoided because it is placed on the same level as the "geometral" dimension: it is considered as something *to be seen* (by the subject), whereas—as Lacan has most convincingly shown—the gaze is the point from which the *subject* is seen, the point from which he is *"photo-graphed."*

What was systematically avoided and concealed by all the suggested kinds of experiments, is the traumatic fact that the gaze (of the Other) precedes our seeing and our "being conscious of what we see." There is the construction of a fantasy that aims to "synchronize" what fundamentally cannot be synchronized. The anteriority of the gaze in relation to consciousness is seen as something that could be suspended and synchronized with this consciousness by means of *staging*—in the present or in the future, the hypothetical point of the successful encounter of the gaze and the consciousness—of their mutual recognition. It is apparent that the "original fantasy" is always the fantasy of the origins.[31]

The scenario in Condillac's and Merian's "science fiction" experiments incarnates perfectly what Lacan called *"the window of fantasy."* Its aim is to enable the subject—via the "object" of the experiment (the child, the blind man, or the statue)—to *see himself seeing himself*, to fix, in his own field of vision, the gaze of the Other and to "synchronize" his consciousness with it. Yet this conception still doesn't properly describe and account for everything that is at stake in those experiments. It soon becomes clear, on closer scrutiny, that the respective roles of the "subject" (the philosopher or the scientist) and the "object" (the child, the blind man, or the statue) of the experiment are not only highly ambiguous, but are actually reversed during the experiment. In Condillac, the statue is, so to speak, what represents the subject, the philosopher, within the window of fantasy. We saw how, from Locke on, the locus at which one could perceive *pure sensations* is conceived as a place where no being can survive any length of time. It is the "window of fantasy" that frames this place. Now, the more the "object" of the experiment (the statue, for instance) loses its rigidity, the more the "subject" (the observer) himself becomes rigid, trapped by the sight that he sees, petrified with fascination, chained to his voyeuristic point of view, mesmerized by the fantasy scene that he has himself constructed. To say simply that the blind men and the children are reduced by these "metaphysical experiments" to mere objects would be to miss the point. For what is at stake here is precisely their subjectivation, their emergence *qua* pure subjects. It is the observer who could be said to be reduced to a "mere object," to the (impossible) pure gaze witnessing the subject's own coming into being.

This is most evident in Merian's text. Although all the discussed authors agree on the point that "pure sight" is something that we have always already lost, what we have left behind us somewhere *in the past*, Merian's strategy of attaining this past differs considerably from everybody else's. The main difference lies in what we may call the "acknowledgment of the ideological stakes" involved in such experimenting. If, in other authors, the search for purely visual perceptions is just a way, a means of attaining another, more general and more important goal—to find perceptions not yet influenced by prejudices, opinions, and habits—Merian is a different case. Although he also commends all sorts of useful results that his experiment could bring to the science, he seems to enjoy the suggested experiment for itself. What is more, he makes it clear that the only way of attaining an "unprejudiced" state of mind is to fill the children's heads with all kinds of prejudices ("Since their spirit is, so to speak, in our hands, so that we can knead it like soft wax and develop its knowledge in such succession as we please, we have the possibility of taking every precaution and of varying the experiment in all imaginable ways").[32] In other words, if the children (or any other subjects) know nothing, *we will have learned nothing*. If the experiment is to function, its subject has to know what he should see when first opening his eyes.

So philosophers, following the path inaugurated by Locke, finally reached the point at which, like in the famous Möbius strip, continuing the same path led them to its reverse side, to elaborating all the "seeds" that have to be planted in our souls if we are to discover *pure* perception. Not only Merian but also Diderot comes right to Locke's starting point—on its reverse side:

> I don't understand, I confess, what they expect from a man who has just been subjected to a painful operation on the most sensitive organ.... I would listen with more satisfaction to the theory of the senses coming from a metaphysician, who was familiar with the principles of physics, the elements of mathematics and the conformation of the parts, rather than listen to a man with no education and knowledge, whose sight has been restored by a cataract operation.... If one wanted to give some certitude to these experiments, it would at least be necessary for the subject to be prepared long beforehand, to be educated, and possibly to be made a philosopher.[33]

The Future of an Illusion: Illusion as Transcendental

Thoughts without content are empty, intuitions without concepts are blind.
—Immanuel Kant, *Critique of Pure Reason*

In the second half of the eighteenth century, the figure of the blind man seems slowly to disappear from the stage of philosophy. Yet did it really disappear? Or, more precisely, did the "structural problem" that required its introduction into philosophy simply vanish?

The efforts to find pure perceptions—with no "alloys" coming from (other) senses or understanding—ended in a certain time paradox, in the gap between "not yet" and "no longer," in the missed encounter between the (pure) object and the (pure) subject of knowledge. Either the subject—when first encountering the object—was *not yet* a true (self-conscious) subject, or the object was *no longer* pure but loaded with "alloys." The "blind man" was mobilized in order to fix this elusive point of a "happy encounter."

Immanuel Kant's "Copernican revolution in philosophy" turned upside down the fundamental proposition of this (and not only this) philosophy. From now on, objects are no longer to be seen as the "cause" of a subject's knowledge, it is the subject's "faculty of knowledge" that has to be the "cause" of the objects, that is, that only constitutes them as objects. And yet, even in this new approach, the old problem reemerges, although on a different level. It appears in the form of the relation between intuition and concept, between the originally given manifold of intuition and the unity which can only be provided by a concept.

Kant defines intuition in terms of a *wholly determined representation*, which, as such, includes the infinite multitude of particularities. On the other hand, the concept is a general representation, and consequently determined only in certain aspects (those which concern the characteristics shared by several representations). Intuition contains an infinite number of determinations, whereas a concept is always finite ("nonwhole"). The problem is that the "wholly determined representation" is always already lost for us. Before understanding, with its creative power of giving form to diversity, approaches the intuitions, these are not only *blind*, but utterly "obscure" and actually "nonrepresentative." However, after understanding takes them in hand, the clear representation is no longer intuition, but concept. Insofar as intuitions are really intuitions, they are confused, but once they become clear, they are already concepts (i.e., partially determined finite representations). Intuition can be seen both (1) as a *material* for forming concepts, as something that contains an inexhaustible wealth of particular determinations and will result, after understanding has finished its job, in wholly determined knowledge; and (2) as the *result* of the process of knowledge, whereby all the sensitive material is "transformed" into concept—thus we arrive at the "complete concept"; but acquiring this kind of knowledge is an infinite task, and at this hypothetical point of wholly determined knowledge, the concept loses its universality and coincides with intuition:

> Thus, in a first approach, intuition can be situated at two equally paradoxical points of the process of knowledge: at its starting point, which is always already surpassed, insofar as we are dealing with representations, and at its final point, which can never be reached, insofar as we are human. It is, simultaneously, always already surpassed and never reached.[34]

In relation to knowledge, intuition functions as a potential aid to complete determination. However, a concept, as long as it remains a concept, cannot be completely determined but remains general. *Understanding* handles such concepts, but has to pay the price of loosening the tie with the thing itself (not the thing in itself, the noumenon, but the thing in its complete determination and infinity of particular features). This is where the other direction of the process of knowledge starts, the one that is the domain of *reason*. The always already lost singularity and complete determination are replaced by something else: the "complete concept" becomes the "idea" or the "ideal" of reason that requires the representations to be wholly determined—adding "in thought," as it were, the missing part: "The complete determination is thus a concept, which, in its totality, can never be exhibited *in concreto*. It is based upon an idea, which has its seat solely in the faculty of reason—the faculty which prescribes to the understanding the rule of its complete employment."[35] One could say that, in a very specific sense, Kant's theory of transcendental ideas (along with his discussion of "transcendental illusion") deals with the same "structural problem" as the figure of the blind man in the philosophy of his predecessors. It provides an answer to the "time loop" involved in the emergence of consciousness; it tackles the problem of the *always already lost part of the object*—the part that has to be lost if the object is to be constituted as object (for the subject).

Although Kant's solution of this problem differs considerably from what has just been discussed, they nevertheless have one common feature: Kant accompanies his conceptualizations with the constant use of metaphors explicitly referred to an "optical context" and which establish an analogy between transcendental ideals and laws that govern the logic of the scopic field.

Let us now examine one of the transcendental ideas, that related to the *paralogism of personality*. This "idea" is especially interesting since it involves a situation in which the object that was lost at its constitution is the subject himself. According to Kant, a subject can only appear to himself as an object of the inner sense. The subject's relation to himself does not allow any "shortcut," is of the same nature as the subject's relation to all other objects.

In his *Opus postumum*, in the section dealing with transcendental ideas, Kant reminds us that "person also means a mask."[36] This etymological link is also pointed out by Lacan in his "Remarks on the report by Daniel Lagache: 'Psychoanalysis and structure of personality.'" Lacan stresses that there is more than an etymological play involved: "What is at stake is the evocation of the ambiguity of the process in which the concept came to embody a unity that is supposed to assert itself in the being [*être*]."[37] It is difficult to overlook the Kantian echo of these words, which describe in their own way precisely the notion of the transcendental idea: a *concept* that embodies a *unity* that is *as if* it existed in the being.

What does the paralogism of personality consist of? Kant formulates it as follows: *That which is conscious of the numerical identity of itself at different times is insofar a person.* It is important to stress that this paralogism is part of what Kant calls "illusion" [*Schein*] but is nevertheless an "inevitable" and "necessary" conclusion of reason. In other words, the "inference" [*Schluss*] about personality is a "spontaneous ideology" of the thinking subject.

According to Kant's critique of this paralogism, the conclusion about our identity amounts to this: in the whole time in which I am conscious of myself, I am conscious of this time as belonging to the unity of myself; and "it comes to the same whether I say that this whole time is in me, as individual unity, or that I am to be found as numerically identical in all this time."[38] The point is, I cannot think one without the other. But if I want to observe the mere "I" in the change of all representations, I have no other *correlatum* to use in my comparisons except again myself. The identity of the consciousness of myself at different times is only a formal condition of my thoughts and their coherence (transcendental identity of apperception), and "identity of person in nowise follows from the [logical] identity of the 'I.'"[39] Of course, it would be a different matter if this identity could appear and be seen "outside," in the form of the "outer sense," but this is not the case, even if we introduce a second "person":

> But if I view myself from the standpoint of another person (as object of his outer intuition), it is this outer observer who first represents *me in time,* for in the apperception *time* is represented, strictly speaking, only *in me.* Although he admits, therefore, the "I", which accompanies, and indeed with complete identity, all representations at all times in *my* consciousness, he will draw no inference from this to the objective permanence of myself. For just as the time in which the observer sets me is not the time of my own but of his sensibility, so the identity which is necessarily bound up with my consciousness is not therefore bound up with his, that is, with the consciousness which contains the outer intuition of my subject.[40]

To put it simply: the fact that somebody else views me as an object of his outer intuition does not permit me yet to draw a conclusion about my identity. This inference would only be possible in a case in which I were able to put *myself* in the very place from which I am being observed, if *I* were able to view myself *at the same time* as object of inner and outer intuition, that is, if *I* were able to *see myself the way the other sees me.*

Thus we have arrived, on the one hand, at the Lacanian conceptualization of the ego-ideal as "the way I see the Other seeing me,"[41] and, on the other hand, at the transcendental idea which corresponds to the paralogism of personality.

It should be pointed out, however, that this constellation is not confined just to "psychological ideas," but is—at least in one aspect— paradigmatic for transcendental ideas in general. Whenever Kant speaks about transcendental ideas in general he does so by using some "optical metaphors" that describe precisely the discussed configuration. Transcendental ideas all express a certain relationship between understanding and reason. The creation of concepts and series of concepts on the one hand, and the ordering and uniting of these concepts on the other, are two distinct tasks distributed between understanding and reason. Understanding is absorbed in the creation of concepts and therefore never has *in view* (the expression is Kant's) their totality, it escapes its sight. The totality can only be seen from the "point of view" of reason.

Yet, if the standpoint of reason is to have any impact on the process of knowledge (as it always has, although only in a "regulative form"), this conception of two mutually exclusive "points of view" is not sufficient. On the contrary, understanding has to perform its job as if it shared, "with one of its eyes," the point of view of reason. If reason is to have any impact on the work of understanding—via transcendental ideas as "regulative principles"—the transcendental idea in its most general sense can be nothing but the *way understanding sees itself being seen by reason*. Consider the following passage from the chapter "The Regulative Employment of the Ideas of Pure Reason":

> [Transcendental ideas] have an excellent, and indeed indispensably necessary, regulative employment, namely, that of directing the understanding towards a certain goal upon which the routes marked out by its rules converge, as upon their point of intersection. This point is indeed a mere idea, a *focus imaginarius*, from which, since it lies quite outside the bounds of possible experience, the concepts of the understanding do not in reality proceed; none the less it serves to give to these concepts the greatest possible unity combined with the greatest possible extension. Hence arises the illusion that the lines have their source in a real object lying outside the field of empirically possible knowledge—just as objects reflected in a mirror are seen as behind it. Nevertheless this illusion is indispensably necessary if, . . . besides the objects which lie before our eyes, we are also to see those which lie at a distance behind our back.[42]

Is there any better way of conceiving the situation described by Kant than to refer it to the famous Lacan's optical device? It is a contraption that Lacan borrowed from Bouasse, with some modifications, and used on several occasions to illustrate some of his concepts (the difference between ideal ego and ego-ideal and the passage from the imaginary to the symbolic) (see figure 3). Let us first examine the left part of the scheme, the section on the left side of the flat mirror (O). There is a spherical mirror (x, y) in front of which a prop is placed with flowers fixed on it. Given that this schema could be seen as a purely conceptual model, it is possible to substitute the flowers with what interests us in the present discussion. Let us imagine that the flowers stand for a series of concepts created by understanding or for the assemblage of the multiple "I thinks" that accompany (in different times) each of my representations.

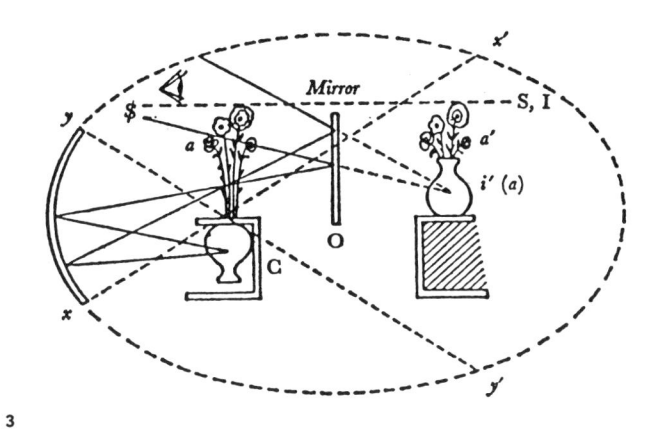

Inside the prop there is a vase turned upside down, that is, the "nothing with something around" that is not a bad representation of what Kant calls the transcendental unity of apperception, insofar as it is only formal or logical. It is the unity, the one thought that I can never "see" as an independent thought, because everything that I think, I think "through" it, and it can therefore never be an object of my immediate consideration. If one were to place an observer (ourselves, for instance) in the right upper corner of this half of the scheme (i.e., somewhere above the flat mirror), the vase would appear, by the effect of the spherical mirror, on the prop and unite the flowers in a "whole," providing a totality for the series of concepts, make a "real" unity out of the logical unity of our self. According to both Kant and Lacan, this configuration is at work in the Cartesian foundation of *cogito*. However, the problem lies in the very fact that neither Lacanian nor Kantian subject can occupy the position of such an ideal observer (of oneself). As a subject, I am necessarily situated "somewhere among the flowers" (Lacan), I am a part of what the spherical mirror unites in a totality. In Kant, the reason for this is of course that he admits no "intellectual intuition": I cannot "contemplate myself contemplating myself."

Now we introduce a second (this time a flat) mirror (O), which opens up the "virtual space," the right part of the scheme. What happens with this intervention? Although I, the subject, still find myself "somewhere among the flowers," I now see before me what always stands behind my back (the totality of myself included). I can now see in the flat mirror the "coherence" and "unity" that are an effect of the spherical mirror. Or, to return to the problem of the complete determination of the concept: what is always already behind me, the part of the object that is necessarily lost when the subject of knowledge approaches it, now appears projected before the subject, as if it could be reached in the future elaboration of the object. It is with this "projected unity" (Kant) in view that the subject has to put to use his faculties of knowledge (according to regulative principles).

In other words, what happens with the intervention of the second mirror is precisely what Kant describes ("Hence arises the illusion that the lines have their source in a real object lying outside the field of empirically possible knowledge—just as objects reflected in a mirror are seen as behind it"). The "I think" as a pure form of transcendental apperception transforms itself—via the notion of personality implied by this configuration—into an identity which appears *as if* it were asserted in the being.

In order for this "illusion," as Kant calls it, to occur, the subject has to be situated between two mirrors in such a way that he discerns in the second mirror the "effect" he (or any other object) has on the first one, the one that is situated behind his back. The function of the transcendental idea is to give frame to this configuration. In the case of the idea of personality it embodies the virtual point from which the subject would see himself as he/she is seen by the other. Analogically, on a more general level, the transcendental idea articulates the relationship between understanding and reason. It is, as already mentioned, the way understanding sees itself as seen by reason.

Lacan's scheme, which we used here in relation to Kant, can also be seen as an elaboration of the scheme of vision composed of two superimposed triangles. This elaborated scheme demonstrates clearly how the "subject of representation" turns himself into a picture under the gaze (of the Other). Thus, strictly speaking, the geometric dimension and its corresponding illusion of consciousness seeing itself seeing itself is not prior to the appearance of the gaze but, on the contrary, its effect. Yet, in order for this "illusion" to function, the subject has to be blind to the object in the very core of his subjective identity. Berkeley's suggestion that we should "take in our thoughts [the case of] one born blind" is, so to speak, the always already realized "ontological condition" of the thinking subject.

Notes

All English translations have been done by the author, with the exception of those cited in the notes.

1. See René Descartes, "La Dioptrique," in *Discours de la méthode* (edition includes extracts from *La Dioptrique, Les Météors, Baillet's Vie de Descartes, Le Monde, L'Homme*, and letters) (Paris: Garnier-Flammarion, 1966), 101, 102.
2. See chapters 6-9 in Jacques Lacan, *The Four Fundamental Concepts of Psycho-Analysis*, trans. Alan Sheridan (Harmondsworth: Penguin Books, 1979).
3. Cf. ibid., 106.
4. Ibid., 93.
5. Ibid., 73.
6. Ibid., 144.
7. See Alain Grosrichard, "Une Expérience psychologique au dix-huitième siècle," in *Cahiers pour l'Analyse* 1-2 (Paris: Seuil, 1966), 104.
8. John Locke, *An Essay Concerning Human Understanding* (New York: Dover, 1959), vol. 1, 211.
9. Ibid., vol. 1, 40.
10. Grosrichard, "Une Expérience," 105.
11. Locke, *Essay*, vol. 2, 37.
12. Ibid., vol. 2, 360.
13. See George Berkeley, "An Essay towards a New Theory of Vision," in *Philosophical Works* (Totowa: Rowman and Littlefield, 1975), par. 50-51.
14. Ibid., par. 51.
15. Ibid., par. 147. Underlined by A.Z.
16. Cf. Grosrichard, "Une Expérience," 106.
17. Berkeley, "Essay," par. 92.
18. Grosrichard, "Une Expérience," 107.
19. When, in 1728, Boullier declares that animals, too, have souls, he bases his conclusion on the analogical structure of human and animal bodies. "In certain aspects," Boullier adds, "animals are everything that man is," and thus, by crediting animals with a certain level of the human, he marks out the limit of the realm that reflective analysis can no longer attain: the realm of the "sensitive soul," as distinguished from the "reasonable soul" which is only given to man. The experiment *inside the understanding* thus loses its justification. From now on an opacity makes it impossible for understanding, experimenting about its own origins, to carry out the analysis all the way to simple elements. Faced with this opacity now threatening the kingdom of understanding "from the inside," philosophy invented a new technique that would make possible an equivalent of Molyneaux's experiment inside the understanding. Cf. Grosrichard, "Une Expérience," 109-10.
20. Etienne Bonnot, abbé de Condillac, *Traité des sensations: Traité des animaux* (Paris: Fayard, 1987), 11.
21. Cf. ibid., 15.
22. Ibid., 104.

23 "So far as the statue places its hand only on itself, it is, in this respect, as if the statue were everything there is. But if it touches a strange body, the ego [*le moi*], which feels modified in the hand, doesn't feel modified in this body. If the hand says *me*, it does not receive the same reply. This way the statue judges its modes of being as existing entirely outside itself. In the same way it formed its own body, the statue forms all other objects. The sensation of solidity that gave them consistency in the first case endows them with it also in the other case; the difference being that the ego that replied to itself no longer replies." Ibid., 105.
24 Ibid., 170.
25 Ibid., 204.
26 Grosrichard, "Une Expérience," 112.
27 Chevalier de Merian, "Histoire de problème de Molyneaux" (Huitième mémoire), in *Cahiers pour l'Analyse* 1-2 (Paris: Seuil, 1966).
28 Ibid., 118, underlined by A.Z.
29 Ibid., 122-23, underlined by A.Z.
30 Denis Diderot, "Additions à la lettre sur les aveugles," in *Oeuvres philosophiques* (Paris: Garnier, 1961), 153.
31 As to interpretation of this point, see the chapter "The 'Missing Link' of Ideology" in Slavoj Žižek, *For They Know Not What They Do* (London: Verso, 1991).
32 Merian, "Histoire," 119.
33 Diderot, "Lettre sur les aveugles," in *Oeuvres philosophiques*, 126-27.
34 Zdravko Kobe, "Mesto nezavednega v transcendentalnem idealizmu," in *Filozofija skoz psihoanalizo* 7 (Ljubljana: Analecta, 1993), 197.
35 Immanuel Kant, *Critique of Pure Reason*, trans. Norman Kemp Smith (London: Macmillan, 1992), B601.
36 Immanuel Kant, *Gesammelte Schriften* (Akademie-Ausgabe), vol. 21 (Berlin: Walter de Gruyter, 1936), 142.
37 Jacques Lacan, "Remarque sur le rapport de Daniel Lagache: 'Psychanalyse et structure de la personalité,'" in *Écrits* (Paris: Seuil, 1966), 671.
38 Immanuel Kant, *Critique*, A362.
39 Ibid., A365.
40 Ibid., A362-63.
41 For an elaborate interpretation of the ego-ideal, see Slavoj Žižek, *For They Know Not*, 11-16.
42 Immanuel Kant, *Critique*, A644-45/B672-73.

Elisabeth Bronfen

3
Killing Gazes,
Killing in the Gaze:
On Michael Powell's
Peeping Tom

As regards the eye, we are in the habit of translating the obscure psychical processes concerned in the repression of sexual scopophilia and in the development of the psychogenic disturbance of vision as though a punishing voice was speaking from within the subject, and saying: "Because you sought to misuse your organ of sight for evil sensual pleasures, it is fitting that you should not see anything at all any more", and as though it was in this way approving the outcome of the process. The idea of talion punishment is involved in this, and in fact our explanation of psychogenic visual disturbance coincides with what is suggested by myths and legends. The beautiful legend of Lady Godiva tells how all the town's inhabitants hid behind their shuttered windows, so as to make easier the lady's task of riding naked through the streets in broad daylight, and how the only man who peeped through the shutters at her revealed loveliness was punished by going blind.—Sigmund Freud, 1910

In classical psychoanalysis, scopophilia, that is, sexual stimulation or satisfaction through gazing or exposing oneself to the gaze of another, is considered one of the primary perversions. It consists in a deviation from the so-called normal sexual act, which is to say, from "coitus with a person of the opposite sex directed towards the achievement of orgasm by means of genital penetration" (Laplanche and Pontalis 1973, 306). Implicitly referring to the writings of Sigmund Freud, the psychoanalyst in Michael Powell's film *Peeping Tom* (1960), who has been called to a crime scene where the body of a murdered woman has been found, describes this reversal of "normal" sexual desire contained within voyeurism as "the morbid urge to gaze." What is so to speak turned the wrong way, twisted, in the behavior of the peeping Tom, who in an old English legend is punished with blindness for his scopophilia, is the fact that his gaze lingers over the activities preparatory to sex, turning them into new sexual aims that can take the place of the normal one (Freud 1905, 156). The act of gazing, meant to be traversed rapidly as the subject moves on in his or her trajectory toward the final aim of sexual activity, namely coitus, is itself transformed into the aim of sexual activity, with sexual satisfaction gained exclusively from this act of gazing. Freud, however, distinguishes between the perversion of gazing and the normal act of lingering over "the intermediate sexual aim of looking that has a sexual tinge to it." The latter, he suggests, "offers . . . a possibility of directing some proportion of . . . libido on to higher artistic aims" (Freud 1905, 55ff.). Specific to the former, to perverse gazing, is the fact that it limits itself exclusively to one part of the body and that it involves surmounting a sense of disgust. Above all, far from preparing for the normal aim of sexual activity, perverse gazing represses this aim. For the scopophile or the exhibitionist, the eye corresponds to an erogenous zone, emerging as a surrogate for the genitals. Gazing takes the place of touching, indeed becomes an independent process, acting on its own, leading to a twisted form of penetrating the other—in Powell's *Peeping Tom,* to a penetration of the other by virtue of gazing or/and to penetration with a murderous knife that stands in for the male sexual organ.

Apodictically speaking, perversion arises with people whose desires "behave exactly like sexual ones but who at the same time entirely disregard the sexual organs or their normal use" (Freud 1940, 152). To this definition Freud, however, adds that the urge to gaze and to be gazed at can be present in two versions, namely as an active and sadistic (masculine) desire to gaze and a passive, masochistic (feminine) one "from the former of which curiosity branches off later on and from the latter the impulsion to artistic and theatrical display" (Freud 1909a, 44).

The Self-Sufficient Gaze: Whore, Pinup, Stand-in

It is precisely this curious meshing of an urge to gaze and an urge to inflict pain that emerges as the structuring principle in Michael Powell's story of the focus-puller Mark, who suffers from having to film everything he sees. Because of this psychosis, he perceives the world either through the intermediary agency of his camera's viewfinder or as a cinematic duplication, projected onto his private screen in the darkroom adjacent to his living quarters. This psychic disturbance, however, turns out to be fatal because he is working on a documentary film about death anxiety. While he at first chooses to depict three beautiful women who offer themselves willingly to the gaze of the voyeur, he ultimately discovers that he can fulfill his cruel *Gesamtkunstwerk* only by turning to his own dying body. In his effort to fix death into an image, that is to say, to capture an image of the fleeting moment of death, by photographing female faces that are marked by death anxiety just before death sets in, Mark takes the cliché that the gaze can kill literally. He lives a very particular version of scopophilia; not the clinically more common urge to see naked the feminine body that the pervert has invested with his twisted sexual desire (Freud 1909b, 163), as his customers desire to do, for example, when they buy the "views" Mark takes in the studio on the second floor of the tobacco store where these pornographic photographs are clandestinely sold. Rather, his perverse fantasy, tinged with a sense of disgust, performing the gesture of exposure as disclosure, consists in observing through the lens of sexuality the anxiety of death shared by every human being. His aim is to capture this insight into the deepest realm of human existence in the form of a sight, a cinematic view. Imitating his professional activity at the film studio, he tries in his spare time to focus the experience of death, which for the living person invariably exists only as a presentiment of death. One can, therefore, speak of Mark's effort at documentary filmmaking as a perverse form of focus-pulling, of focus turned the wrong way—from sexuality to mortality.

In order to set the mood for the role she is to play in his documentary film, he describes to one of his victims, the stand-in Vivian, the scenario he has thought up for this fatal project: "Imagine a man coming towards you, who wants to kill you regardless of consequences . . . a mad man, but he knows it and you don't, and just to kill you isn't enough for him." He then proceeds to show her that a spike is hidden in one of the legs of his tripod, adding, "but there is something else." Significantly, Mark can only *show* Vivian this "something else," this surplus that marks what is specifically perverse about his documentary project. He can *find words* for this twisted attachment only once he is forced to confront a woman he could love instead of his camera. This woman is Helen. Because she insists that he give her answers to the images of horror she has seen on

1

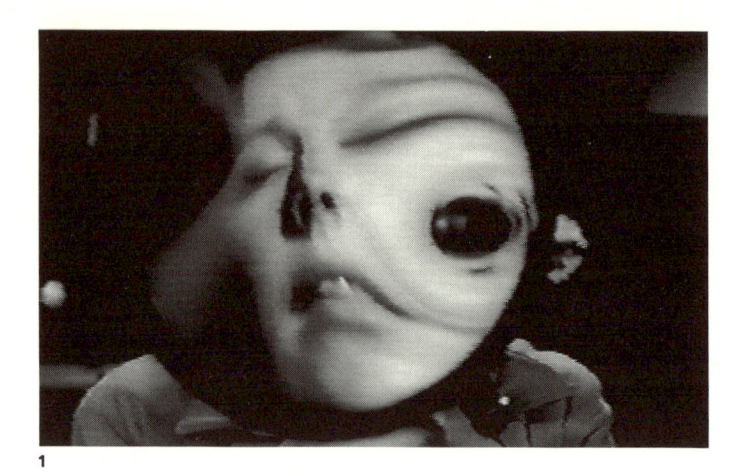

the screen of his private cinema, he offers her the following explanation: "Do you know what the most frightening thing in the world is? It's fear. So I did something very simple." Having then proceeded to show her the convex mirror he has mounted on one side of his camera (photo 1), he concludes, "When they felt the spike touching their throat and knew I was going to kill them, I made them watch their own deaths. I made them see their own terror as the spike went in. And if death has a face, they saw that too."

Mark's particular perversion thus consists not only in his tarrying with the gaze, in his sexualization of the gaze, just as it doesn't only refer to the transformation of gazing into killing. Rather, what makes his perversion specific is above all the significant addition of a relay of gazes, where the victims of murder are forced to watch themselves in the act of being killed. The beautiful women who were so willing to cede themselves to the gaze of the voyeur are themselves forced into the voyeuristic position. As a result, the figure of voyeurism, once it has turned the wrong way, breaks down completely, given that observing the other as a version of oneself and observing oneself as a version of the other are gestures that collapse into each other. Of course, by staging this scenario, Michael Powell also self-consciously questions his own activity as filmmaker. For the implication is that he and his audience are caught, at least in a figural sense, in a similarly perverse relay of gazes. In any act of filming—so runs Powell's self-critical message—death is at stake.

For even if the intention is not explicitly murderous, the depicted body is always framed, transformed into a deanimated body, an absent body that is made present again by virtue of a substitute, the image.

At the beginning of the film we see a closed eye that suddenly opens in horror, then a prostitute, standing in front of a shop window, apparently waiting for her next customer. A man approaches her, filming her as he walks up to her. His camera is hidden under his coat, just above his hip. From the moment he catches sight of her, we will see the prostitute only as the chosen object of his gaze, to be precise, we will see her only through a mediated gaze, namely through the viewfinder of his camera. This field of vision, in which the woman has figuratively been caught only to be deanimated into an image, is, furthermore, partitioned into four parts and a central point by the black cross that structures the viewfinder. The camera crops the empirical world, determines the distance to the gazed-at body, chooses the detail it wishes to focus on; it repeatedly shifts from her back to her legs, her feet, and then to her face. Crucial, however, is the fact that the camera will now no longer allow the woman to escape from its field of vision. In a sense, the woman has already been figurally nailed to the cross of the viewfinder, even though she is still apparently moving, undulating across the street, entering a door, and beckoning her customer to follow her, climbing the stairs to her room in the uppermost floor of the building.

This act of gazing, with which we are from the beginning of the film complicitous, is, however, not the disinterested gaze of the cineast. Only in the course of the film will we discover that the woman, caught in this activity of gazing, is part of a documentary film that self-reflexively refers to its own process of re-presenting absent bodies on celluloid. Through the viewfinder we see the man commenting on his perverse activity, given that he also films himself throwing away the wrapping of his film cartridges. Such explicit reference to the act of filming marks a break in the conventional mode of commercial cinematic language, which traditionally avoids as far as possible drawing attention to its own medium of representation (Bordwell and Thompson 1979). What we then see is the woman, consciously giving herself up to the gaze of her client, undressing, lying on her bed. She explicitly stages her body as a commodity meant to satisfy the customer. What this woman doesn't, however, know is that in addition to giving herself as a prostitute, she

2

is also offering herself to the gaze of the filming pervert. A small additional element, a supplement, the ominous "something else," suddenly appears in the guise of a light reflection above her head. Her gaze is now no longer marked with the boredom of routine, rather it signifies horror. The camera, armed with its fatal attachments, the hidden knife and the mirror that the film audience has not yet seen, approaches the figure of the prostrate prostitute. The reversal of normal sexual penetration ends in a scream. We see her face distorted in anguish, disgust, and fright (photo 2).

The conventional situation of exchange implied by prostitution has been markedly transformed. The prostitute no longer controls the gaze of her client, rather, his gaze masters her. Gazing has now quite literally become the act of taking possession. We, the audience, are as confined as the gazed-at woman, like her reduced to the field of vision offered by Mark's viewfinder. At the climax of each rendition of the scene of murder, Michael Powell chooses to cut just before the spike concealed in the leg of the tripod is about to penetrate the neck of the victim, so that it is precisely in and through this cinematic cut that what cannot be shown—death and the fear of death—occurs. As such, the sought-for image of death comes to be articulated precisely as an ellipsis. After the cut, ending with an image of the prostitute's scream, Powell presents a repetition of the scene, its field of vision similarly confined. As the opening title and credits move across the screen, we see the filmmaker Mark,

3

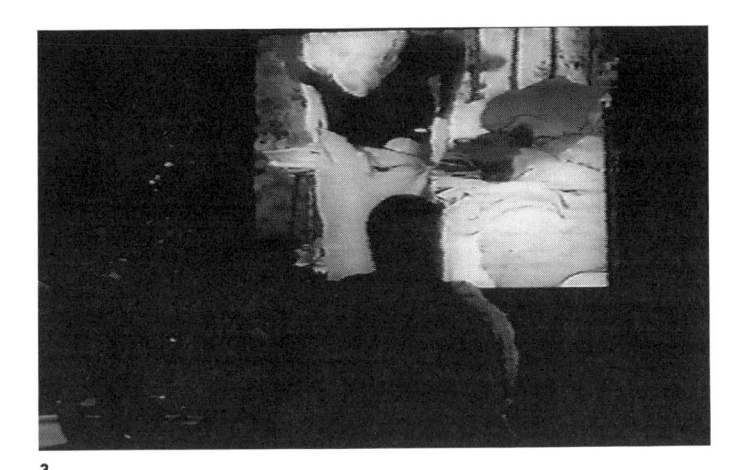

watching the previous scene on the screen of his private cinema, now significantly without the cross in the viewfinder (photo 3).

Projected onto a screen, the scene of murder appears even more mediated than it did seen through Mark's viewfinder, yet at the same time, this second rendition exposes an uncanny paradox. What follows upon the literally killing gaze of the camera is a resurrection of the dead woman. On the screen, the murdered prostitute is once again alive, and as a figure in a film, she can repeat endlessly the gestures of the previous scene—undressing for her client, suddenly emitting her scream of horror, her terrified eyes anticipating death. The represented death is double, therein lies the deconstruction offered by Powell's film. The prostitute is dead in a figural sense, because she is bodily absent and only present as an image. But she is also dead in a real sense, because she has been stabbed to death with the attachment on Mark's camera. The exchange between gazing and killing thus traces the following trajectory: An act of gazing that kills its object in a figural sense by turning its victim's body into a commodity, leads to real death, but is superseded, in turn, by a gaze whose point of departure is this real death, only to arrest death in an endless play of visual doublings.

This first murderous film sequence is given a narrative resolution. Mark films the policemen, carrying the prostitute's corpse out of her apartment building. In part we see this corpse once again through the cross in his camera's viewfinder and are thus again bound to his gaze.

In part, however, we also see this corpse through the gaze of a third party, the implied filmmaker Michael Powell himself, who waits until this moment to establish a narrative distance between himself and his perverse double. In other words, Powell points to the difference between his and Mark's gazing and filming activity only after a complicity with this twisted act of filming has unmistakably been established. For it is only at this moment that Powell shows Mark for the first time from an external point of view, that is to say, shows Mark while he is filming quasi-objectively rather than through the initially employed technique of the subjective camera.

In order to describe the aporia inherent in any relationship between representation and death, Michel Foucault coined the resilient metaphor of a mirror reflecting to infinity and erected against death. He explains, "[B]efore the imminence of death, language rushes forth, but it also starts again, tells of itself . . . headed toward death, language turns back upon itself; it encounters something like a mirror; and to stop this death which would stop it, it possesses but a single power: that of giving birth to its own image in a play of mirrors that has no limits. From the depths of the mirror where it sets out to arrive anew at the point where it started (at death) but so as finally to escape death, another language can be heard—the image of actual language, but as a miniscule, interior, and virtual model" (Foucault 1963, 54).

To a certain degree Michael Powell already deconstructs *avant la lettre* what Foucault proclaims rather euphorically as the virtual power of self-reflexive poetic language. For Powell uses the murder scenes of the three beautiful women that Mark has chosen as the objects for his perverse documentary, to depict what might be the logical consequence of a cinematic language that represents itself on the border of death. Representing at the point of death invariably entails an aporetic gesture. Mark's perverse attempt to arrest and capture the moment of killing in cinematic language, circumventing death even as his production of images feeds on death, proves to be a dangerous repetition and doubling compulsion. For Powell, the other possible cinematic language, emerging from a play of reflections at the border to death, is that of evasive withdrawal but also of duplication. On the one hand, Mark is forced to repeat incessantly his fatal filmmaking, given that his images of death bring him to the border of cinematic language, only to strike back without allowing him to transgress this border. "The lights," he explains, "fade too soon." At least on the diegetic level of the film, this failure calls for real victims. On the other hand, Powell himself can only partially withdraw from this fatal circuit. For his *Peeping Tom* develops precisely that other language emerging within a virtual space, which Foucault evokes with his metaphor of a mirror erected on the border of death and against death. However, this productive virtuality of the film, itself profiting from the arrestation and fixation of death, is staged as a self-critical doubling of the depicted killings.

In the middle of the film a second murder takes place. One evening after work, Mark and the stand-in Vivian decide to stay at the locked studio they both work for, fully aware that they are involved in a prohibited activity. They want to make a clandestine screen test of Vivian, so that she can convince the producer Jarvis of her acting talents. Vivian is vain, self-consciously beautifies herself for the shooting, simulates the masculine gaze by skillfully transforming herself into its desired object. But once again a performance of the feminine body, where the woman involved believes she can control and master the masculine gaze, takes the wrong turn and transforms into a scene of utter feminine disempowerment. While Vivian dances, pleased with herself in the guise of a star, indeed, exhibiting endless self-sufficient narcissistic pleasure, Mark scrupulously builds a setting with props, lights up the scene, points his spotlights and his camera onto the woman, and marks the spot where she is to stand with a cross. They even rehearse the postmortal posture. Laughing, Vivian lies down in the suitcase that will later bar her flight from the murderous camera and serve as her coffin (photo 4).

In contrast to the first murder scene, with its fortuitous quality, Mark has calculated every detail of this second attempt to capture the image of death. This time he wants to leave nothing up to chance. "The result," he explains, "must be so perfect that even he . . ." The performance is consciously directed to another spectator, a third subject in the exchange of murderous gazes. But while Vivian explicitly displays her body for the producer Jarvis, Mark implicitly addresses his father. For his documentary about the perfect likeness of the fear of death in fact represents his perverse answer to the research undertaken by his dead father. As a behavioral scientist, the father had attempted to produce as complete as possible a documentation of the life of a child—Mark—

68   Bronfen

4

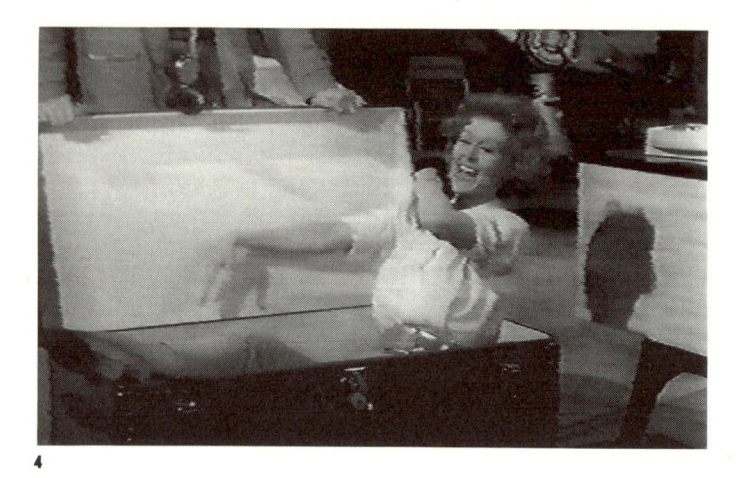

growing up. Because of the double address of the staged scene—Jarvis and the dead father—Mark requires two cameras; on the one hand, the official camera, which the focus-puller Mark seems to usurp from his boss, and on the other, his own, private, murderous camera. Once again Powell stages a self-reflexive break in the narrative flow. Vivian decides to stand behind the camera of the official "father" while Mark films her doing so with his perverse camera, thus staging a reflection of the relay of camera gazes. He explains, "I'm photographing you photographing me." He then asks Vivian to "stand on your cross," so that she can play her star role, namely the scene of death anxiety, to which Mark must compulsively return again and again. The aporia inherent in his obsession with perfect rendition consists in the fact that for Vivian, simulation transforms into reality. She literally dies of her fear of death. However, a likeness of this fear, its facial expression, can neither be calculated nor caught in the cinematic image. Death appears as expectation and addendum while the actual moment of death recedes from any representation—for Mark, because once again the lights fade too soon, for the film audience owing to the fact the Powell once again ends the scene just before death occurs, with another self-consciously staged cut.

In his desperation, Mark finally falls back on the pinup Milly. In the scenes prior to Vivian's murder, Milly, who modeled for the pornographic views Mark makes in the studio above the tobacco store, had repeatedly given herself quite consciously to his camera, simulating feminine seductiveness, fully aware of her power to transform herself into a desirable image. In the very first photo session, for example, she wishes to use the camera's ability to deceive so as to satisfy her own interests. She asks Mark to obliterate the blue patches on her body, "Can you fix my bruises so they don't show?" Powell thus stages two ways of seeing. The first, a socially sanctioned way of gazing, employs pornographically staged, simulated scenes of eroticism and the artificiality of these images to cover up and beautify real violence, for which Milly's bodily injuries are representative signs. The second way of gazing, with which Powell aligns cinematic language, precisely seeks what is ugly, what disfigures the beautiful surface of the image, so as to disrupt the aesthetic coherence of the film image. This other way of gazing is excluded from any sanctioned economy of viewing and exchanging views. Thus one of the most disturbing ironies of the film consists in the fact that the pornographic gaze, given that it deanimates the feminine body by turning it into an image of masculine desire, reifies this body—either the woman's body (the whore) or the woman's image (the stand-in, the pinup) serves as a commodity. In so doing, the pornographic gaze figurally kills off the feminine body. However, only a sexualized gazing that drops out of the conventionally sanctioned circuit of viewing, namely, the filming of which Mark says "some things I photograph for nothing," actually kills in a literal sense. In the end Milly, too, cannot escape this other cinematic language. At first she is still lying on the bed in the photo studio, lightly dressed. Simulating the pose of a prostitute, she self-sufficiently gazes at Mark and implicitly at us, who at this moment still share Mark's point of view. In the next take, Powell's camera has jumped to the other side of the bed, on which Milly is now lying naked, her gaze still directed toward Mark, who is approaching the bed with his camera. As though Powell wanted to use cinematic language to represent for his audience a transgression about to take place, we now, for the first time, no longer see the image of the victim. Rather, we share the position of the victim, watch with her, as for a split second her murderer approaches her and implicitly us (photo 5).

Freud offers two explanations for why a drive may turn into its opposite, "a change from activity to passivity, and a reversal of its content." This explanation might serve as an answer to the question why the fatal economy of the perverted gaze must at first be played out over

5

the bodies of three feminine victims. "Examples for the first process," Freud argues, "are met with two pairs of opposites: sadism–masochism and scopophilia–exhibitionism. The reversal affects only the *aims* of the instincts. The active aim (to torture, to look at) is replaced by the passive aim (to be tortured, to be looked at). Reversal of *content* is found in the single instance of the transformation of love into hate" (Freud 1915, 127). Mark's choice of three beautiful women as victims of his torturous gaze reveals the complementarity of voyeur and exhibitionist, for only those women that support his fatal economy of gazing can act in his documentary project. At the end of the film, in the final image of Mark's corpse, Powell then stages the complete collapse of the active, masculine scopophilic drive and passive, feminine one.

Mark's perversion, which the film is seeking to deconstruct, consists above all in the fact that a symbolic economy of the gaze (Baudrillard 1976) in which the feminine body is exchanged as image and the image as commodity reverts into the register of the Real once it has reached the border with death. The figural killing inherent to reification actually takes place and thus, in more than one sense, disrupts the so-called normal circuit of exchanged gazes. By transferring the feminine body into a second medium, the cinematic image, in the process of which it is killed twice, Mark hopes to arrest an enigma, namely death. He hopes to expose an image of death in the face of the dying woman. In doing so, however, he also reached the limit of his representational system.

Repeatedly he fails, and repeatedly he is forced to undertake this murderous activity—"the lights fade too soon."

A further explanation for Mark's choice of victims can perhaps be found in the traditional Western cultural economy of gazes, about which John Berger argues that "men act and women appear. Men look at women. Women watch themselves being looked at. The surveyor of woman in herself is male: the surveyed female. Thus she turns herself into an object—and most particularly an object of vision: a sight" (Berger 1972, 47). In *Peeping Tom* the reification Berger refers to becomes an actual event. For the three beautiful women fit into Mark's monstrous *Gesamtkunstwerk* precisely because they are vain, because they consciously simulate the femininity, beauty, and seductiveness addressed to the masculine gaze that Berger speaks about, because they willingly allow themselves to be transformed into an image—for money, but also for fame (Vivian) and embellishment and beautification (Milly, Vivian). For all three, to engage in Mark's perverse economy of gazing means entering into a transgressive space—the dark nocturnal street, the locked film studio at night, the locked room above the tobacco store. They come to serve as such useful material for Mark's project because, to a certain degree, they themselves desire the murderous reification of their bodies into an image. In that sense the actual murder is only a consequent. In these three scenes of murder, the beloved self-image, so narcissistically pleasurable to each woman, becomes literally fatal. These women can and must die, because they are willing to look into the mirror Mark holds up to their horrified and astonished gaze, and there, at the limit of their own reflection, at the vanishing point of their beautiful self-image, they see death. Powell here indirectly refers to the iconography of the vanitas tradition so prevalent in European Baroque art, more precisely to the traditional allegory of vanity, where the man or woman seeking to confirm their immaculate, eternal beauty instead see death reflected in the mirrored image.

These feminine corpses are beautiful, seductive, because they represent a repetition of the false mother. In the home movie of his childhood, which Mark shows to Helen on her birthday, we find the model of all subsequent feminine victims—the second wife of his father, stepping Venus-like out of the waves of the ocean. What above all, however, characterizes these feminine corpses, and what Powell stages as a reversal of the conventional feminine gaze into the mirror, is precisely a disruption of this classical feminine beauty. For the gaze that they give themselves up to in such a fatal manner, once they are forced to look at not the mediating gaze of the man filming them but rather their own gaze, ricocheted back from their mirrored self-image, is an anamorphotic gaze (Lacan 1973). These women are forced to look into a convex mirror, and there they already see death analeptically, insofar as the reflection, meant narcissistically to support their sense of self-sufficiency, already subverts this mirrored rendition, owing to the distorted picture it produces. In a sense, the mirror double figuratively already heralds what the spike, hidden in the leg of the tripod, will perform. In the seconds before the actual killing occurs that will render the distortion in the mirror real, the three women already see their fragmented body.

This uncanny reversal of beauty also remains to haunt the spectators of the dead. The policemen notice that these dead women are different from other corpses owing to the horrified gaze that rigor mortis has frozen onto their faces: "Never seen such fear on anyone's face as on this girl's." Here the epitome of the beautiful, exhibited feminine body—purchasable and frameable—has become radically ugly. The reversed process, which is to say the perverse exchange of gazes Mark initiates, thus traces the following trajectory: all three women give themselves to the masculine gaze, whether this is the bodily eye or the mechanical photo and film lens. Over the bodies of these beautiful corpses the process of deanimation and killing implied by reification becomes literal. However, two aspects disrupt this economy of gazing. First, Mark never achieves the image he is seeking. The perfection of the image meant to bind death into this economy is impossible. Traumatic material can never be fixed completely into an image. A part mercilessly recedes from representation. Secondly, the beautiful corpse wears the face of horror. While the feminine corpse might serve as the perfect rendition of woman fulfilling her function as privileged object of the masculine gaze, the facial expression these dead bodies exhibit disturbs any reassurance they are meant to effect. The turning has not only gone the wrong way, the twist has gone too far, becoming real. But the desired surplus, the "something else" Mark incessantly seeks, nevertheless recedes.

The Rejecting Gaze: Dead Mother, Blind Mother

In contrast to the gaze of the beautiful women, neither the absent gaze of the dead mother nor the dull gaze of Helen's mother, the blind Mrs. Stevens, can be bound into Mark's perverse economy. A scene from one of the documentary films about his childhood (photo 6), which Mark shows to Helen, depicts him taking leave of his dead mother. Significantly, we are shown the full body of the boy as well as the hands of the corpse but never the face of the mother.

Mark fast-forwards the scenes that immediately follow, of her funeral and burial. The next images he is willing to show Helen are of what replaces the mother—his father's new lover exhibiting her beauty during a trip to the beach. On the morning of his honeymoon the father presents his son with the gift of a camera, so that Mark, acting as the paternal representative, may perceive and register his surroundings in an indirect manner, through the viewfinder of this camera. The camera is, of course, also quite explicitly a representative of the paternal eye, reminding the son of the father's law even in his absence. What thus comes to fill the position within Mark's psychic topography that, with the death of the mother, became empty is significantly not the real stepmother, but rather the camera, and connected with it, the paternal gaze. The function of the real stepmother is merely that of witness. She films the exchange of camera from father to son, she is the first to film the son as he begins to film the world.

Mark tries but fails to kill Helen's blind mother and this failed attempt also stages an economy of gazing diametrically opposed to the traditional maternal gaze. Usually the child seeks to draw onto itself the gaze of the mother so as to find itself mirrored there. It uses this image reflection of an intact subject to support its fragile narcissism. Mrs. Stevens cannot, however, satisfy his desire to finish his documentary film about the fear of death precisely because she cannot return a gaze of horror in reaction to the distorted rendition of her face in the convex mirror. Rather, she can reflect back to Mark only a dead gaze (photo 7). She cannot fulfill what Mark projects on the screen in his private cinema before her dull eyes. She cannot double the terror distorting Vivian's face. Her gaze marks precisely the gesture of receding, which Mark repeatedly finds himself confronted with in his effort to film the edge of death.

6

Her gaze signifies a refusal, a lost motion. Perversion, and with it also the murder of a woman, is here arrested because no reversal is possible.

Here, something has gone awry, but what in this case fails is, above all, the psychic state psychoanalysis calls narcissism, namely the fantasy of unity, which the gaze of the mother and its surrogate, the gaze of the beloved, is meant to offer to the subject. For the so-called normal development of the child traces the following trajectory: only after this illusion of plenitude has been attained, in the course of primary narcissism, is a disruption of the imaginary self-image meant to occur, to be more precise, a breaking up of the mother-child dyad through the father, as representative of authority, of the laws of culture and of the consistency of the symbolic. Of course this "intact" image of the self, transmitted through the maternal gaze, already contains an alienating difference, on the one hand, because the reflected image of the self can never be entirely identical with the represented body (Lacan 1966a), and on the other hand, because the image implies the absence of the body (Bronfen 1992). For the "healthy" psychic development of the subject to take place, this fantasy of integrity and unity, along with the difference inherent to it, must be given up. It nevertheless returns in adult life as a means of mitigating the narcissistic wound contingent upon giving up the maternal body, above all in the guise of the constitutive deception and pleasurable illusion of love relationships.

Classical psychoanalysis specifies a second phase of gazing, which is in turn bound to the father. As representative of a third agency, the

7

father teaches the child the castrating prohibitions and laws of culture, even as these prohibitions allow the child to enter the symbolic order. Psychoanalytically speaking, the father symbolically negotiates the renunciation of the maternal body and castration, both of which come to be understood as cultural achievements. Accepting the paternal gaze, the paternal metaphor, as a prohibition of the mother and as a substitute for her gaze (which had transmitted an ambivalent form of plenitude) allows the subject to attain a new, different kind of stability. The authority coterminous with the forbidding gaze of the father renders an inconsistent universe consistent. The imaginary image of the body of plenitude is replaced by an acceptance of the split within the subject, fantasies of complete satisfaction are deferred, boundaries are drawn between body and image, thoughts and their realization. Culture thus comes to mean displacing fantasies of destruction, plenitude, and completion into the realm of signs; for the narrative of *Peeping Tom*, into the realm of science and art. Crucial to the film, however, is not only Powell's deconstruction of the disruption, the perverse reversal of this so-called normal circuit but rather his argument that Mark's perversion results from the fact that the position of the mother was never adequately filled. Owing to this failure, the disruption of the mother-child dyad, which the gaze of the father brings about, occurs at the start because of an empty position. At the same time Mark's primary narcissism is never allowed to develop sufficiently.

Significantly, Helen's blind mother is the only person who has any insight into the danger of Mark's scopophilia. She warns him, "Instinct is a wonderful thing. Pity *it* can't be photographed. If I'd listened to it years ago, I might have kept my sight. I wouldn't have let a man operate I had not faith in. So I'm listening to my instinct, Mark. And it says, all this filming isn't healthy. You need help. Get it Mark." She then forbids him to see Helen again until he has found medical help. Because she is blind, she can recognize the dangers of photographing, even as her loss of sight is what also forbids her to fill the empty position of the mother within Mark's psychic topology, thus making it impossible for her to give him the maternal gaze that would offer a soothing illusion of plentitude. This lack must, therefore, be negotiated elsewhere, namely in the opposition between Mark's private camera and the one potential beloved, Helen.

The Curious Gaze: The Camera, the Beloved

In the confrontation between camera and beloved we find both a continuation and a significant disruption of the paternal project. As already noted, Mark's documentary is the articulation of perversion precisely because it represents a reversed completion of the documentary of a growing child, which his father worked on all his life. Helen is herself working on a book about a magical camera and what it photographs, and this book is a counterproject to the paternal one. Helen, living with her mother as one of the tenants in Mark's house, is established from the start as the one character in the film who seems to move outside Mark's fatal economy of gazing. On her twenty-first birthday she approaches Mark, asking him to join her in her birthday festivities. When he declines, she decides to follow him upstairs to his rooms, disturbing him while he is watching his deathly films, so as to bring him a piece of the birthday cake. She is the one who repeatedly interrupts Mark's perverse gazing. On the evening of her birthday, she not only asks to be let into his darkroom, but, as a kind of birthday gift, she also demands to see his films. Significantly Mark does not show her one of his own documentaries, but one of his father's. That is to say, while he does not show her the symptoms of his perversion, he does display the primal scene of his trauma; not the object of his murderous gaze, killed twice over by the image, but rather his own body as the object of another's gaze and another's film.

This gift implies exchanging positions of gazing. Helen is allowed to share Mark's position of the surveyor, and, with him, she watches the child Mark and the torture that the parental experiment inflicted upon him—the nocturnal blinding, the sudden awakening, and the terror, when, for example, he discovers that a lizard has been thrown onto his bed. In contrast, however, to the beautiful, narcissistically self-sufficient, other women, Helen will not support this economy of gazing. Mark wishes to film her while she is watching this documentary film, so as to place her into the passive position of being the object rather than the subject of surveillance, that is, into the position he so traumatically found himself placed repeatedly during his childhood. Helen, however, rejects this murderous circuit of gazing and image-making, seeking not to duplicate the represented scenario but rather to interrupt it by understanding it. She does not give herself to Mark's camera, indeed, she holds her hand in front of the lens so as to shield herself from its gaze.

Furthermore, while watching these images of early childhood torture, she repeatedly demands explanations, putting into question the propriety and usefulness of the paternal project, until she finally turns off the projector, while Mark is rendered motionless and can only helplessly watch these scenes from his childhood. Her decision to turn off the projector significantly occurs at the point where the father hands over the camera to his son, as he is about to embark on his honeymoon, and where Mark points the lens of this new gift, meant implicitly to be an extension of his childish gaze, at the lens of the paternal camera filming him (photo 8).

In the final scene of *Peeping Tom*, Helen does ultimately watch Mark's murderous documentary film, but she does so alone and in defiance of his prohibition. Furthermore, her gazing brings about his explanatory confession. Also significant for the confrontation between camera and beloved is the fact that at this point in the narrative we see only Helen's reaction to the expression of horror on the faces of the women about to die and to the images of their corpses, but no longer the cinematic images themselves. Powell thus illustrates once more that within Mark's perverse psychic topography, his love objects either fall into the position of women who support his murderous economy of gazing, who allow themselves to be filmed or want to film themselves, or women, like Helen's blind mother, who can still at least partially partake in his

78   Bronfen

8

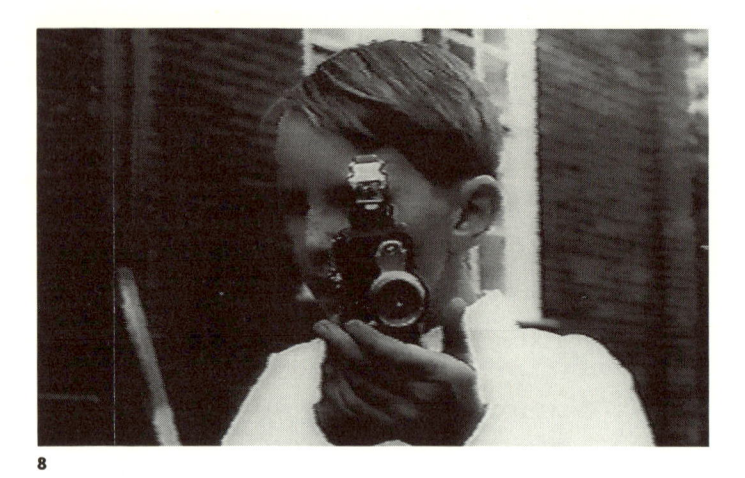

phantasma, and Helen, who radically disrupts this circuit of exchanged gazes.

Her children's book about a magic camera, for which Mark is to take the photographs, is meant as a counterproject, illustrating another, nonmurderous gaze. In her story the camera belongs to a little boy, and the pictures it takes seek to expose the submerged traces of childlike features in the faces of adults. She explains, "It sees grown-ups as they were, when they were children." Her project is thus diametrically opposed to Mark's. Powell stages this contrast as a sequence, where in two separate rooms parts of these two projects are simultaneously developed. While the strips of film representing Mark's horrific images of Vivian's dying are being developed in his darkroom, Helen begins to develop her plans for her children's book speaking to Mark in his living room. The analogy between these two projects consists furthermore in the fact that Helen, too, seeks to capture the remnants of the child in the adult, not, however, like Mark, the traces of childhood trauma, the experiences of fear and despair, but rather the state of happiness and unconditional wonder, covered up in the process of adulthood but never entirely obliterated. In other words, in the physiognomy of the adult, she seeks the traces of primary narcissism, so seminally connected to the maternal gaze. For Helen, retrieving a childlike state in the midst of adulthood does not, therefore, imply a scene where the child, as object of the gaze of the paternal other, is reified and deanimated, as it does for Mark. Rather, it implies a scene where the child is animated by the gaze of the Other.

9

Helen represents the gaze of the Other as one that sustains a supportive intersubjectivity rather than a deanimation of the gazed-at child: Powell stages her in an almost overdetermined manner as a mother surrogate. She lives in the room of the dead mother and milk is repeatedly presented as her attribute. Before she goes out to dinner with Mark, she takes away his camera and locks this rival into her bedroom (i.e., into the maternal room). Once he is without this camera, Mark can entertain a so-called normal relationship to a love object. Having returned to the house with Helen, he can kiss her for the first time. Mark himself articulates this rivalry between camera and beloved when he explains to Helen "It will never see you. . . . Whatever I photograph I always lose." Helen can, therefore, survive the scene of confession precisely because she neither looks into the camera nor into the convex mirror (photo 9). She thus comes to represent an unmitigated gazing, based on presence and meant to disrupt the murderous economy of gazing that feeds upon a play of absence and duplication.

Significant for the argument of the film, however, is the fact that both projects of representation prove to be impossible—Mark's attempt to expose in the facial expression of his victims an image of the fear of death and Helen's attempt to expose in the facial expression of adults those traces that let them look like children. Both representational efforts—the perfect rendition of death and the perfect rendition of happiness—fail, because the empty maternal position can neither be filled with a normal surrogate (Helen as a life-sustaining alternative to Mark's camera) nor with the perverted repetition of this lack (the beautiful women and their fatal relationship to Mark's camera).

What in contradistinction does not fail, and this is what makes Powell's message so disturbing, is that the production of images emerges from paternal authority. Because Mark was always the object of his father's gaze he could not develop a healthy narcissism. By sympathetically presenting us with his story, *Peeping Tom* documents the danger and the pain that arises from a psychic disturbance, scopophilia, that dooms one constantly to gaze at the world, to relate to one's surroundings exclusively by means of gazing. To do so, Powell's film offers an analogy between voyeur and murderer, developing a psychic scenario where the camera takes the place of the beloved and where a murderous relationship to filming that Mark calls "work" occurs in lieu of so-called normal sexual intercourse.

Powell, however, almost more compellingly documents the pain involved in constantly being gazed at and always being conscious of the Other's gaze as well. Perhaps the murders committed by Mark are not the most terrifying acts that *Peeping Tom* illustrates, given that from the start the subjective camera Powell so skillfully uses asks us to have sympathy with his pervert's psychic state. Above all, by choosing to include Helen as a figure of identification for the audience's reaction, Powell makes it quite evident that what is far more disturbing than the murderous acts themselves is the fact that Mark was under constant surveillance by his father, who registered every minute of his son's early years; and, as a result of this primal trauma, Mark has so completely internalized the gaze of the Other that he is compelled to repeatedly watch and listen to these representations of himself. The deadliness of this compulsion to repeat consists in the fact that Mark is, in turn, compelled to include the people he comes in contact with in this circuit of gazes, hoping finally to reach closure. In an effort to put an end to his psychic trauma, one could say, Mark feels compelled to let others, namely beautiful feminine victims, meant to serve as figures of identification for himself, repeatedly perform the primal scene of his trauma, so that he can repeatedly watch his own victimization refracted in the rendition of the victimization of others. For the seminal surplus, the significant "something else," around which this perverse scenario turns is the fact that his victims must watch themselves while they are dying, that is, at the edge of death they meet their own gaze. At precisely this point Powell stages the collapse of active into passive that Freud designated as one of the aims of perversion. According to this logic, both the subject that gazes and the subject that is gazed at will be punished. In the same gesture that Mark seeks to confirm his masculine sadism by sacrificing a feminine, masochistic body, he invariably falls into the passive position himself.

Crucial to Powell's staging of Mark's perversion is the fact that his failure to achieve any sense of narcissictic wholeness, his inability to construct an illusory plenitude within his fantasy world, is contingent upon the fact that from the start of his conscious existence, Mark was forced to include the father as a third element in his self-constructions. In so doing he prematurely entered into the symbolic order, which is to say, before he could distinguish this symbolic realm from the imaginary register he could have negotiated over the maternal gaze. As a result, he perversely inundates the symbolic with imaginary activity. In his perversion he repeats the disruption of the mirror phase, of an intact image of self-identity, concomitant with the maternal gaze (Lacan 1966a), that is, he repeats the fragmentation of his self-image based on paternal intervention precisely by forcing his victims to confront such a fragmented self-image. Thus he can mirror himself in them and thus they reflect back to him his own vulnerability. This perverse circuit can, however, be maintained endlessly. Mark is thus finally forced to recognize that he will never be able to complete his documentary project as long as he has recourse to the other, feminine body. Only once he returns to his own body as object of both the externally determined paternal gaze and his internally motivated self-gaze can closure be attained. Liberation from the system can occur only in the gesture of short-circuiting.

From Feminine Corpse to the Suicide of the Voyeur

Let us return once more to Freud's discussion of the voyeur and the exhibitionist and to the way we find these two positions articulated within the language of perversion. Freud distinguishes three phases: (1) looking as an activity directed toward an extraneous object; (2) giving up the object and turning the scopophilic instinct toward a part of the subject's own body and, concomitant with this, a transformation to passivity and a setting up of a new aim, namely that of being looked at; and (3) the introduction of a new subject to whom one displays oneself in order to be looked at by him (Freud 1915, 129). Freud, however, specifies these stages by explaining that at the beginning of its activity, the scopophilic drive is autoerotic, "it has indeed an object, but that object is part of the subject's own body" (130). Only later, by a process of comparison, is the drive led to exchange this object for an analogous part of someone else's body. Put another way, the primary act of gazing at oneself (the preliminary autoerotic stage) results in two possibilities: to gaze at an object foreign to oneself (masculine scopophilia) or to be the object gazed at by a person foreign to oneself (feminine exhibitionism). For Freud, the former is the active, the latter the passive expression of the drive that begins in autoeroticism.

In *Peeping Tom,* Powell radically reverses the pattern of development presented by Freud, even as he uses Freud's writings as the explicit intertext for his film, not only because of the title but also because the absent father is a psychologist and the person called to the scene of murder in the film studio by the police is a psychoanalyst. For the seminal disruption within Mark's psychic development evolves from the fact that he never was in the first phase. While the preliminary stages of scopophilia, during which the urge to gaze transforms the subject's body into an object, belongs to the area of narcissism, the active articulation of the urge to gaze implies leaving the narcissistic position, while the passive urge to gaze is a holding onto a narcissistic formation. Mark's biography, however, offers narcissism as an empty position. In other words, Powell takes over from Freud the notion "that the instinctual vicissitudes which consist in the instinct's being turned round upon the subject's own ego and undergoing reversal from activity to passivity are dependent on the narcissistic organization of the ego and bear the stamp of that phase" (Freud 1915, 132). His film, however, stages a postmodern deconstruction of this trajectory. For in his narrative this position of origin is empty. Before any possible narcissistic formation we invariably find the castrating voice and the authoritarian gaze of the father. In the case of Mark, any autoeroticism was always already inscribed by an awareness of the punitive gaze of the Other.

The second equally significant reversal of Freud undertaken by Powell consists in showing that the initial urge to gaze, resulting from the relay of gazes between the father and the child, is not exclusively sexual in nature, that is, not aimed at the subject's sexual body parts or the sexual activities of its parents. Rather, it emerges as a cross between sexuality and a threat to the integrity of the body. In his attempt to present a complete documentation of the development of a child, Mark's father did not privilege childish joy, pleasure, or happiness, but rather the reaction of the child's nervous system to fear. Thus the second key explanation of the film, referring not to Mark's pathological crimes but rather to those of his father, occurs while Mark is explaining to Helen the meaning of the film documenting his childhood. Significantly, Helen had screamed at precisely that moment in the film where she saw someone throw a lizard onto the bed of the little boy and that the animal crept under the blanket just above the boy's genitals, upon which little Mark woke up in terror. Mark explains that his father wanted as perfect as possible a rendition of the development of his child, complete in every detail. Owing to this scientific urge to gaze and register he chose ceaselessly to take notes on his son's behavior, so that Mark never had a moment of privacy. To Mark's exclamation, "He was a brilliant scientist," Helen, however, sceptically responds, "A scientist drops a lizard on a child, and good comes of it?!"

We thus have the following circuit, whose point of origin remains the absent but still powerful father. As a child, Mark was deanimated, figurally turned into a dead body because of the trauma inflicted upon him by the paternal Other, and because he was constantly aware of the representations this paternal Other was producing of him. In the place of a mother, who could have confirmed his narcissism, after its initial wounding through the castrative paternal gaze, indeed as a replacement for the dead mother, he is presented with a camera. This circuit is then repeated in the following manner in his adult life: The urge to capture the fear of death in cinematic images is a displaced externalization of his own fear. So as finally to put closure on this fatal circulation of gazes, he ultimately returns to his own body as the privileged object of his documentary project. Even though his victims were able to see the face of death in the mirror held up to them just before their own demise, his camera was not able to capture this expression. He realizes that he can only receive the image so intensely desired of the fear of death once he chooses to gaze at his own death. For the sight he seeks is radically subjective, the reflection of an observer that cannot be shared by someone occupying a third, mediated position of viewing. Only once Mark has become both the gazing subject and the gazed-at object of this terrifying relay of gazes can he complete the paternal project. What happens, as Mark offers one last turn in the wrong direction, is that the active and the passive poles of perversion collapse into each other, even as the boundary between external, foreign, and internal, own body is dissolved. Mark thus assumes both the position of the child and that of the father from the scenario of his early childhood trauma, so as to repeat them one last time. As he explains to Helen, he had always counted on this suicide, "I've been ready for this for such a long time."

In the scene when the short circuit finally occurs, Mark has the tape recorder simultaneously playing all the voices recorded by his father, while the photoflashes and the camera releases of all the cameras go off one after another. As Mark stabs himself with the spike hidden in his tripod he experiences for the first time the liberating feeling of unmitigated fear. For those surviving him, an expression of this fear of death, however, remains irrevocably inaccessible. At the end of the film, the voices played by the tape recorder replace the circuit of fatal gazes that has been brought to closure by Mark's suicide. Once the reel in Mark's projector has come to the end of its film and begins spinning senselessly because it is no longer transporting any cinematic images, we hear the paternal prohibition, "Don't be a silly boy, there's nothing to be afraid of." Then, when Powell's screen has also gone dark we hear from offscreen, as though it were a hallucination of the film *Peeping Tom* itself, the voice of Mark as a child, responding to the paternal prohibition with a declaration of love, "Good night Daddy. Hold my hand." The circuit closes by confirming the economy of the paternal gaze, even as the Real once again recedes from the image. In the end, Mark can complete the circulation of deanimating images set in motion by the paternal gaze by choosing death itself, in lieu of an image of death. What, however, remains unattainable is the happiness he might have experienced had he been able to choose Helen as representative of the empty place of the mother. This happiness is presented by Powell as a second, but impossible way of putting closure on the perverse circulation of gazes passed down from father to son.

Meant as a self-conscious critique of the voyeurism implicitly inherent in the production and viewing of cinema images, *Peeping Tom* ultimately asks, who is allowed to gaze with impunity? Powell's answer is, the father and the psychoanalyst, in their function as scientists; the director and the film producer, in their function as artists; the police, in their function as representatives of the law; and finally the clients of prostitutes and the consumers of pornography. Not sanctioned, however, are Helen's curious gaze and the perverse gaze of the voyeur Mark. This opens a second set of questions: On the basis of what agency can such a boundary be drawn between the sanctioned and the nonsanctioned? And whose law is thus stabilized? What Powell repeatedly shows is that the enmeshment of killing and the production of images is dependent upon the position of the father. To sustain this relationship, a negotiation of the name of the father, that is, the paternal metaphor proved to be seminal. On the one hand, the agency of the father prematurely undermined the mother-child dyad in such a manner that from the beginning of his childhood, Mark's psychic apparatus was inscribed with the traumatizing paternal gaze in lieu of a supporting maternal one. On the other hand, this paternal gaze made itself independent from any concrete father as its source. Not only did the child Mark know that he was constantly the target of the gaze of his father, even when the latter was not present in his room, but this paternal authority becomes particularly powerful when the father is actually absent, as in his honeymoon and later his death. The deviant reversal of so-called normal gazing set into motion by this paternal absence is dependant upon how the perverse subject deals with this third gaze, whose function it is to give consistency to his world. In other words, Mark's primary narcissism was from the start disrupted by the paternal gaze, so that he could not develop the imaginary activity, normally negotiated through the maternal gaze, in opposition to and in relation with the symbolic realm that stands under the aegis of the father. Rather, in reaction to this twist in Mark's psychic development, the agency of the symbolic came to blot out the register of the imaginary completely so that the foreclosed imaginary psychic energy could only return in the guise of a psychotization of the symbolic.

In "On a Question Preliminary to Any Possible Treatment of Psychosis," Jacques Lacan describes what happens when the paternal metaphor, functioning as the culturally privileged agency that gives consistency to the world, goes awry. The subject, according to Lacan, is presented with the question of its existence in the form of a question articulated by the Other who functions as the representative of this agency assuring consistency: "'What am I there?', concerning his sex and his contingency in being, namely, that, on the one hand, he is a man or a woman, and, on the other, that he might not be, the two conjugating their mystery, and binding it in the symbols of procreation and death" (Lacan 1966b, 194). Deciding the question is, then, contingent upon the existence of such a stabilizing Other. If, however, the paternal metaphor proves to be inadequate, that is to say, if it fails in its function to procure symbolic order, the result is the foreclosure of the signifier, of the law of the Other. With this foreclosure, the entire semiotic process of delimitation comes to be destabilized, that is, the processes of rejection, denial, and affirmation as well as the production of semantic oppositions and culturally codified constructions. The position of the Other, meant to convey coherence, is then no longer perceived as the site of questioning, but rather as a hole in the symbolic, and the lack of a paternal metaphor is replaced by hallucinations in the Real.

The paternal metaphor becomes a delirious metaphor: "It is the lack of the Name-of-the-Father in that place which, by the hole that it opens up in the signified, sets off the cascade of reshapings of the signifier from which the increasing disaster of the imaginary proceeds, to the point at which the level is reached at which signifier and signified are stabilized in the delusional metaphor" (Lacan 1966b, 217). For Powell's *Peeping Tom* one could say that the father's scientific project becomes the son's hallucinatory project, or, to be more precise, it becomes the delusional documentary film, where body and image can no longer be separated from each other, where the figural killing into an image becomes real. The best example for such an appearance of hallucinations in the Real is the scene of confrontation between Mark and Helen, where she refuses to look into the mirror as he explains his murder scenario, while the film audience hears the feminine screams of the victims. Powell does maintain as an aporia the fact that Mark's documentary represents both the most supreme tribute to the paternal metaphor and its psychotic reversal. Equally aporetic is the fact that in a manner diametrically opposed to Mark, the curious Helen also acknowledges the paternal metaphor, that is, the figurally killing scientific project of Mark's father, by reversing it in her version of the delusional metaphor, the book about a magic camera. With her magical narrative, in which the border between childlike and adult expression becomes blurred, she offers herself as an alternative representative of the third agency meant to afford consistency.

What triumphs in the end, however, are not her magical fantasies but rather Mark's hallucinations. After his final sentence to her, "I'm sorry I couldn't find those faces for you," and after he has thrown Helen to the ground, he reverses one last time the symbolic mandate taken over from his father and fulfills in suicide the only successful act open to him. Slavoj Žižek argues that the only authentic position available to the subject consists in taking on one's symbolic mandate performatively, that is, playing the role it has assumed under the aegis of the symbolic to its logical conclusion, so as to reach the border between symbolic reality and real negativity. The withdrawal from the symbolic world, in the course of symbolic suicide, is aimed at excluding the subject from any intersubjective circulation (Žižek 1992). In the act of symbolic suicide in *Peeping Tom*, as this pertains not to Mark's actual killing of himself but rather to the staging of the final images of death, planned by him so minutely and well in advance, three positions collapse that have been structuring his murderous economy of gazing: the gazed-at subject (Mark as child), the gazing subject (the father and then the internalization of the paternal gaze), and the representative of the gazing subject, who has taken on his symbolic mandate (Mark as murderous filmmaker). This authentic act is the moment when the subject performing it suspends the network of symbolic relations and notions that have sustained him in his everyday life and instead confronts the radical negativity underlying all symbolic encodings. This act as an encounter with the Real, as the transgression of a symbolic boundary throws the subject back onto the abyss of the Real, from which all symbolic reality emerges (Žižek 1992). The act, tracing the trajectory from symbolic reality to the Real, stages a short circuit of the symbolic circulation of signs and gazes. One can, therefore, conclude that Mark's act denounces the authority of the symbolic father's mandate, by exposing the nullity of all the roles simulated in his name, without, however, denying how necessary the stabilizing consistency is that the paternal metaphor affords. From this Žižek concludes that the lack which the subject must assume is not his own lack but rather the lack in the Other, which is far more difficult to bear. The biggest illusion consists precisely in the subject's trust in the consistency of the big Other. The freedom Mark experiences in the moment of his own death can be explained if one reads this as the first time that he renounces the support of the paternal Other, no longer addressing himself to the father but rather taking the burden of his existence entirely onto himself. For ultimately what had not only initiated but also sustained Mark's perversion was his limitless and unquestioned trust in the consistency of the Other.

In the end, it appears as though the paternal metaphor and, by implication, the punitive gaze of the father, which Mark had internalized, is once again securely installed in its place. In the last scene of the film, once all the cinematic images have finally faded, and implicitly directed against Mark's delusional and against Helen's fantastic metaphor, we hear the voice of the father, recorded on the tape Mark has preserved, speaking his prohibition, "Don't be a silly boy." Those who gaze in the name of the paternal metaphor remain undamaged, while those who oppose and resist the paternal metaphor (Helen) or who reverse it (Mark) are punished, the latter quite literally destroying himself in the course of this deviant reaction. But even though the paternal agency clearly survives the son's psychotic reversal of the symbolic as well as the son's authentic act, which marks a momentary suspension of the symbolic order, the murderous aspect sustaining the paternal function has also been exposed, by Mark's destructive reversal of his paternal heritage on the one hand and Helen's critical counterproject on the other. What also remains undecidable is whether the voices of the feminine victims do not represent a further hallucination for the film's audience, in which case, at least for the extradiegetic level of the film, the delusional metaphor would not have been arrested. In a similar vein, the representatives par excellence of the agency meant to assure a consistent symbolic order, namely the policemen, are also exposed as being insufficient, for they always come too late. Finally, not even the sanctioned curators of voyeurism, the studios that produce commercial cinema and pornography, remain undamaged by the deconstruction that *Peeping Tom* performs. For in their midst, in a trunk and on a bed, functioning as disturbing signs for an internal difference inextinguishably inscribed into any process of representation, we find the corpses of Vivian and Milly.

Works Cited

All English translations have been done by the author, with the exception of those listed below.

Baudrillard, Jean. 1976. *L'Échange symbolique et la mort*. Paris: Gallimard.
Berger, John. 1972. *Ways of Seeing*. Harmondsworth: Penguin.

Bordwell, David, and Kristin Thompson. 1979. *Film Art: An Introduction*. Reading, Mass.: Addison-Wesley.

Bronfen, Elisabeth. 1992. *Over Her Dead Body: Death, Femininity and the Aesthetic*. Manchester and New York: Manchester UP and Routledge.

Foucault, Michel. 1963. "Language to Infinity." *Language, Counter-Memory, Practice: Selected Essays and Interviews*. Ed. and trans. Donald F. Bouchard and Sherry Simon. Ithaca: Cornell UP.

Freud, Sigmund. 1905. "Three Essays on the Theory of Sexuality." *Standard Edition* 7. Ed. James Strachey. London: Hogarth Press, 1953. 123–245.

———. 1909a. "Five Lectures on Psycho-Analysis." *Standard Edition* 11. Ed. James Strachey. London: Hogarth Press, 1957. 3–55.

———. 1909b. "Notes upon a Case of Obsessional Neurosis." *Standard Edition* 10. Ed. James Strachey. London: Hogarth Press, 1955. 153–318.

———. 1910. "The Psycho-Analytic View of Psychogenic Disturbance of Vision." *Standard Edition* 11. Ed. James Strachey. London: Hogarth Press, 1957. 207–18.

———. 1915. "Instincts and Their Vicissitudes." *Standard Edition* 14. Ed. James Strachey. London: Hogarth Press, 1957. 111–40.

———. 1940. "An Outline of Psycho-Analysis." *Standard Edition* 23. Ed. James Strachey. London: Hogarth Press, 1964. 141–207.

Lacan, Jacques. 1966a. "The Mirror Stage as Formative of the Function of the I." *Écrits: A Selection*. Trans. Alan Sheridan. New York: Norton, 1977. 1–7.

———. 1966b. "On a Question Preliminary to Any Possible Treatment of Psychosis." *Écrits: A Selection*. Trans. Alan Sheridan. 179–225.

———. 1973. *The Four Fundamental Concepts of Psycho-Analysis*. Ed. Jacques-Alain Miller, trans. Alan Sheridan. New York: Norton.

Laplanche, J., and J.-B. Pontalis. 1973. *The Language of Psychoanalysis*. Trans. Donald Nicholson-Smith. London: Karnac Books, 1988.

Žižek, Slavoj. 1992. *Enjoy Your Symptom! Jacques Lacan in Hollywood and Out*. London: Routledge.

4

"I Hear You with My Eyes"; or, The Invisible Master

Slavoj Žižek

Voice and gaze are the two objects added by Jacques Lacan to the list of Freudian "partial objects" (breasts, faeces, phallus). They are *objects,* that is to say, they are not on the side of the looking/hearing subject but on the side of what the subject sees or hears. Let us recall the archetypal scene from Hitchcock: a heroine (Lilah in *Psycho,* Melanie in *The Birds*) is approaching a mysterious, allegedly empty house; she is looking at it, yet what makes a scene so disturbing is that we, the spectators, cannot get rid of the vague impression that the object she is looking at is somehow *returning the gaze*. The crucial point, of course, is that this gaze should not be subjectivized: it's not simply that "there is somebody in the house," we are, rather, dealing with a kind of empty, a priori gaze that cannot be pinpointed as a determinate reality—she "cannot see it all," she is looking at a blind spot, and the object returns the gaze from this blind spot. The situation is homologous at the level of voice: it is as if, when we're talking, whatever we say is an answer to a primordial address by the Other—we're always already addressed, but this address is blank, it cannot be pinpointed to a specific agent, but is a kind of empty a priori, the formal "condition of possibility" of our speaking; so it is with the object returning the gaze, which is a kind of formal "condition of possibility" of our seeing anything at all. . . . What happens in psychosis is that this empty point in the other, in what we see and/or hear, is actualized, becomes part of effective reality: in psychosis, we effectively hear the voice of the primordial Other addressing us, we effectively know that we are being observed all the time. Usually, psychosis is conceived as a form of lack with reference to the "normal" state of things: in psychosis, something is missing, the key signifier (the "paternal metaphor") is rejected, foreclosed, excluded from the symbolic universe and thence returns in the real in the guise of psychotic apparitions. However, the obverse of this exclusion, the inclusion, should also not be forgotten. Lacan pointed out that the consistency of our "experience of reality" depends on the exclusion of what he calls the *objet petit a* from it: in order for us to have normal "access to reality," something must be excluded, "primordially repressed." In psychosis, this exclusion is undone: the object (in this case, the gaze or voice) is *included* in reality, the outcome of which, of course, is the disintegration of our "sense of reality," the loss of reality.[1]

Another way to make the same claim about the quasi-transcendental status of voice and gaze is to say as Lacan does that, in both cases, we are dealing with a "transfinite" object, in Cantor's sense. Why Lacan's unexpected reference to Cantor? The distinction between "transfinite" and "infinite" elaborated by Cantor roughly fits the Hegelian distinction between "true" and "bad" (or "spurious") infinity: within "bad infinity," we never effectively reach the infinite, to every number we can add another unit; "infinity" here refers to this very constant possibility of adding, that is, to the impossibility of ever reaching the ultimate element in the series. What if, however, we treat this set of elements, which is forever "open" to addition, as a closed totality and posit the infinite as an element of its own, as the external frame of the endless set of elements it contains? This is the transfinite: a number or an element with the paradoxical property of being insensitive to addition or subtraction: if we add to it or subtract from it a unit, it remains the same.[2] And was it not in a similar way that Kant constructed the concept of "transcendental object"? One is tempted to risk a pun here: Cantor–Kant. The transcendental object is an object that is external to the endless series of empirical objects: we arrive at it by way of treating this endless series as closed, and positing outside of it an empty object, the very form of object, that frames the series.[3] It is easy to discern a further homology with the *objet petit a,* the Lacanian object cause of desire: the latter is also "transfinite," that is, it is an empty object that frames the endless set of empirical objects. In this precise sense, our two *objets petit a*, voice and gaze, are "transfinite": in both cases, we are dealing with an empty object that frames the "bad infinity" of the field of the visible and/or audible by giving body to what constitutively eludes this field. On this account, the object gaze is a blind spot within the field of the visible, whereas the object voice par excellence, of course, is silence.

Is it possible to conceive of this tension between the *objet a* and the frame of reality at the level of the relationship between the visual and auditory dimensions, so that voice itself would function as the *objet a* of the visual, as the blind spot from which the picture returns the gaze? Therein seems to reside the lesson of talking films. That is to say, what is the effect of adding a soundtrack to silent film? The exact opposite of the expected "naturalization," that is, of an even more "realistic" imitation of life. What took place from the very beginning of the sound film was an uncanny autonomization of the voice, baptized "acousmatisation" by Chion:[4] the emergence of a voice that is neither attached to an object (a person) within diegetic reality nor simply the voice of an external commentator, but a spectral voice, which floats freely in a mysterious intermediate domain and thereby acquires the horrifying dimension of omnipresence and omnipotence, the voice of an invisible master — from Fritz Lang's *Testament des Dr. Mabuse* to the "mother's voice" in Hitchcock's *Psycho*. In the final scene of *Psycho*, the "mother's voice" literally cuts out a hole in the visual reality: the screen image becomes a delusive surface, a lure secretly dominated by the bodiless voice of an invisible/absent Master, a voice that cannot be attached to any object in the diegetic reality — as if the true subject of enunciation of Norman's mother's voice is death itself, that is, the skull that we perceive for a brief moment in the fade-out of Norman's face. . . .

What we have to renounce is thus the commonsense notion of a primordial, fully constituted reality in which sight and sound harmoniously complement each other: the moment we enter the symbolic order, an unbridgeable gap separates forever a human body from "its" voice. The voice acquires a spectral autonomy, it never quite belongs to the body we see, so that even when we see a living person talking, there is always some degree of ventriloquism at work: it is as if the speaker's own voice hollows him out and in a sense speaks "by itself," through him.[5] In his *Lectures on Aesthetics*, Hegel mentions an ancient Egyptian sacred statue, which, at every sunset, as if by miracle, issued a deep reverberating sound—this mysterious sound magically resonating from within an inanimate object is the best metaphor for the birth of subjectivity. However, we must be careful here not to miss the tension, the antagonism, between a *silent* scream and a vibrant tone, that is, the moment when a silent scream *resounds*. The true object voice is mute, "stuck in the throat," and what effectively reverberates is the void: resonance always takes place *in a vacuum*—the tone as such is originally a lament for the lost object. The object is here as long as the sound remains unarticulated; the moment it resounds, the moment it is "spilled out," the object is evacuated, and this voidance gives birth to $, the barred subject lamenting the loss of the object. This lament, of course, is deeply ambiguous: the ultimate horror would be that of an object voice coming *too close* to us, so that the reverberation of the voice is at the same time a conjuration destined to keep the object voice at sufficient distance. We can now answer the simple question "Why do we listen to music?": *in order to avoid the horror of the encounter of the voice qua object*. What Rilke said for beauty goes also for music: it is a lure, a screen, the last curtain, which protects us from directly confronting the horror of the (vocal) object. When the intricate musical tapestry disintegrates or collapses into a pure unarticulated scream, we approach voice *qua* object. In this precise sense, as Lacan points out, voice and silence relate as figure and ground: silence is not (as one would be prone to think) the ground against which the figure of a voice emerges; quite the contrary, the reverberating sound itself provides the ground that renders visible the figure of silence. We have thus arrived at the formula of the relationship between voice and image: voice does not simply persist at a different level with regard to what we see, it rather points toward a gap in the field of the visible, toward the dimension of what eludes our gaze. In other words, their relationship is mediated by an impossibility: *ultimately, we hear things because we cannot see everything*.

The next step is to reverse the logic of voice as the filler of the body's constitutive gap: the obverse of the voice that gives body to what we can never see, to what eludes our gaze, is an image that renders present the failure of the voice—an image can emerge as the placeholder for a sound that doesn't yet resonate but remains stuck in the throat. Munch's *Scream,* for example, is by definition silent: in front of this painting, we "hear (the scream) *with our eyes.*" However, the parallel is here by no means perfect: *to see what one cannot hear is not the same as to hear what one cannot see.* Voice and gaze relate to each other as life and death: voice vivifies, whereas gaze mortifies. For that reason, "hearing oneself speak" [*s'entendre-parler*], as Derrida has demonstrated, is the very kernel, the fundamental matrix, of experiencing oneself as a living being, while its counterpart at the level of gaze, "seeing oneself looking" [*se voir voyant*], unmistakably stands for death: when the gaze *qua* object is no longer the elusive blind spot in the field of the visible but is included in this field, one meets one's own death. Suffice it to recall that, in the uncanny encounter of a double (Doppelgänger), what eludes our gaze are always his eyes: the double strangely seems always to look askew, never to return our gaze by looking straight into our eyes—the moment he were to do it, our life would be over. . . . [6]

It was Schopenhauer who claimed that music brings us in contact with the *Ding an sich:* it renders directly the drive of the life substance that words can only signify. For that reason, music "seizes" the subject in the real of his/her being, bypassing the detour of meaning: in music, we hear what we cannot see, the vibrating life force beneath the flow of *Vorstellungen.* What happens, however, when this flux of life substance itself is suspended, discontinued? At this point, an image emerges, an image that stands for absolute death, for death beyond the cycle of death and rebirth, of corruption and generation. Far more horrifying than to see with our ears—to hear the vibrating life substance beyond visual representations, this blind spot in the field of the visible—is to hear with our eyes, that is, to see the absolute silence that marks the suspension of life, as in Caravaggio's *Testa di Medusa:* Is not the scream of Medusa by definition silent, "stuck in the throat"? Does this painting not provide an image of the moment at which the voice fails? [7]

Against this background of "hearing what one cannot see" and "seeing what one cannot hear," it is possible to delineate the illusory locus of the "metaphysics of presence." Let us return for a brief moment to the difference between "hearing oneself speaking" and "seeing oneself looking": only the second case involves *reflection* proper, that is, the act of recognizing oneself in an (external) image, while in the first case we are dealing with the illusion of an immediate auto-affection that precludes even the minimal self-distance implied by the notion of recognizing oneself in one's mirror image. In contrast to Derrida, one is

"I Hear You with My Eyes" 95

tempted to assert that the founding illusion of the metaphysics of presence is not simply that of "hearing oneself speaking," but rather a kind of short circuit between "hearing oneself speaking" and "seeing oneself looking": a "seeing oneself looking" *in the mode of "hearing oneself speaking,"* a gaze that regains the immediacy of the vocal self-affection. That is to say, one should always bear in mind that, from Plato's *theoria* onward, metaphysics relies on the predominance of *seeing*—so how are we to combine this with "hearing oneself speaking"? "Metaphysics" resides precisely in the notion of a self-mirroring seeing that would abolish the distance of reflection and attain the immediacy of "hearing oneself speaking." In other words, "metaphysics" stands for the illusion that, in the antagonistic relationship between "seeing" and "hearing," it is possible to abolish the discord, the impossibility, that mediates between the two terms (one hears things because one cannot see it all, and vice versa) and to conflate them in a unique experience of "seeing in the mode of hearing" . . .

How does this "seeing in the mode of hearing" affect the logic of power? Let us begin with Orson Welles who, in his movie version of Kafka's *Trial,* accomplished an exemplary antiobscurantist operation by way of reinterpreting the place and the function of the famous parable on "the door of the Law." In the film, we hear it twice: at the very beginning, it serves as a kind of prologue, read and accompanied by (faked) ancient engravings projected from lantern slides; then, shortly before the end, it is told to Josef K. not by the priest (as in the novel) but by K.'s lawyer (played by Welles himself), who unexpectedly joins the priest and K. in the cathedral. The action now takes a strange turn and diverges from Kafka's novel—even before the lawyer warms up in his narrative, K. cuts him short: "I've heard it. We've heard it all. The door was meant only for him." What ensues is a painful dialogue between K. and the lawyer, in which the lawyer advises K. to "plead insanity" by claiming that he is persecuted by the idea of being the victim of the diabolical plot of a mysterious state agency. K., however, rejects the role of victim offered to him by the lawyer: "I don't pretend to be a martyr." "Not even a victim of society?" "No, I'm not a victim, I'm a member of society. . . ." In his final outburst, K. then asserts that the true conspiracy (of power) consists in the very attempt to persuade the subjects that they are victims of irrational impenetrable forces, that everything is crazy, that the world is absurd and meaningless. When K. thereupon leaves the cathedral, two plainclothes policemen are already waiting for him; they take him to an abandoned building site and dynamite him. In Welles's version, the reason K. is killed is therefore the exact opposite of the reason implied in the novel—*he presents a threat to power the moment he unmasks, "sees through," the fiction upon which the social link of the existing power structure is founded.*

Welles's reading of *The Trial* thus differs from both predominant approaches to Kafka, the obscurantist-religious approach as well as the naive, enlightened, humanist one. According to the former, K. is effectively guilty: what makes him guilty is his very naive protestation of innocence, his arrogant reliance on naive-rational argumentation. The conservative message of this reading that perceives K. as the representative of the enlightened questioning of authority is unmistakable: K. himself is the true nihilist, who acts like the proverbial bull in a china shop—his confidence in public reason renders him totally blind to the mystery of power, to the true nature of bureaucracy. The court appears to K. as a mysterious and obscene agency bombarding him with "irrational" demands and accusations exclusively on account of K.'s distorted subjectivist perspective: as the priest in the cathedral points out to K., the court is in fact indifferent, it wants nothing from him. . . . In the contrary reading, Kafka is a deeply ambiguous writer who staged the phantasmatic support of the totalitarian bureaucratic machinery, yet was himself unable to resist its fatal attraction. Therein resides the uneasiness felt by many "enlightened" readers of Kafka: in the end, did he not participate in the infernal machinery he was describing, thereby strengthening its hold instead of breaking its spell?

Although it may seem that Welles aligns himself with the second reading, things are by no means so unequivocal: he, as it were, adds another turn of the screw by raising "conspiracy" to the power of two—as K. puts it in Welles's version of his final outburst, the true conspiracy of power resides in the very notion of conspiracy, in the notion of some mysterious agency that "pulls the strings" and effectively runs the show, that is to say, in the notion that, behind the visible, public power, there is another obscene, invisible, "crazy" power structure. This other, hidden law acts the part of the "Other of the Other" in the Lacanian sense, the part of the metaguarantee of the consistency of the big Other (the symbolic order that regulates social life). The "conspiracy theory" provides a guarantee that the field of the big Other is not an inconsistent bricolage: its basic premise is that, behind the public Master (who, of course, is an impostor), there is a hidden Master who effectively keeps everything under control. "Totalitarian" regimes were especially skilled in cultivating the myth of a secret parallel power, invisible and for that very reason all-powerful, a kind of "organization within the organization"—KGB, freemasons, or whatever—that compensated for the blatant inefficiency of the public, legal power and thus assured the smooth operation of the social machine: this myth is not only in no way subversive, it serves as the ultimate support of power. The perfect American counterpart to it is (the myth of) J. Edgar Hoover, the personification of the obscene "other power" behind the president, the shadowy double of the legitimate power. He held on to power by means of secret files that allowed him to keep the entire political and power elite in check, while he himself regularily dressed up as a woman. . . .

K.'s lawyer offers to him, as a desperate last resort, this role of the martyr-victim of a hidden conspiracy; K., however, turns it down, being well aware that by accepting it, he would walk into the most perfidious trap of power. This obscene mirage of the other power brings into play the same phantasmatic space as the famous publicity spot for Smirnoff vodka, which also deftly manipulates the gap between reality and the "other surface" of the fantasy space: the camera wanders around the deck of a luxurious ocean liner; every time it passes an object, we first see this object as it is in reality, and then, when, for a brief moment, the transparent glass of the bottle comes between our gaze and the object, we see it distorted, in its fantasy dimension—two gentlemen in black evening attire become two penguins, the necklace around a lady's neck a living snake, stairs a set of piano keys, and so on. The court in Kafka's *Trial* possesses the same purely phantasmagorical existence; its predecessor is Klingsor's castle in Wagner's *Parsifal*. Since its hold upon the subject is entirely phantasmatic, it is sufficient to break its spell via a gesture of distantiation, and the court or castle falls to dust. Therein resides the political lesson of *Parsifal* and of Welles's *Trial*: if we are to overcome the "effective" social power, we have first to break its phantasmatic hold upon us.[8]

To avoid the reproach of committing a *petitio principii* by resorting to an example from literary fiction in order to prove that violence emerges when a fiction is threatened, let us evoke another exemplary case of evil which, although it passed into fiction, originated in "real life": the unfortunate Captain Bligh of the *Bounty*. We are dealing here with a true enigma: why was this exemplary officer, obsessed with the safety and health of his sailors, elevated into one of the archetypal figures of evil in our popular culture? Successive changes in the predominant image of Bligh serve as a perfect index to shifts in hegemonic ideology—each epoch had its own Bligh. It suffices to mention the three principal cinema portraits: the decadently aristocratic Charles Laughton in the thirties, the coldly bureaucratic Trevor Howard in the sixties, the mentally tortured Anthony Hopkins in the eighties.

Even more interesting than these vicissitudes is, however, the enigma of the origins: what did "happen really" on HMS *Bounty?* What was the "true cause" of the mutiny?[9] Our first temptation, of course, is to propose a countermyth to the official myth: Bligh was a severe, overzealous, and pedantic, yet profoundly fair and caring, captain of impeccable personal integrity. The mutiny against him resulted from a coalition of spoiled young officers of aristocratic descent—put out because Bligh, their superior, was not a real gentleman, not "one of them," but of lower descent and equitable in dealing with ordinary sailors—and the *lumpenproletarian* sailors-criminals who were also disturbed by Bligh's sense of justice, which led him to restrain their terrorizing of decent common sailors. His "progressive" attitude, unusual for his time, was attested again when, two decades after the *Bounty* mutiny, in the only case of a military coup in the entire English history, he was forceably deposed as governor of Australia. The corrupt officers of New South Wales overthrew him because of his politics: Bligh threatened to break their illegal monopoly on the rum trade; after the prisoners had served their term, he endeavored to integrate them into normal social life and even gave them employment in government agencies, and so on.

This countermyth, however, provides a much too simplified picture of the affair. The element of truth in it is that Bligh was perceived as "not a proper gentleman," as somebody who did have power (as the ship's commander, he had the right to make decisions and give orders, a right he took full advantage of), yet did not radiate real authority (the charisma, the *je ne sais quoi* that could arouse respect and make him a natural leader). All descriptions converge on this point: Bligh was somehow "stiff," lacking the sensitivity that tells a good leader when and how to apply rules, how to take into account the "organic," spontaneous network of relations between his subordinates, and so on. However, even this analysis is not precise enough: Bligh's mistake was not simply that of being insensitive to the concrete network of "organic" relations among the sailors, his crucial limitation consisted in the fact that he was completely "blind" to the structural function of the ritualized power relations among the sailors (the right of older, more experienced sailors to humiliate the younger and inexperienced ones, to exploit them sexually, to submit them to ordeals, etc.). These rituals provided an ambiguous supplement to the public-legal power relations: they acted as their shadowy double, apparently transgressing and subverting them, yet actually serving as their ultimate support. Consider the business of "Crossing the Line," an extremely cruel and humiliating ordeal to which those who were crossing the equator for the first time were subjected (they were tied to a rope, thrown into the ocean, and trailed for hours, made to drink sea water, etc.):

> It was that Line that divided [the world] into hemispheres, the equator. That Line marked entry into a topsy-turvy world—into an antipodes, a place of mirror opposites, where seasons were reversed, where even the unchanging heavens were different. . . . Across time and between nationalities, the ceremonies differed, but their expressions had a common character. Firstly, they played out a reversed world in which for a time the true authority of the ship belonged to those who had already Crossed the Line, and not to any by right of their commissions or warrants or appointments. . . . A second common quality was that the theatre of the ceremony was always a grotesque satire on institutions and roles of power. The satire could be about the sacraments of the state—the accolade of a knight—or the sacraments of the church—baptism by the priest. On English ships in the late eighteenth century, the satire was of kingship and the power over life and death. . . . The trial was full of insults, humiliations, injustices, erotic oaths, and compromising choices.[10]

Again, one must be attentive to the deeply ambiguous character of these rituals: they are a satire on the legal institutions, an inversion of public power, yet they are a transgression that consolidates what it transgresses. In his blindness to the "stabilizing" role of these rituals, Bligh prohibited them, or at least took their edge off by changing them into a harmless folkloristic exercise. Caught in the Enlightenment trap, Bligh was able to perceive only the worst aspect of this ritual ("of all customs it is the most brutal and inhuman," he wrote), not the satisfaction it brought about. Henningsen[11] found observers using the following words to describe the ceremony of "Crossing the Line": ridiculous, childish, foolish, stupid, silly, ludicrous, bizarre, grotesque, crazy, repulsive, burlesque, profane, superstitious, shameless, outrageous, revolting, tiresome, dangerous, barbarous, brutal, cruel, coarse, rapacious, vindictive, riotous, licentious, mad—are not all these words eventually so many synonyms for *jouissance*? The mutiny—violence—broke out when Bligh interfered with this murky world of obscene rituals that served as the phantasmatic background of power.

Does one not encounter the same set of unwritten rules at the other end of modern English history, in the life of English public schools as depicted in numerous memoirs and, among others, in Michael Anderson's film *If*? Beneath the civilized, open-minded, liberal surface of the daily life in these schools, with their dull but charming atmosphere, there is another world of brutal power relations between younger and older pupils—a detailed set of unwritten rules prescribes the ways older pupils are allowed to exploit and to humiliate in different ways their younger peers, all of this pervaded with "prohibited" sexuality. We do not have the public "repressive" rule of law and order undermined by undercover forms of rebellion—mocking the public authority, and so on—but rather its opposite: the public authority maintains a civilized, gentle appearance, whereas beneath it there is a shadowy realm in which the brutal exercise of power is itself sexualized. And the crucial point, of course, is that this obscene shadowy realm, far from undermining the civilized semblance of the public power, serves as its inherent support. It is only by way of the initiation into the unwritten rules of this realm that a pupil is able to participate in the benefits of the school life—the penalty for breaking these unwritten rules is much harsher than for breaking the public rules.

This distance between the public, written law and its obscene superego counterpart also enables us to demonstrate clearly where cynicism, or cynical distance, as the predominant form of ideological attitude of the late capitalist subject, falls short: a cynic mocks the public law from the position of its obscene underside which, consequently, he leaves intact. Insofar as the enjoyment that permeates this underside is structured in fantasies, one can also say that what the cynic leaves intact is the fantasy, the phantasmatic background of the public, written ideological text. Cynical distance and full reliance on fantasy are thus strictly codependent: the typical subject today is the one who, while displaying cynical distrust of any public ideology, indulges without restraint in paranoiac fantasies about conspiracies, threats, and excessive forms of enjoyment of the Other.

Here, however, one should be careful to avoid a fateful confusion: the set of obscene unwritten rules misrecognized by Bligh has nothing whatsoever to do with the so-called implicit, impenetrable background of our daily activity, that is, as Heideggerians would have put it, with what we, finite human beings, do, being always "thrown" into a situation and having to find ourselves in it, in a way that can never be formalized into a set of explicit rules. Let us recall another film that stages this obscene ritual of power: Stanley Kubrick's *Full Metal Jacket*. What we get in the first part of the film is the military drill, bodily discipline, saturated by a blend of sexualization, a humiliating display of power, and blasphemy (at Christmas, the soldiers are ordered to sing "Happy birthday, dear Jesus . . .")—in short, the superego machine of power at its purest. As to the status of this obscene machine with respect to our everyday life-world, the lesson of the film is clear: the function of this underworld of unwritten rituals is not to enable the official "public" ideology to "catch on," to start to function as a constituent of our actual social life, that is, this obscene underworld does not "mediate" between the abstract structure of symbolic law and the concrete experience of the actual life-world. The situation, rather, is inverse: we need a "human face," a sense of distance, in order to be able to accommodate ourselves to the crazy demands of the superego machine. The first part of the film ends with a soldier who, on account of his overidentification with the military ideological machine, "runs amok" and shoots first the drill sergeant, then himself—the radical, unmediated identification with the superego machine necessarily leads to a murderous *passage à l'acte*.[12] The second, main part of the film ends with a scene in which a soldier (Matthew Modine) who, throughout the film, has displayed a kind of ironic "human distance" toward the military machine (e.g., on his helmet, the inscription "Born to kill" is accompanied by the peace sign), kills out of compassion the wounded Vietcong sniper girl—he is the one in whom the interpellation by the military big Other has fully succeeded, he is the fully constituted military subject.

Insofar as the obscene superego machine displays the structure of the unconscious and thus exemplifies in an outstanding way Lacan's thesis that the Master is unconscious, there is a more general conclusion to be drawn from it. The paradoxical achievement of Lacan, which usually passes unnoticed even with his advocates, is that, on behalf of psychoanalysis, he returns to the modern age, "decontextualized," rationalist notion of subject. Recall that one of the commonplaces of today's American appropriation of Heidegger is to emphasize how he, alongside with Wittgenstein, Merleau-Ponty, and others, elaborated the conceptual framework that enables us to get rid of the rationalist notion of subject as an autonomous agent who, excluded from the world, processes in a computerlike way data provided by the senses. Heidegger's notion of "being-in-the-world" points toward our irreducible and insurpassable "embeddedness" in a concrete and ultimately contingent life-world: we are always already *in* the world, engaged in an existential project within a background that eludes our grasp and remains forever the obscure horizon into which we are "thrown" as finite beings. And it is customary to interpret the opposition between consciousness and the unconscious along the same lines: the disembodied ego stands for rational consciousness, whereas the "unconscious" is synonymous with the opaque background that we cannot ever fully master, since we are always already part of it, caught in it. . . . Lacan, however, in an unheard-of gesture, claims the exact opposite: the Freudian "unconscious" has nothing whatsoever to do with the structurally necessary and irreducible opaqueness of the background, of the life context in which we, the always already engaged agents, are embedded; the "unconscious" is, rather, the disembodied rational machine that follows its path irrespective of the demands of the subject's life-world, it stands for the rational subject insofar as it is originally "out of joint," in discord with its contextualized situation: "unconscious" is the rupture on account of which the subject's primordial stance is not that of "being-in-the-world." This way, one can also provide a new, unexpected solution to the old phenomenological problem of how it is possible for the subject to disengage itself from its life-world and (mis)perceive itself as a disembodied rational agent: this disengagement can only occur because there is from the very outset something in the subject that resists its full inclusion into its life-world context, and this "something," of course, is the unconscious as the psychic machine that disregards the requirements of the "reality principle."

A further feature to be noted is the inherently vocal status of these unwritten rules, of this shadowy paralegal domain, which can teach us a lot about the voice. True, the experience of *s'entendre-parler*, of hearing-oneself-speaking, grounds the illusion of the transparent self-presence of the speaking subject. Is, however, the voice not at the same time that which undermines most radically the subject's self-presence and self-transparency? I hear myself speaking, yet what I hear is never fully myself but a parasite, a foreign body in my very heart. This stranger in myself acquires positive existence in different guises, from the voice of conscience and the opaque voice of the hypnotist to the persecutor in paranoia. Voice is that which, in the signifier, resists meaning, it stands for the opaque inertia that cannot be recuperated by meaning. It is only the dimension of writing that accounts for the stability of meaning, or, to quote the immortal words of Samuel Goldwyn, "A verbal agreement isn't worth the paper it's written on." As such, voice is neither dead nor alive: its primordial phenomenological status is rather that of the living dead, of a spectral apparition that somehow survives its own death, that is, the eclipse of meaning. In other words, it is true that the life of a voice can be opposed to the dead letter of a writing, but this life is the uncanny life of an undead monster, not the "healthy" living self-presence of meaning....

In order to render manifest this uncanny voice, it is sufficient to cast a cursory glance at the history of music—it reads as a kind of counter-history to the usual story of Western metaphysics as the domination of voice over writing. What we encounter in it again and again is a voice that threatens the established order and that, for that reason, has to be brought under control, subordinated to the rational articulation of spoken and written word, fixed into writing. In order to designate the danger that lurks here, Lacan coined the neologism *jouis-sense*, enjoyment-in-meaning—the moment at which the singing voice cuts loose from its anchoring in meaning and accelerates into a consuming self-enjoyment. The problem is thus always the same: how are we to prevent the voice from sliding into a consuming self-enjoyment that "effeminates" the reliable masculine Word?[13] The voice functions here as a "supplement" in the Derridean sense: one endeavors to restrain it, to regulate it, to subordinate it to the articulated Word, yet one cannot dispense with it altogether, since a proper dosage is vital for the exercise of power (it suffices to recall the role of patriotic-military songs in the building-up of a totalitarian community). However, this brief description of ours can give rise to the mistaken impression that we are dealing with a simple opposition between the "repressive" articulated word and the "transgressive" consuming voice: on the one hand, the articulated Word that disciplines and regulates the voice as a means of asserting social discipline and authority, and on the other hand, the self-enjoying voice that acts as the medium of liberation, of tearing apart the disciplinary chains of law and order. . . . But what about the U.S. Marine Corps's mesmeric "marching chants"—are their debilitating rhythm and sadistically sexualized nonsensical content not an exemplary case of the consuming self-enjoyment in the service of power? The excess of the voice is thus radically undecidable.

Our argument can be briefly summarized as follows: the outbreak of "real" violence is conditioned by a symbolic deadlock. *"Real" violence is a kind of acting out that emerges when the symbolic fiction that guarantees the life of a community is in danger.*[14] And we obtain the same answer when we approach the problem from the other end: what is the *target* of the outbursts of violence? What are we aiming at, what do we endeavor to annihilate when we exterminate Jews or beat up foreigners in our cities? The first answer that offers itself again involves symbolic fiction: is not the ultimate aim of the rapes in the Bosnian war, for example— beyond direct physical pain and personal humiliation—to undermine the fiction (the symbolic narrative) that guarantees the coherence of the Muslim community? Is not a consequence of extreme violence also that "the story the community has been telling itself about itself no longer makes sense" (to paraphrase Richard Rorty)?[15] This destruction of the enemy's symbolic universe, this "culturocide," however, is in itself not sufficient to explain an outburst of ethnic violence—its ultimate cause (in the sense of driving force) is to be sought at a somewhat deeper level. What does our "intolerance" toward foreigners feed on? What is it that irritates us in them and disturbs our psychic balance? Even at the level of a simple phenomenological description, the crucial characteristic of this cause is that it cannot be pinpointed to some clearly defined observable property: although we can usually enumerate a series of features that annoy us with "them" (the way they laugh too loudly, the bad smell of their food, etc.), these features function as indicators of a more radical strangeness. Foreigners may look and act like us, but there is some unfathomable *je ne sais quoi*, something "in them more than themselves" that makes them "not quite human" ("aliens" in the precise sense this term acquired in the science-fiction films of the fifties).[16] Our relationship to this unfathomable traumatic element that "bothers us" in the Other is structured in fantasies (about the Other's political and/or sexual omnipotence, about "their" strange sexual practices, about their secret hypnotic powers, etc.). As we have already seen, Jacques Lacan baptized this paradoxical uncanny object that stands for what in the perceived positive, empirical object necessarily eludes my gaze and as such serves as the driving force of my desiring it, *objet petit a*, the object cause of desire; another name for it is *plus-de-jouir*, the "surplus enjoyment" that designates the excess over the satisfaction brought about by the positive, empirical properties of the object. At its most radical level, violence is precisely an endeavor to strike a blow at this unbearable surplus enjoyment contained in the Other.

So even when violence is "merely verbal," as in the case of injurious words ("hate speech"), one has to reach beyond the domain of meaning in order to account for its impact. A good way to begin is to recall Lacan's thesis according to which the aim of a sadist is *faire exister l'Autre*: by means of my victim's pain, I make the Other exist. The victim's pain has the weight of an ontological proof: it demonstrates that the Other exists in the real, beyond symbolic fiction, in the fullness of his/her being.[17] Pain is by definition experienced as a meaningless real, and this, precisely, is what an insult reckons with: the speaker aims at emitting a word that the other (its addressee) will not be able to "subjectivize," to integrate in his field of meaning, a word that will cause the other's universe of meaning to collapse momentarily—*jouissance* emerges at this very point of the *aphanisis* of meaning. An injurious word aims at bringing about in the other the breakdown of argumentation: its wound "corners" the other to such an extent that he is at a loss and can only counter my injurious word by having recourse to a violent *passage à l'acte*. This moment of perplexity, of the breakdown of the symbolic fiction, is the proof for me that the other exists in the real. When, to take the most elementary case, I shout at somebody, "You stupid bitch!" the victim makes herself ridiculous the moment she sets to refute my charge by means of rational argumentation, since she thereby already falls into the trap of taking my insult seriously. Therein resides the double bind of the injurious word: it discredits in advance the victim's attempt to refute it *via* counterargumentation.[18]

As Lacan pointed out in his seminar 3 on *Psychoses,* the psychotic kernel of the injurious word resides in the way it perturbs the "normal" scheme of communication in which I, the speaker, receive from the other my own message in its inverted-true form: when I say to another person, "You're my master!" I thereby posit myself as his servant or pupil, that is, my assertion as it were stakes out the field of possible response to it, it delineates its symbolic context. Although, in a first approach, the statement "You stupid bitch!" looks similar to the statement "You're my master!" the respective logic of the two statements differs profoundly: the injurious word lacks, or rather actively suspends, its context, it pops up as the Real of an answer bereft of a question delineating its symbolic context—this lack of a context accounts for the shocking impact of the injurious word.[19] One of the most repulsive racist rituals from the American Old South was to force the African American cornered by a white gang to commit the first gesture of insult; while the African American was held tightly by the white racist thug's associates, the white shouted at him "Spit on me! Tell me I'm filth!" and so on, in order to extort from him the "occasion" for a brutal beating or lynching—as if the white racist wanted to set up retroactively the proper dialogical context for his violent outburst. Here we encounter the *perversity* of the injurious word at its purest: the proper order of succession and implication is perverted; in a mocking imitation of the "normal" order, I compel the victim to insult me voluntarily, that is, to assume the discursive position of the offender and thereby to justify my violent outburst. The mechanism of injury is therefore inconceivable without the distinction between the actual speaker *qua* flesh-and-blood person and the virtual/symbolic position of enunciation he assumes in a concrete discourse.[20] More precisely, an injurious word not only entraps the victim into a humiliating position of enunciation; over and above, by means of its perplexing impact, it renders it impossible for him to assume an adequate position of enunciation at all, so that the victim is bereft of his symbolic identity and is reduced to a pure $\$$ confronted with the obscene object.

Since hatred is thus not limited to the "actual properties" of its object but targets its real kernel, *objet a,* what is "in the object more than itself," the object of hatred is *stricto sensu indestructible:* the more we destroy the object in reality, the more powerfully it rises in front of us. This paradox was long ago recognized as the dragon's teeth of the Jews in Nazi Germany: the more they were ruthlessly exterminated, the more horrifying were the dimensions acquired by the remainder. . . . This phantasmatic element that, the more it is annihilated in reality, the stronger it returns in its spectral presence, points toward the Freudian problematic of the castration complex. The notion of the castration complex has been the target of feminist criticism for years: only if we silently accept "having the phallus" as the standard by which we measure both sexes, does "not having the phallus" appear as a lack, that is, is the woman perceived as "castrated." In other words, the notion of feminine castration ultimately amounts to a variation on the notorious old Greek sophism "What you don't have, you have lost; you don't have horns, so you have lost them." It is nonetheless too hasty to dismiss this sophism (and thereby the notion of castration) as inconsequential false reasoning. To get a presentiment of the existential anxiety that may pertain to its logic, recall the Wolf-Man, Freud's Russian analysand, who was suffering from a hypochondriacal *idée fixe*: he complained that he was the victim of a nasal injury caused by electrolysis; however, when thorough dermatological examinations established that there was absolutely nothing wrong with his nose, this triggered an unbearable anxiety in him: "Having been told that nothing could be done for his nose because nothing was wrong with it, he felt unable to go on living in what he considered his irreparably mutilated state."[21] This "irreparable mutilation," of course, stands for castration, and the logic is here exactly the same as that of the above-quoted Greek sophism: if you do not have horns, you lost them; if nothing can be done, then the loss is irreparable. Within the Lacanian perspective, of course, this sophism points toward the fundamental feature of a structural/differential order: the unbearable absolute lack emerges at the very point when the lack itself is lacking.

According to Freud, the attitude of the male subject toward castration involves a paradoxical splitting: I know that castration is not an actual threat, that it will not really occur, yet I am nonetheless haunted by its prospect. And the same goes for the figure of the "conceptual Jew": it doesn't exist (as part of our experience of social reality), but for that reason I fear him even more—in short, *the very nonexistence of the Jew in reality functions as the main argument for anti-Semitism.* That is to say, the anti-Semitic discourse constructs the figure of the Jew as a phantomlike entity that is to be found nowhere in reality, and then uses this very gap between the "conceptual Jew" and the reality of actually existing Jews as the ultimate argument against Jews. We are thus caught in a kind of vicious circle: the more things appear to be normal, the more suspicion they arouse, and the more panic-stricken we become. In this respect, the Jew is like the maternal phallus: there is no such thing in reality, but for that very reason, its spectral presence gives rise to an unbearable anxiety. Therein consists also the most succinct definition of the Lacanian Real: the more my (symbolic) reasoning tells me that X is not possible, the more its specter haunts me—like the proverbial courageous Englishman who not only did not believe in ghosts, he was not even afraid of them.

A homology imposes itself here between the "conceptual Jew" and the "Name of the Father": in the latter case, we are also dealing with the splitting between knowledge and belief ("I know very well that my father is actually an imperfect, confused, impotent creature, yet I nonetheless believe in his symbolic authority"). The empirical person of the father never lives up to his Name, to his symbolic mandate—insofar as he *does* live up to it, we are dealing with a psychotic constellation (a clear case of a father who did live up to his Name was Schreber's father from the case analyzed by Freud). Is therefore the "transubstantiation," the "sublation" [*Aufhebung*] of the real father in the Name of the Father not strictly homologous to the "transubstantiation" of the empirical Jew into (the form of appearance of) the "conceptual Jew"? Is the gap that separates effective Jews from the phantasmatic figure of "conceptual Jew" not of the same nature as the gap that separates the empirical,

"I Hear You with My Eyes" 109

always deficient person of the father from the Name of the Father, from his symbolic mandate? Is it not that, in both cases, a real person acts as the personification of an irreal, fictitious agency—the actual father is a stand-in for the agency of symbolic authority and the actual Jew a stand-in for the phantasmatic figure of "conceptual Jew"?

Convincing as it may sound, this homology has to be rejected as deceptive: in the case of the Jew, the standard logic of symbolic castration is *reversed*. In what, precisely, does symbolic castration consist? A real father exerts authority only insofar as he posits himself as the embodiment of a transcendent symbolic agency, that is, insofar as he accepts that it is not himself, but the big Other who speaks through him, in his words—like the millionaire from a film by Claude Chabrol who inverts the standard complaint about being loved only for his millions: "If only I were to find a woman who would love me only for my millions, not for myself!" Therein resides the ultimate lesson of the Freudian myth of the parricide, of the primordial father who, after his violent death, returns stronger than ever in the guise of his Name, as a symbolic authority: *if the real father is to exert the paternal symbolic authority, he must in a way die alive*—it is his identification with the "dead letter" of the symbolic mandate that bestows authority on his person, or, to paraphrase the old antiaboriginal American slogan: "Only a dead father is a good father!"[22]

The trouble with the critics of Lacan's "phallocentrism" is that, as a rule, they refer to "phallus" and/or "castration" in a preconceptual, commonsense metaphoric way: in the standard feminist film studies, for example, every time a man behaves aggressively toward a woman or asserts his authority over her, one can be sure that his act will be designated as "phallic"; every time a woman is framed, rendered helpless, cornered, and so on, one can be sure that her experience will be designated as "castrating." What gets lost here is precisely the paradox of phallus as the signifier of castration: if we are to assert our (symbolic) "phallic" authority, the price to be paid is that we have to renounce the position of agent and consent to function as the medium through which the big Other acts and speaks. Insofar as phallus *qua* signifier designates the agency of symbolic authority, its crucial feature therefore resides in the fact that it is not "mine," the organ of a living subject, but a place at which a foreign power intervenes and inscribes itself onto my body, a place at which the big Other acts through me—in short, the fact that phallus is a signifier means above all that it is structurally an organ without a body, somehow "detached" from my body.[23] This crucial feature of the phallus, its detachability, is rendered visible in the use of the plastic artificial phallus (dildo), as, for example, in lesbian practices, where one can play with it, where it circulates—a phallus is far too serious a thing for its use to be left to stupid creatures like men.[24]

There is, however, a pivotal difference between this symbolic authority guaranteed by phallus as the signifier of castration and the spectral presence of the "conceptual Jew": although in both cases we are dealing with the split between knowledge and belief, the two splits are of a fundamentally different nature. In the first case, the belief concerns the "visible" public symbolic authority (notwithstanding my awareness of the father's imperfection and debility, I still accept him as a figure of authority), whereas in the second case, what I believe in is the power of an invisible spectral apparation.[25] The phantasmatic "conceptual Jew" is not a paternal figure of symbolic authority, a "castrated" bearer-medium of public authority, but something decidedly different, a kind of uncanny double of the public authority that perverts its proper logic: he has to act in the shadow, invisible to the public eye, irradiating a phantomlike, spectral omnipotence. On account of this unfathomable, elusive status of the kernel of his identity, the Jew is—in contrast to the "castrated" father—perceived as *uncastratable:* the more his actual, social, public existence is cut short, the more threatening becomes his elusive phantasmatic ex-sistence.[26]

This phantasmatic logic of an invisible and for that very reason all-powerful Master was clearly at work in the way the figure of Abimael Guzman, "Presidente Gonzalo," the leader of Sendero Luminoso in Peru, functioned prior to his arrest: the fact that his very existence was doubted (people were not sure if he effectively existed or was just a mythical point of reference) added to his power. The most recent example of such a Master *qua* invisible and for that reason all-powerful agency is provided by Bryan Singer's *The Usual Suspects,* a film centered on the mysterious "Keyser Söze," a master criminal about whom it is not clear if he exists at all: as one of the persons in the film puts it, "I don't believe in God, but I'm nonetheless afraid of him." People are afraid to see him or, once forced to confront him face-to-face, to mention this to others—his identity is a highly kept secret. At the end of the film, it is disclosed that Keyser Söze is the most miserable of the group of suspects, a limping, self-humiliating wimp, like Alberich in Richard Wagner's *Ring des Nibelungen*. What is crucial is this very contrast between the omnipotence of the invisible agent of power and the way this same agent is reduced to a crippled weakling, once his identity is rendered public. The phantasmatic feature that accounts for the power exerted by such a master figure is not his symbolic place but an act by means of which he displayed his ruthless will and readiness to sever all ordinary human links (Keyser Söze supposedly shot in cold blood his wife and children in order to prevent the members of an enemy gang blackmailing him by threatening to kill them—an act strictly homologous to Alberich's renunciation of love).

In short, the difference between the Name of the Father and the "conceptual Jew" is that between symbolic *fiction* and phantasmatic *specter*: in Lacanian algebra, between S_1, the master signifier (the empty signifier of symbolic authority) and the *objet petit a*.[27] When the subject is endowed with symbolic authority, he acts as an appendix of his symbolic title, that is, it is the big Other who acts through him: it suffices to recall a judge who may be a miserable and corrupted person, but the moment he puts on his robe and other insignia, his words are the words of law itself. . . . In the case of the spectral presence, in contrast, the power I exert relies on something "in me more than myself" that is best exemplified by numerous science-fiction thrillers from *Alien* to *Hidden*: an indestructible foreign body that stands for the presymbolic life substance, a nauseous mucous parasite that invades my interior and dominates me.[28] So, back to Chabrol's joke about the millionaire: when somebody says that he loves me not because of myself but because of my symbolic place (power, wealth), my predicament is decidedly better than when I am told that I am loved because somebody feels the presence in me of "something more than myself." If a millionaire loses his millions, the partner who loved him for his wealth will simply lose his interest and abandon him, no deep traumas involved; if, however, I am loved because of "something in me more than myself," the very intensity of this love can easily convert into no less passionate hatred, into a violent attempt to annihilate the surplus object in me that disturbs my partner.[29] One can therefore sympathize with the poor millionaire's plight: it is far more comforting to know that a woman loves me because of my millions (or power or glory)—this awareness allows me to maintain a safe distance, to avoid being caught in the game too deeply, to expose to the other the very kernel of my being. The problem arises when the other sees *in me* "something more than myself"—the path is then wide open for the paradoxical short circuit between love and hate for which Lacan coined the neologism *l'hainamoration*.[30]

According to the standard notion of the difference between the sexes, man's identity hinges on his symbolic title, on what he is "for the others," whereas the center of gravity of woman's identity resides in what she is in her concrete reality, beyond (or, rather, beneath) her symbolic titles. However, it is man's very attachment to the symbolic mandate that propels him in the illusory search for some kernel of the real beyond the public mandate ("I want to be loved not for my public titles, but for what I really am as an individual, beneath my titles"), whereas a woman is far more aware of the unsettling fact that *there is nothing, no hidden treasure, beneath the symbolic mandate*.[31]

This difference between (symbolic) fiction and fantasy is of crucial importance for the psychoanalytical theory of ideology. In his recent book on Marx, Jacques Derrida brought into play the term "specter" in order to indicate the elusive pseudomateriality that subverts the classic ontological oppositions of reality and illusion, and so on.[32] And, perhaps, it is here that we should look for the last resort of ideology, for the preideological kernel, the formal matrix, onto which are grafted various ideological formations: in the fact that there is no reality without the specter, that the circle of reality can be closed only by means of an uncanny spectral supplement. Why, then, is there no reality without the specter? Lacan provides a precise answer to this question: (what we experience as) reality is not the "thing itself," it is always already symbolized, constituted, structured by way of symbolic mechanisms—and the problem resides in the fact that symbolization ultimately always fails, that it never succeeds in fully "covering" the real, that it always involves some unsettled, unredeemed symbolic debt. *This real (the part of reality that remains unsymbolized) returns in the guise of spectral apparitions.* Consequently, "specter" is not to be confused with "symbolic fiction," with the fact that reality itself has the structure of a fiction in that it is symbolically (or, as some sociologists put it, "socially") constructed; the notions

"I Hear You with My Eyes" 113

of specter and (symbolic) fiction are codependent in their very incompatibility (they are "complementary" in the quantum-mechanical sense). To put it simply, reality is never directly "itself," it presents itself only *via* its incomplete, failed symbolization, and spectral apparitions emerge in this very gap that forever separates reality from the real, and on account of which reality has the character of a (symbolic) fiction: the specter gives body to that which escapes (the symbolically structured) reality.

The preideological "kernel" of ideology thus consists of the *spectral apparition that fills up the hole of the real*. This is what all the attempts to draw a clear line of separation between "true" reality and illusion (or to ground illusion in reality) fail to take into account: if (what we experience as) "reality" is to emerge, something has to be foreclosed from it, that is, "reality," like truth, is by definition never "whole." *What the specter conceals is not reality but its "primordially repressed," irrepresentable X on whose "repression" reality itself is founded*. It may seem that we have thereby lost our way in speculative murky waters that have nothing whatsoever to do with concrete social struggles—is, however, the supreme example of such a "real" not provided by the Marxist concept of *class struggle*? The consequent thinking out of this concept compels us to admit that there is no class struggle "in reality": "class struggle" designates the very antagonism that prevents the objective (social) reality from constituting itself as a self-enclosed whole.[33]

This interpretation of social antagonism (class struggle) as real, not as (part of) objective social reality, enables us to counter the worn-out line of argumentation according to which one has to abandon the notion of ideology since the gesture of distinguishing "mere ideology" from "reality" implies the epistemologically untenable "God's view," that is, access to objective reality as it "truly is." The question of the suitability of the term "class struggle" to designate today's dominant form of antagonism is here secondary, it concerns concrete social analysis; what matters is that the very constitution of social reality involves the "primordial repression" of an antagonism, so that the ultimate support of the critique of ideology—the extraideological point of reference that authorizes us to denounce the content of our immediate experience as "ideological"—is not "reality" but the "repressed" real of antagonism.[34]

In order to clarify this uncanny logic of antagonism *qua* real, let us recall Claude Lévi-Strauss's exemplary analysis, from his *Structural An-

thropology, of the spatial disposition of buildings in the Winnebago, one of the Great Lake tribes. The tribe is divided into two subgroups ("moieties"), "those who are from above" and "those who are from below"; when we ask an individual to draw on a piece of paper, or on sand, the ground plan of his/her village (the spatial disposition of cottages), we obtain two quite different answers, depending on which subgroup he/she belongs to. Both perceive the village as a circle; but for one subgroup, there is within this circle another circle of central houses, so that we have two concentric circles, while for the other subgroup, the circle is split into two by a clear dividing line. In other words, a member of the first subgroup (let us call it "conservative-corporatist") perceives the ground plan of the village as a ring of houses more or less symmetrically disposed around the central temple, whereas a member of the second ("revolutionary-antagonistic") subgroup perceives his/her village as two distinct heaps of houses separated by an invisible frontier. . . .[35] The central point of Lévi-Strauss is that this example should in no way entice us into cultural relativism, according to which the perception of social space depends on the observer's belonging in a group: the very splitting into the two "relative" perceptions implies a hidden reference to a constant—not the objective, "actual" disposition of buildings but a traumatic kernel, a fundamental antagonism the inhabitants of the village were unable to symbolize, to account for, to "internalize," to come to terms with, an imbalance in social relations that prevented the community from stabilizing itself into a harmonious whole. The two perceptions of the ground plan are simply two mutually exclusive endeavors to cope with this traumatic antagonism, to heal its wound *via* the imposition of a balanced symbolic structure. (Is it necessary to add that things stand exactly the same with respect to sexual difference: "masculine" and "feminine" are like the two configurations of houses in the Lévi-Straussian village? And in order to dispel the illusion that our "developed" universe is not dominated by the same logic, suffice it to recall the splitting of our political space into Left and Right: a leftist and a rightist behave exactly like members of the opposite subgroups of the Lévi-Straussian village. They not only occupy different places within the political space; each of them perceives differently the very disposition of the political space—a leftist as the field that is inherently split by some fundamental antagonism, a rightist as the organic unity of a community disturbed only by foreign intruders.)[36]

"I Hear You with My Eyes" 115

Common sense tells us that it is easy to rectify the bias of subjective perceptions and to ascertain the "true state of things": we rent a helicopter and take a snapshot of the village directly from above. What we obtain this way is the undistorted view of reality, yet we miss completely the real of social antagonism, the unsymbolizable traumatic kernel that found expression in the same distortions of reality, the fantasized displacements of the "actual" disposition of houses. This is what Lacan has in mind when he claims that *the very distortion and/or dissimulation is revealing:* what emerges *via* the distortions of the accurate representation of reality is the real, that is, the trauma around which social reality is structured. In other words, if all the inhabitants of the village were to draw the same accurate ground plan, we would be dealing with a nonantagonist, harmonious community. However, if we are to arrive at the fundamental paradox implied by the Marxist notion of commodity fetishism, we have to accomplish a step further and imagine, say, two different "actual" villages, each of which realizes, in the disposition of its dwellings, one of the two fantasized ground plans evoked by Lévi-Strauss: in this case, the structure of social reality itself materializes an attempt to cope with the real of antagonism.[37] That is to say, what one should never forget is that "commodity fetishism" does not designate a (bourgeois) theory of political economy but a series of presuppositions that determine the structure of the very "real" economic practice of market exchange—in theory, a capitalist clings to utilitarian nominalism, yet in his own practice (of exchange, etc.) he follows "theological whimsies" and acts as a speculative idealist. "Reality" itself, insofar as it is regulated by a symbolic fiction, conceals the real of an antagonism, and it is this real, foreclosed from the symbolic fiction, that returns in the guise of spectral apparitions—exemplarily, of course, in the guise of the "conceptual Jew."

In other words, the real is not accessible directly, as that which underlies the delusive realm of fictions and/or fantasies: what renders the real accessible is, rather, the splitting between the two kinds of fictions, symbolic fictions proper and spectral fantasies: they are not on the same level, their relationship is "convoluted," that is, fantasy emerges in order to fill in the void, the failure, of the symbolic fiction.[38] *The proof that "all is not fiction" thus resides in the very redoubling of the domain of fictions,* in the fact that both symbolic fiction and spectral fantasy turn on the same "absent Cause," symbolic fiction approaching it endlessly, spectral fantasy directly filling out its void—the real is this very "absent Cause," the invisible gap that keeps them apart.³⁹

This duality of symbolic fiction and spectral apparition can be discerned also *via* the utter ambiguity of the notion of fantasy. That is to say, the notion of fantasy offers an exemplary case of the dialectical *coincidentia oppositorum:* on the one hand, fantasy in its beatific side, in its *stabilizing* dimension, the dream of a state without disturbances, out of reach of human depravity; on the other hand, fantasy in its *destabilizing* dimension, whose elementary form is envy—all that "irritates" me about the Other, images that haunt me of what he or she is doing when out of my sight, of how he or she deceives me and plots against me, of how he or she ignores me and indulges in an enjoyment that is intensive beyond my capacity of representation, and so on and so forth (this, for example, is what bothers Swan apropos of Odette in *Un Amour de Swan*). And does the fundamental lesson of so-called totalitarianism not concern the codependence of these two aspects of the notion of fantasy? Those who alleged fully to realize fantasy¹ (the symbolic fiction) had to have recourse to fantasy² (spectral apparitions) in order to explain their failure—the foreclosed obverse of the Nazi harmonious *Volksgemeinschaft* returned in the guise of their paranoiac obsession with "the Jewish plot." Similarly, the Stalinists' compulsive discovery of ever-new enemies of socialism was the inescapable obverse of their pretending to realize the ideal of the "new socialist man." Perhaps freedom from the infernal hold of fantasy² provides the most succint definition of a saint.

Fantasy¹ and fantasy², symbolic fiction and spectral apparition, are thus like front and back of the same coin: insofar as a community experiences its reality as regulated, structured, by fantasy¹, it has to disavow its inherent impossibility, the antagonism in its very heart—and fantasy² (the figure of the "conceptual Jew," for example) gives body to this disavowal. In short, the effectiveness of fantasy² is the condition for fantasy¹ to maintain its hold.⁴⁰ Lacan rewrote Descartes's "I think, therefore I am" as "I am the one who thinks 'therefore I am' "— the point being, of course, the noncoincidence of the two "am"s, that is, the phantasmatic nature of the second "am." One should submit the pathetic assertion of ethnic identity to the same reformulation: the moment "I am French (German, Jew, American . . .)" is rephrased as "I am the one who thinks 'therefore I am French,'" the gap in the midst of my self-identity becomes visible—and the function of the "conceptual Jew" is precisely to render this gap invisible.

What, then, is fantasy? One should always bear in mind that the desire "realized" (staged) in fantasy is not subject's own but the *other's* desire. That is to say, fantasy, phantasmatic formation, is an answer to the enigma of "Che vuoi?" [What do you want?], which renders the subject's primordial, constitutive position. The original question of desire is not directly "What do I want?" but "What do *others* want from me? What do they see in me? What am I for the others?" A small child is embedded in a complex network of relations, he serves as a kind of catalyst and battlefield for the desires of those around him, his father, mother, brothers, and sisters, and so on, fight their battles around him, mother sending a message to father through her care for the son, and the like. While being well aware of this role, the child cannot fathom what, precisely, for an object he is for the others, what the exact nature is of the games they are playing with him; and fantasy provides an answer to this enigma—at its most fundamental, fantasy tells me what am I for my others. It is again anti-Semitism, the anti-Semitic paranoia, which renders visible in an exemplary way this radically *intersubjective* character of fantasy: fantasy (social fantasy of the Jewish plot) is an attempt to provide an answer to "What does society want from me?" that is, to unearth the meaning of the murky events in which I am forced to participate. For that reason, the standard theory of "projection," according to which the anti-Semite "projects" onto the figure of the Jew the disavowed part of himself, is not sufficient: the figure of "conceptual Jew" cannot be reduced to the externalization of my (anti-Semite's) "inner conflict"; on the contrary, it bears witness to (and tries to cope with) the fact that I am originally decentered, part of an opaque network whose meaning and logic elude my control.

On that account, the question of *la traversée du fantasme*, of how to gain the minimum of distance toward the phantasmatic frame that organizes one's enjoyment, of how to suspend its efficiency, is crucial not only for the concept of the psychoanalytic cure and its conclusion: today, in our era of renewed racist tensions, of universalized anti-Semitism, it is perhaps the foremost *political* question. The impotence of the attitude of traditional Enlightenment is best exemplified by the antiracist who, at the level of rational argumentation, produces a series of convincing reasons against the racist Other, but is nonetheless clearly *fascinated* by the object of his critique—and, consequently, all his defense disintegrates in the moment of real crisis (when "the fatherland is in danger," for example), as in the classical Hollywood film in which the bad guy, although "officially" condemned and ruined at the end, is nonetheless the focus of the spectator's libidinal investment (it was Hitchcock who emphasized that a film is only as alluring as its bad guy). The foremost problem is not how to denounce and rationally defeat the enemy—a task that can easily result in strengthening its hold upon us—but *how to break its (phantasmatic) spell upon us*. The point of *la traversée du fantasme* is not to get rid of *jouissance* (in the mode of the old leftist Puritanism): the distance toward fantasy means, rather, that I as it were "unhook" *jouissance* from its phantasmatic frame and acknowledge it as that which is properly *undecidable*, as the *indivisible remainder* that is neither inherently "reactionary," the support of historical inertia, nor the liberating force that enables us to undermine the constraint of the existing order.

Notes

All English translations have been done by the author, with the exception of those cited in the notes.

1 Insofar as this object is the elementary phantasmatic object (see Lacan's mathem of fantasy, $ ◇ a), another way to make the same point is also to say that our sense of reality disintegrates the moment reality approaches too much our fundamental fantasy. We should be attentive not to miss the paradox here: when, exactly, does the experience of the "loss of reality" take place? Not, as one would expect, when the abyss that separates "words" and "things" grows too large, so that "reality" no longer seems to fit the frame or horizon of our symbolic pre-understanding, but, on the contrary, when "reality" fits "words" too closely, i.e., when the content of our words is realized in an excessively "literal" way. Suffice it to recall Freud's uncanny reaction when, after long years of fantasizing about the Acropolis, he for the first time visited it: he was so amazed by the fact that all he was reading about from his early youth really existed and looked exactly like it was described in the books, that his first reaction was an overwhelming feeling of the "loss of reality"—no, this cannot be real . . .

2 In a first approach, it may appear that we are here as far as possible from Hegel: Does Cantor's concept of the transfinite as that which persists outside the finite, which stands side by side with it, which is exempted from it as its external frame, not provide an exemplary case of what Hegel calls the "abstract infinite," which, insofar as

it is externally opposed to the finite and excludes it, is in itself again finite? And is not, in contrast to this transfinite, the Hegelian "true infinite" immanent to the finite, is it not the very organic totality of the finite in its movement of self-sublation? It is, however, precisely such an "organic" notion of the infinite as the living totality of the finite that remains at the level of substance since, in it, the infinite is not yet *for itself*: it is crucial for Hegel that the infinite must appear, that it be "posited as such," in its difference to the finite—only thus do we pass from substance to subject. For Hegel, "subject" *qua* the power of absolute negativity designates the point at which the infinite is posited as such, in its negative relationship to everything finite.

3 Strictly speaking, the same goes also for the *transcendental* dimension as such. The field of our experience is in principle "open," infinite, there is always something to be added to it; we arrive at the transcendental dimension when we decide to treat this "open" field of experience as a closed, framed totality, and to render thematic the frame that, although not part of our experience, a priori delineates its contours.

4 See Michel Chion, *La Voix au cinéma* (Paris: Cahiers du Cinéma, 1982).

5 The point is therefore not only that voice fills out the hole in the image: the voice simultaneously *cuts out* this hole. What we encounter here is again the fundamental paradox of fantasy, which fills out the gap it itself opens up: the element that conceals is simultaneously that which reveals, i.e., the very process of concealing creates the concealed content, it creates the impression that there is something to conceal. A scene from Mel Brooks's *High Anxiety* takes place at a psychoanalytical conference, with a couple of young children occupying seats in the first row. The speaker, scrutinized by these inquisitive children, feels embarrassed when he is about to talk about perversions, phallus, castration, etc., so he eludes the impasse by translating the complex psychoanalytical jargon into "childspeak" ("Papa threatens to cut off the little boy's pipi," etc.). The blunder of this tactic resides in the fact that the very endeavor to adapt the content to the horizon of the children (and thus to neutralize its traumatic impact) renders it accessible to them—if the speaker were simply to read his text, the children would have no idea about its content.

6 However, although it is not possible to "see oneself looking," it is, for that very reason, possible to "see oneself [being] seen" [*se voir être vu*]—therein, in *seeing* oneself being exposed to the other's gaze, consists the exhibitionist's enjoyment. On the other hand, the very possibility of "hearing oneself speaking" renders it impossible to "hear oneself being heard" [*s'entendre être entendu*]—as Lacan points out, the subjects who *do* "hear themselves being heard" are precisely those who "hear voices," psychotics with audiohallucinations (see Jacques Lacan, *Le Séminaire*, book 8: *Le Transfert* [Paris: Éditions du Seuil, 1991], 360).

7 Georges Balanchine staged a short orchestral piece by Webern (they are all short) so that, after the music is over, the dancers continue to dance for some time in complete silence, as if they had not noticed that the music that provides the substance for their dance is already over—like the cat in a cartoon who simply continues to walk over the edge of the precipice, ignoring that she no longer has ground under her feet. The dancers who continue to dance after the music is over are like the living dead who

dwell in an interstice of empty time: their movements, which lack vocal support, allow us to see not only the voice but silence itself.

8   What if there is—and there certainly always is—an actual conspiracy or corruption scandal in which the state power itself is involved? The phantasmatic logic of conspiracy effectively hinders the public revelation of actual conspiracies, corruption cases, etc. The efficiency of the phantasmatic logic of conspiracy demands that the enemy remains an unfathomable entity whose true identity can never be fully disclosed.

9   We are relying here on the excellent book by Greg Dening, *Mr. Bligh's Bad Language: Passion, Power and Theatre on the Bounty* (Cambridge: Cambridge UP, 1994), especially 55–87.

10 Ibid. 77–79.

11 See Henning Henningsen, *Crossing the Equator: Sailor's Baptisms and Other Initiation Rites* (Munksgaarde, 1961), quoted in Dening, *Mr. Bligh's Bad Language,* 77.

12 *Full Metal Jacket* successfully resists the temptation to "humanize" the drill sergeant, in opposition to *An Officer and a Gentleman,* for example, which performs the ideological gesture of letting us know that, beneath his cruel and demanding appearance, the drill sergeant is a warm, fatherlike figure.

13 For a more detailed account of this status of the voice, see, in the present volume, Mladen Dolar's "The Object Voice."

14 This thesis—that violence emerges when the fundamental symbolic fiction that holds together a social edifice is (perceived as) endangered—is relevant also for the revolutionary process. In his "Really-Existing Marxism" (unpublished manuscript), Fredric Jameson draws a parallel between the role of terrestrial wealth in early capitalist Protestantism and the role of violence in a revolutionary experience. In the Protestant universe of divine predestination, terrestrial wealth—although not *in itself* good—nonetheless serves as a "sign of grace": it indicates that the subject is among the chosen. In a homologous way, in a revolutionary process, the outbreak of violence (i.e., the violent resistance of the ruling classes, their state apparatuses, and their ideologues to the process of revolutionary change) serves as a key index of the authenticity of the revolutionary change: it bears witness to the fact that we have effectively "touched the nerve" of the existing social order. The point is thus not that, in a revolution, violence is in itself good: it emerges as a kind of "essential by-product" of the revolutionary process, as a surprised "reaction" of the existing power structure to the revolutionary measures that, as a rule, have the form of a "peaceful" program of reforms.

15 The example of Bosnia provides an exemplary case of how the connection between violence and symbolic fiction runs also in the opposite direction: the very exposure of a subject (a community) to extreme "real" violence can instigate the formation of symbolic identity. Prior to the recent war and the torments they were exposed to, Bosnian Muslims were arguably the most "cosmopolitan" ethnic element in the former Yugoslavia, with practically no sense of national identity—it is the very fact of extreme violence that set in motion a prolific process of the constitution of symbolic identity, i.e., it is in reaction to violence that Bosnian Muslims began to perceive

themselves as an entity with a clear sense of national identity. See Renata Salecl, *The Spoils of Freedom* (London: Routledge, 1994).

16 Let me recall a rather personal experience, that of my own mother. Her best friend is, as the saying goes, an old Jewish lady; after some financial transaction with her, my mother told me, "What a nice lady, but did you notice the strange way she counted the money?" In my mother's eyes, this feature, the way the Jewish lady handled the money, functioned exactly like the mysterious feature from the science-fiction novels and films that enables us to identify aliens who are otherwise indistinguishable from ourselves (a thin layer of transparent skin between the third finger and the little finger, a strange gleam in the eye).

17 One has to be attentive here not to miss the key point: the other that the pervert aims to *faire exister* is *not* the big Other *qua* the virtual symbolic order, but the *real other*, the other from which the big Other (the "wall of language") separates us forever. The pervert's aim is to render palpable, via the other's unbearable pain, which obliterates the symbolic dimension, the hard kernel of the real that eludes symbolization.

18 For a more detailed account of the libidinal economy of "hate speech," see Renata Salecl, "See No Evil, Speak No Evil," in Joan Copjec, ed., *On Radical Evil*, S series, vol. 2 (London: Verso, 1996).

19 Insofar as this context is the big Other *qua* the formal structure that regulates communication, one can also put it in the following way: "castration" stands for the impossibility of hearing directly the big Other as such — the Other is the "absent Cause," the empty structure which "runs the show" and for that very reason cannot be heard. The injurious word, in contrast, is experienced as the suspension of (symbolic) castration: it is as if, in it, *the big Other directly makes itself heard* — this direct intervention of the Other renders (counter)argumentation impossible.

20 *Mutatis mutandis,* the same goes also for the discourse analysis of works of fiction: its proper object is the proto-Popperian "third world," which is *neither* the world of diegetic reality (in this case, one treats persons from diegetic reality as real persons and analyzes their psychic complexes — "Was Hamlet an obsessional neurotic or not?" etc.) nor the psychic reality of the reader or spectator (in this case, one studies the psychic impact of a work of fiction on him/her, the fantasies this work sets in motion, etc.), but the intermediate level of positions of enunciation and/or identification that constitute the "dialogue" between a work of fiction and its consumer — say, in Hitchcock's *Psycho,* the complex interplay of different positions constructed, "set up," for the spectator.

21 Muriel Gardiner, *The Wolf-Man and Sigmund Freud* (Harmondsworth: Penguin, 1973), 287.

22 For that reason, our experience of the paternal figure necessarily oscillates between lack and surplus: there is always "too much" or "not enough" of the father, never the right measure of him — "either he is wanting as presence or, in his presence, he is all too much here" (Jacques Lacan, *Le Séminaire,* book 8: *Le Transfert* [Paris: Éditions du Seuil, 1991], 346). On the one hand, we have the recurrent motif of the *absent* father, his absence being blamed for everything including the crime rate among ado-

lescents; on the other hand, as soon as the father is effectively "here," his *presence* is necessarily experienced as disturbing, vulgar, boastful, indecent, incompatible with the dignity of the parental authority, as if his presence as such is already an obtrusive excess.

This dialectics of lack and excess accounts for the paradoxical inversion in our relationship to a figure of power: when this figure (father, king . . .) no longer successfully performs his function, when he no longer fully exerts his power, *this lack is necessarily (mis)perceived as an excess,* i.e., the ruler is reproached with "amassing too much authority," as if we're dealing with a "brutal excess of power." This paradox is typical of the prerevolutionary situation: the more a regime (say, the ancien régime in France in the years before 1789) is uncertain of itself, of its legitimacy, the more it hesitates and makes concessions to the opposition, the more it is attacked by the opposition as an illegitimate tyranny. The opposition, of course, acts here as a hysteric, since its reproach of excessive exercise of power covers its exact opposite—the true reproach of the opposition is that the regime *is not strong enough,* that it doesn't live up to its mandate of power.

23 If we were to indulge in speculation on why the phallus *qua* organ has been chosen to function as the phallic signifier, then the characteristic that "predisposes" it for this role would be the feature evoked by Saint Augustine: the phallus is an organ of power-potency, yet an organ whose display of potency essentially eludes the subject's control—with the alleged exception of some Hindu priests, one cannot bring about erection at will, so that erection bears witness to some foreign power at work in the very heart of the subject.

24 The other (mis)reading, closely linked to the first, concerns the opposition between the phallic economy and the polymorphous plurality of subject positions: according to the standard view, the task of the phallic economy is to mould the pre-Oedipal dispersed plurality of subject positions into a unified subject who is subordinated to the rule of the Name of the Father (bearer and relay of social authority) and is as such the ideal subject of (social) power. What one has to call in question here is the underlying assumption that social power exerts itself via the unified oedipal subject entirely submitted to the phallic paternal law, and, inversely, that the dispersion of the unified subject into a multitude of subject positions as it were automatically undermines the authority and exercise of power. Against this commonplace, one has to point out again and again that power always interpellates us, addresses us, as *split* subjects, that, in order to reproduce itself, it relies upon our splitting: the message the power discourse bombards us with is by definition inconsistent, there is always a gap between public discourse and its phantasmatic support—far from being a kind of secondary weakness, a sign of the power's imperfection, this splitting is constitutive for its exercise. With regard to the so-called postmodern form of subjectivity that befits late capitalism, one has to go even a step further: the postmodern subject is directly, at the level of the public discourse itself, constituted as an inconsistent bundle of multiple "subject positions" (economically conservative but sexually "enlightened" yuppie, etc.).

25 For a classic statement of the different versions of "I know very well, but still . . ." see Octave Mannoni, "Je sais bien, mais quand même . . . ," in *Clefs pour l'imaginaire* (Paris: Seuil, 1968); for a political reading of it, see chapter 6 of Slavoj Žižek, *For They Know Not What They Do* (London: Verso, 1991).

26 The same logic seems to be at work in the anti-Communist right-wing populism that is recently gaining strength in the former socialist East European countries: its answer to the present economic and other hardships is that, although they lost legal, public power, Communists continue to pull the strings, to dominate the levers of effective economic power, to control the media and state institutions. Communists are thus perceived as a phantasmatic entity *à la* Jew: the more they lose public power and become invisible, the stronger their phantomlike all-presence, their shadowy effective control. . . . This *idée fixe* of the populists, according to which what is now emerging in postsocialist countries is not "true" capitalism but a false imitation in which actual power and control remain in the hands of ex-Communists dressed up as newly baked capitalists, also offers an exemplary case of the illusion whose mechanism was laid bare for the first time by Hegel: what they fail to recognize is that their opposition to this "false" capitalism is effectively opposition to capitalism *tout court*, i.e., that they, not the ex-Communists, are the true ideological inheritors of socialism—no wonder that the populists are compelled to resuscitate the old Communist opposition between "formal" and "true" democracy. In short, we are dealing with yet another example of the irony that pertains to the revolutionary process, the irony already described by Marx: all of a sudden, the amazed revolutionaries perceive that they were mere vanishing mediators whose "historical role" was to prepare the terrain for the old masters to take over in new guises.

27 Incidentally, another homology that has to be rejected for the same reasons is that between the Name of the Father and the phantasmatic Woman. Lacan's "Woman doesn't exist" [*la Femme n'existe pas*] (see Jacques Lacan, *Le Séminaire,* book 20: *Encore* [Paris: Éditions du Seuil, 1975], 68) does not mean that no empirical, flesh-and-blood woman is ever "She," that she cannot ever live up to the inaccessible ideal of Woman (in the way that the empirical, "real" father never lives up to his symbolic function, to his Name). The gap that forever separates any empirical woman from Woman is not the same as the gap between an empty symbolic function and its empirical bearer who can never fully live up to it: the problem with woman is, on the contrary, that it is not possible to formulate her empty ideal-symbolic function—*this* is what Lacan has in mind when he asserts that "Woman doesn't exist." The impossible "Woman" is not a symbolic fiction, but again a phantasmatic specter whose support is *objet a*, not S_1. The one who "doesn't exist" in the same sense as Woman is the primordial father enjoyment, which is why his status is correlative to that of Woman.

28 An exemplary case of this opposition between symbolic authority and the spectral invisible Master is provided by Wagner's *Das Rheingold,* in the guise of opposition between Wotan and Alberich—see, in the present volume, my essay "There Is No Sexual Relationship."

29 The millionaire's position is in fact even more complex. That is to say, when a woman

says to a man "I don't love you for your millions (or power . . .) but for what you really are!" what does this amount to? The more she "means it sincerely," the more she is the victim of a kind of perspective illusion, failing to notice how *the very fact that (people know that) I am a millionaire (or a man of power) affects people's perception of what I am "in myself," irrespective of this property of mine.* As long as I remain rich, people perceive me as a strong, independent personality, whereas the moment I lose my millions, they all of a sudden see in me a dull weakling (or vice versa, for that matter). In short, the paradox resides in the fact that only a woman who (knows that she) loves me on behalf of my millions is able to perceive me the way I truly am, since my wealth no longer distorts her perception.

James Ivory's film *Remains of the Day* presents an interesting variation on this standard illusion of a woman in love with a man "not for his (symbolic) status but for what he really is": in the film, Emma Thompson is in love with the rigid, obsessive butler (Anthony Hopkins); in her perception of the situation, she loves him *in spite of* his symbolic mask of obsessive rigidity and his inability to find an outlet for his emotions, whereas she in fact loves him *on account of* his obsessive rigidity—this very obsessive mask gives rise to the idea that, beneath it, there must be a warm human person waiting to be let free. . . . For that reason, it is in the vital interest of her love that their relationship remains unconsummated, i.e., that Hopkins does *not* respond to her calls: if he were to "set himself loose," he would instantly cease being her love object. (See, in the present volume, Renata Salecl's "I Can't Love You Unless I Give You Up.") And, incidentally, a homologous misrecognition seems to be at work in the public perception of Pope John Paul II: one is usually impressed by his charisma, his moral inner conviction and firmness, yet one regrets his "extremist" standpoints (in the matters of abortion, contraception, divorce, etc.)—as if it were possible to separate the two sides, i.e., as if this intransigence were not the crucial constituent of the Pope's charisma. Therein resides the paradox of the Pope's charisma: what appears as a stain on it, an obstacle to it, is in fact its inherent condition—the Pope does not irradiate charisma *in spite of* his extreme inflexibility but *because of it*.

30 See Jacques Lacan, *Le Séminaire,* book 20: *Encore* (Paris: Seuil 1975), 84. This problematic enables us to approach Wagner's *Lohengrin* in a new way: what is ultimately at stake in this opera is precisely the impasse of Chabrol's unfortunate millionaire, namely the status of that something "in him more than himself" that the woman perceives in the hero; for a more detailed account of it, see, in the present volume, my essay "There Is No Sexual Relationship."

31 For a more detailed account of these paradoxes, see chapter 2 of Slavoj Žižek, *The Indivisible Remainder* (London: Verso, 1996).

32 See Jacques Derrida, *Spectres de Marx* (Paris: Galilée, 1993).

33 This notion of antagonism is, of course, due to Ernesto Laclau and Chantal Mouffe, *Hegemony and Socialist Strategy* (London: Verso, 1985).

34 Perhaps this notion of the real also accounts for the key feature of the "new wave" of documentaries from the late eighties and early nineties whose exemplary case is *The Thin Blue Line* (see the nonpareil analysis by Linda Williams in her "Mirrors without

Memories—Truth, History, and the New Documentary," *Film Quarterly* 46, no. 3, [spring 1993]: 9–21): these films, although they leave behind the naive reference to reality that allegedly persists "out there," outside the cinematic fiction, also avoid the "postmodernist" trap of the boundless game of simulacres in which the very notion of "referent" disappears, is dismissed as the last remnant of metaphysical illusion. In *The Thin Blue Line*, the referent is well operative: the entire film turns on "what really happened" on the night of the killing; the film is as far as possible from any kind of pseudo-*Rashomon* ideology in which reality evaporates into the multiplicity of points of view. However, this real kernel, this "hard core," is simultaneously closer and further away than the traditional "realist" referent: it is further away since it is presupposed as inherently unrepresentable, as something that a priori eludes and resists integration into the narrative (the film can only offer faked dramatizations of the different hypotheses of what "really happened"); it is closer since the film conceives of itself as an intervention into what it describes (the filmmaker clearly endeavors to lay ground for the retrial). We can see here how radical transcendence (the positing of the real as unrepresentable, beyond the reach of our representations) coincides with radical immanence (with the fact that between "us" and the real there is no clear distance that allegedly separates the represented content from the perceiving-registering subject: the subject directly intervenes into, is part of, the unrepresentable content, which therefore *remains unrepresentable on account of this same overproximity*). It is the same with Claude Lanzmann's *Shoah*: the film alludes to the trauma of holocaust as something that is beyond representation (it can only by discerned via its traces, surviving witnesses, remaining monuments); however, the reason for this impossibility of representing the holocaust is not simply that it is "too traumatic," but rather that we, observing subjects, are still involved in it, are still part of the process that generated it (recall the scene from *Shoah* in which Polish peasants from a village near the concentration camp, interviewed now, in our present time, continue to find Jews "strange," i.e., repeat the very logic that brought about the holocaust). This coincidence is properly Hegelian and is, as such, to be opposed to the logic of Disneyland denounced years ago by Baudrillard: the trap of Disneyland does not reside in its attempt to convince us of the authenticity of its faked attractions, it rather resides in the attempt to convince us that the world *outside* Disneyland, the world we (re)enter when we leave the theme park, is "true reality" and not a fake. In other words, the true deception resides in the fact that the staged appearance *offers itself as a fake*, thereby guaranteeing the authenticity of "reality" outside itself—this is, according to Hegel, the true deception involved in the notion of appearance.

35 Claude Lévi-Strauss, "Do Dual Organizations Exist?" in *Structural Anthropology*, trans. Claire Jacobson and Brooke Schoepf (New York: Basic Books, 1963), 131–63; the drawings are on pp. 133–34.

36 Here we have an exemplary case of how the difference *qua* the real of antagonism paradoxically *precedes* the two terms it differentiates: these two positive terms (the political "Left" and "Right") are the two endeavors to formulate within the symbolic the difference (the antagonism) that eludes the symbolic order.

37 The domain of architecture is here of special interest: do great architectural and urban projects not always bear witness to the endeavor to materialize—in the very disposition of the social space of buildings, public spaces, free-time facilities, etc.—an imagined solution to social antagonisms? Is, for example, the modernist functionalism not an attempt to construct a transparent and rationally organized social space guaranteeing the harmonious coordination of all aspects of social life (work, free time, administration)? Architecture is perhaps the clearest example of how the very "real" materiality (of the disposition of buildings) always gives body to an ideological project.

38 In a strictly homologous way, the proof that the dimension of law does not cover the entire field of ethics resides in the very fact that there are *two* laws, the public symbolic law and its obscene superego underside: each of these two laws (the public law regulating the "service of goods," the peaceful coexistence of subjects, as well as its counterpart, the obscene injunction to enjoyment) involves a way to "compromise our desire," i.e., it entices the subject to betray the ethical dimension of "not giving way as to one's desire." For more on these two sides of the law, see chapter 3 of Slavoj Žižek, *Metastases of Enjoyment* (London: Verso, 1994).

39 This problematic also enables us to formulate the gap that separates Althusser and Lacan: in the Althusserian theoretical edifice, there is no place for the difference fiction/fantasy. Althusser operates with only two terms—the (symbolic) *structure* and the *imaginary* experience of its (mis)recognition—whereas Lacan requires a minimum of three: although fantasy is imaginary, it occupies the place of the real. That is to say, on the one hand, of course, we have the imaginary misrecognition of the symbolic machine; on the other hand, however, this machine is in itself impeded, structured around a constitutive blockage, in a word, around the real of an impossibility, and fantasy is the imaginary scenario that functions as a kind of stand-in for this void, i.e., it simultaneously bears witness to it and conceals it. For the same reason Lacan, in clear contrast to Althusser, not only maintains the term "alienation" but even uses it in two meanings not to be confused: on the one hand, alienation *qua* imaginary identification with the mirror-other which blinds me to the symbolic mediation and, on the other hand, my—the subject's—identification with the signifier that represents me for others, i.e., my constitutive alienation in the signifying structure itself.

40 For a more detailed elaboration of the logic of anti-Semitism with regard to its specific function in capitalism, see chapter 1 of Slavoj Žižek, *The Sublime Object of Ideology* (London: Verso, 1989), chapter 3 of Slavoj Žižek, *Enjoy Your Symptom!* (New York: Routledge, 1992), as well as chapter 4 of Slavoj Žižek, *Tarrying with the Negative* (Durham, N.C.: Duke University Press, 1993).

PART II | **love objects**

Mladen Dolar

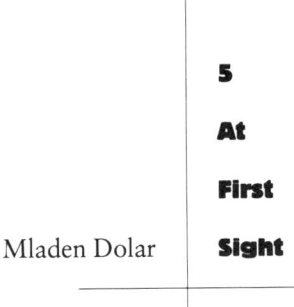

5
At First Sight

The paradox of love can perhaps best be formulated in the following terms: *the junction of a contingent exterior with the most intimate interior.* To put it in these terms points toward that essential dimension for which Lacan has coined the excellent word, *extimacy,* the dimension so crucial to psychoanalytic discovery and which, maybe, contains the key to psychoanalytic concepts of the subject and the object.[1]

Let us first consider a very simple case, a paradoxical kind of social requirement, which could be called "injunctions of love," such as, love your parents, love your family, your home, your native soil, your country, your nation, and love your next-door neighbor. The paradox is, of course, that love is prescribed where there is actually no choice as to its object—it seems self-evident that one cannot choose one's parents or native soil, and so on. The contingent circumstances of one's birth are transformed into an object of prescribed love; what is unavoidable and offers no possibility of a choice becomes ethically sanctioned. The given is tacitly assumed to be an object of a supposed choice and of one's inner consent—the choice that one has never made, or rather, that has "always already" been made. If there is a choice, it is a forced one; it is decided in advance. These injunctions actually preserve the content of the given and change only its form, but this purely formal difference is essential: the natural links are undone as natural, but they are tied together as the signifying ties. The subject can only be liberated from its natural bonds by being tied to the chains of the signifier (the current neutral term "the signifying chain" is perhaps not so innocent).

This common process can be seen as a triple device of subjectivation—three things happen simultaneously: first, the passage from a contingent exterior into an object of inner acceptance; second, the purely formal change where the contents remain the same and there is only a shift in the subject's position; third, the forced choice where the given is presented as what one has chosen, although one was never granted a situation of "free choice." The forced choice is not simply an absence of choice: the choice is offered and denied in the same gesture, but this empty gesture is what counts for subjectivity.

One of the most famous formulations of the forced choice was given by Lacan in his seminar on *The Four Fundamental Concepts of Psycho-Analysis* (Lacan 1979, 212). Lacan takes a very drastic example, that of being presented with a choice of "Your money or your life" ("La bourse ou la vie"). The peculiar thing in this choice is that, if taken seriously, there is no choice at all: one can only choose to hold to one's life and thus lose only the money; holding on to the money would entail losing both. One can only choose one alternative, and even this one is curtailed (life deprived of money), whereas the other alternative is void (money without life). In any case, one loses the intersection of both (life with money)—which can be illustrated by the simple scheme of two intersecting circles that Lacan was so fond of (Lacan 1979, 211-12).

The formal aspect of this model may serve as a pattern of subjectivation: one is presented with a choice that is decided in advance, and by choosing, one suffers a loss. To put it roughly, the subject, in its insertion in the social, is subject of a choice, but a forced one, and of a loss. The example is also designed to demonstrate the price one has to pay for the entry into symbolic—something that we can provisionally leave aside. This experience is very common, not confined to dark and solitary alleys. Love, in its many various forms,[2] has this mechanism of forced choice always attached to it. To put it simply, one is compelled to choose love and thereby give up the freedom of choice, while by choosing freedom of choice, one loses both.[3] There is an angle from which "love your parents" comes close to "money or your life."

I have started with the simplest and the most common example, something that everybody has to undergo in order to become a social being. But love in its most emphatic and glorified form, "erotic" love, the traditionally celebrated love between a man and a woman, involves precisely the same device. It would seem that there has to be an autonomy of a free choice—indeed one cannot speak of love if there is no freedom of choice (if the choice is made, e.g., by parents, as was the common practice until quite recently). Yet to take a closer, or even a very superficial, look at the centuries of effusions about love, it is obvious that love and autonomy of the subject rule each other out. All melodramas know that; the pattern could be described as follows: A young hero quite *by coincidence* and *through no endeavor of his* meets a young girl in some more or less extraordinary circumstances. What happened unintentionally and by pure chance is in the second stage recognized as the realization of his innermost and immemorial wishes and desires. The contingent miraculously becomes the place of his deepest truth, the sign of fate given by the Other. It is the Other that has chosen, not the young man himself who was powerless (and who has to face heroically, in the third stage, the consequences of his nonchoice: the opposition of the parents or the society, the intrigues, the bad fortune, the illness, etc., with various possible combinations and outcomes). It turns out that the pure chance was actually no chance at all: the intrusion of the unforeseen turned into necessity, the *tyche* turned into the *automaton*. The moment of subjectivation is precisely that moment of suspension of subjectivity to the Other (fate, providence, eternal plan, destiny, or whatever one might call it), manifesting itself as the pure contingency of the Real. Indeed, the strange force of love reputedly rules out any other considerations; it does not permit deliberation, the balance of gains and losses, pondering the advantages of a certain choice—it just demands the unconditional surrender to the Other. All melodramas also know very well that the moment one stops to reason about the viability of a certain choice, the moment one starts to calculate the advantages and disadvantages, one is heading for disaster. If one doesn't surrender unconditionally to fate, fate will inexorably revenge itself.[4]

The situation is obviously contradictory, since it presupposes the freedom of an autonomous choice and at the same time demands its suppression. This contradiction can only be reconciled in a strange logic of *post festum*: the young man has chosen only by recognizing that the choice has already been made, regardless of his freedom of choice; he could only endorse and corroborate the decision of the Other by accepting the unavoidable as his own inner essence. In other words, the choice here has to be conceived as a retroactive category: it is always in the past tense, but a special kind of *past that was never present*. The moment of choice can never be pinpointed, one cannot pin it down to a presence of a conscious and autonomous decision, it passes directly and immediately from a "not yet" to an "always already." It is past by its very nature. Falling in love means submitting to the necessity—there is always the moment when the Real, so to speak, begins to speak, its opacity turns into transparence, the senseless sign becomes the embodiment of the highest sense, and the subject is reduced to recognizing it after the fact. This is the moment of the glorified miracle of love.

Their Eyes Met

There is hardly any myth that has shown such an obstinate persistence as the myth of the first encounter, "the first sight." It is present in all our narrations, from the legends of times immemorial throughout the bulk of the world literature to its modern versions in cinema. It has crossed millennia and traversed all boundaries between cultures, it permeates both the highest achievements of the "elite" culture and the lowest forms of popular culture and entertainment. Its core has remained remarkably the same, the quasi-mechanic repetition of one and the same story: the chance encounter has miraculous consequences, it becomes the foundational moment that has the power to entirely transform the subjects who assume the contingent as the very essence of their being, something to rule their destiny, and no power can be equal to it.

One could imagine the alluring task of setting up a catalogue of that precise moment of falling in love, taking the world literature, plus the cinema, from its highest to its lowest forms, as the evidence in the matter. The task was actually remarkably carried out, at least for the bulk of French literature, by Jean Rousset (1984), who has undertaken an extensive phenomenology of "the scene of the first sight in the novel" (as the subtitle of his book goes, the title being *Their Eyes Met*). "Their eyes met"—the simple sentence is taken from Flaubert's *Sentimental Education*, surely one of the greatest love novels, but it could have been taken from thousands of other examples. It epitomizes the gaze, the return of the gaze, as the crucial moment of that foundational myth of encounter. It is a moment of recognition: one recognizes what has "always already" been there, since the beginning of time, and the whole previous existence retroactively acquires the sense of leading just to this moment. (All the examples I give are chosen at random; one could choose myriads more):

> Surely it was lovers who discovered astrology. Nothing less than the great chamber of the stars could be large and steady enough to be context, origin, and guarantee of something so eternal. I realized now that my whole life had been determinedly travelling towards this moment. Her whole life had been travelling towards it, as she played and read her school books and grew and looked in the mirror at her breasts. This was a predestined collision. But it had not only just happened, it had happened aeons ago, it was of the stuff of the original formation of earth and sky. When God said 'Let there be light' this love was made. It had no history. (Murdoch 1975, 206)

The sudden recognition implies that *the first time is already repetition,* one realizes what one has always already known. It is foundational insofar as it creates its own prehistory, the "original" moment is the "reproduction" of what was already there, but which was nevertheless retroactively created by it—for it was not there before its "reproduction." Seeing the beloved for the first time, one recognizes him/her as somebody one has always known:

> *Sieglinde:* A marvel stirs in my memory:
> although you came but today,
> I've seen your face before!
> *Siegmund:* I know your dream
> I feel it too:
> in ardent yearning
> you were my dream! (Wagner 1977, 92)[5]

In the same way as the encounter creates its prehistory, it also founds its future: the subject's life is entirely transfigured and acquires a new destination; there is a sudden transubstantiation of his or her entire existence, where every detail is transformed by a new light. Life is henceforward to be governed by fidelity to what emerged in the accident of that passing instant. There is a paradigmatic opposition between the briefness of a moment (and as a rule it has to be a brief and sudden instant) and its definitive character, which aims at eternity, metamorphosing radically both past and future.

The modalities of this instant can of course vary greatly. The happy encounter of two strangers, albeit the guiding image, is just the extreme case of the myth. There can be an abrupt recognition in relation to someone one has known for a long time. There can be a mutual dislike at first sight retroactively changing into recognition (as in *Pride and Prejudice*, for instance). There can be a one-sided miracle, leading to the tortures of unrequited love. But "Their eyes met" is nevertheless the paradigm: there is an exchange of the gaze, *the Real has returned the gaze*, even if the other person didn't respond, or was unaffected by it, or even unaware of it. The lack of sense of a contingent fate, the haphazard string of events, was in that moment suddenly filled by the gaze, that Lacanian paramount evocation of what he called the object *a*. For once, one saw instead of just looking. For once one ceased to be blind, the gaze was returned—or is it that one sees only at the price of blindness, as common sense would have it, always associating love and blindness, a blindness more radical than what went before? If the gaze comes to fill the lack of sense in that senseless fortune, it also creates it by filling it, for it is only looking backward that one sees the lack, and only as a lack destined to be filled. Life didn't "make sense" before, but now, suddenly, it does.

The contingency that lies at the bottom of this emergence of love is remarkably aligned around the gaze. The evidence is overwhelming, the hand of fate seems to operate primarily by the gaze. It can be, in some rather rare cases, deflected toward the voice (the other Lacanian object): a few sentences overheard in the dark, as in the first encounter of Count Andrei and Natasha in *War and Peace;* a singing voice responding in the night as in Balzac's *L'Enfant maudit;* but it always seems to function as a preparatory stage for the exchange of the gaze, its prefiguration. To be sure, this exchange of the gaze can take all kinds of strange forms: falling in love with a portrait (e.g., *The Magic Flute*); falling in love with a veiled stranger, and so on. One of the most exquisite contemporary examples is given in the opening chapter of Salman Rushdie's *Midnight's Children*, where a young Indian doctor can only examine a young female patient through a hole in a sheet, for the sake of propriety, one part of her body at a time—this device is enough for them to fall madly in love, the girl inventing always new illnesses and symptoms for the doctor to return and examine her, and it eventually took three years before "their eyes met," when she finally invented the simplest of symptoms, a headache. But the gaze was returned long before their eyes met, the perforated sheet was framing exactly what Lacan called "the window of fantasy." The gaze returned can be metonymically presented by all kinds of contingent objects or circumstances that have acquired the status of the embodiment of fate. The trifling and trivial details are magically transfigured to return the gaze.

The external contingency can thus be ultimately reduced to and epitomized by the gaze, that elusive object, which in the foundational scene of the encounter appears as anything but elusive: it emerges as the firm rock of positivity on which to build one's existence, the authoritative and commanding presence by which to rule one's life, the steadfast support of one's being against all odds. Therefore Lacan can say that love is always returned.

The Mirror

Surely the paramount case of falling in love at first sight, the exchange of the gaze, of the gaze returned, is constituted by the recognition of one's own image in the mirror, the kernel of the famous Lacanian "mirror phase." In that foundational myth as well there is a sudden and miraculous recognition, the emergence of something that was, retroactively, already there, the creation of a prehistory, the sudden insight dissipating the blindness, or rather coinciding with it, the jubilation, the happy love immediately returned, the promise of a radiant future. There is a strange time loop where one becomes what one recognizes oneself always to have been. At the pivotal point of this mythical situation, there is, of course, the gaze.

It may seem that one can get a simple clue to love in this emergence of narcissism, constituting the first recognition and the self — for Lacan, it is precisely from a recognition in the mirror reflection, with the necessary blinding it entails, that the notion of ego can be deduced. Indeed, psychoanalysis has repeatedly insisted on the narcissistic nature of love. One can easily find literal examples:

> *Sieglinde*: The stream has shown
> my reflected face —
> and now I find it before me;
> in you I see it again,
> just as it shone from the stream! (Wagner 1977, 92)

Yet there is a dimension of narcissism that is concealed and occulted by recognition and jubilation, the initial enthusiasm and self-indulgent pleasure. The gaze returned also encloses another message: it points to a thin line between jubilation and the most shattering anxiety. The gaze is at the junction of elation and an impending disaster that threatens to disintegrate reality.

The motive of the double, the alter ego, to which Freud devoted some reflections in his famous paper "The Uncanny," is maybe the simplest way to envision this other side. The motive takes the narcissistic choice of love object literally and thereby destroys it: one meets one's double, a *Doppelgänger,* someone exactly like oneself, and the result is the very opposite of jubilatory self-recognition: one is inexorably heading for a disaster. A profound anxiety emerges as soon as the mirror other becomes independent, when it stops being a "simple reflection" (is the reflection ever simple?). The immediate realization of the narcissistic model brings about its disruption, *the dissociation of the gaze and recognition.* The double displays the ambiguity of narcissistic recognition in the most immediate sense: the mirror image is myself and at the same time the other, and therefore all the more alien; since it constitutes my narcissistic homeliness, at the closest to my core, it is all the more threatening.

The phenomenon also appears as a clinical entity, technically called *autoscopia*—seeing or meeting oneself as another person. Although a rather rare form of mental disorder, it has produced a considerable amount of technical literature since the mid-nineteenth century (see Blumel 1980 for a general survey). But it owes its rather spectacular fame to its abundant use in literature, particularly in an incredible outburst in the Romantic era, which gave birth to a very extensive gallery of doubles.[6]

There are some simple structural features of these stories, which can have a number of complex ramifications with different outcomes: the subject[7] is confronted with his double, the very image of himself (this can be accompanied by the disappearance, or trading off, of his mirror image or his shadow), which immediately produces a frightful anxiety, the crumbling of subject's accustomed reality, the shattering of the bases of his world. Usually only the subject can see his own double, who takes care to appear only privately, or only the subject can realize its significance. The double then produces two seemingly contradictory effects: he arranges things so they turn out badly for the subject, he turns up at the most inappropriate moments, he dooms him to failure; but, on the other hand, he realizes subject's hidden or repressed desires, he does things the subject would never dare to do. In the end, the relation usually gets unbearable, so that the subject, in a final showdown, is compelled to kill his double, but in killing him he kills himself, unaware that his substance and being were concentrated in his double: "You have conquered, and I yield," says William Wilson's double in Poe's story. "Yet henceforward art thou also dead—dead to the World, to Heaven, and to Hope! In me didst thou exist—and, in my death, see by this image, which is thine own, how utterly thou hast murdered thyself" (Poe 1979, 178).

As a rule, all these stories finish badly: the moment one encounters one's double, there seems to be no way out. In the clinical cases of autoscopia as well the forecast is bad, the outcome likely to be tragic. Rank (1989) gives an extensive "phylogenetic" account of the theme of the double in different mythologies and superstitions. They all converge in the result that the shadow and the mirror image are the obvious analogs of the body, its immaterial doubles, and are thus the best means to represent the soul. They survive the body due to their immateriality—reflections constitute our essential selves.[8] The image is more fundamental than its owner, it institutes his substance, his essential being, his "soul," it is his most valuable part, it makes him a human being.[9] It is his immortal part, his protection against death.

In a way, psychoanalysis would agree. After all, this is what Lacan's theory of the mirror phase aims at: it is only by virtue of one's mirror reflection that one can become endowed with an ego, establish oneself as an "I." My "ego identity" comes from my double. But the trouble with the doubles springs from the fact that they seem to stand for all three instances of Freud's "second topic": they constitute the essential part of the ego, they carry out the repressed desires springing from the id, and they also prevent the subject from carrying out his desires with a malevolence typical of the superego—all at one and the same time. So how can the three fit together?

There is a moment in the legend of Narcissus where the blind seer Tiresias gives the prophecy to the beautiful boy's mother: "Narcissus will live to a ripe old age, provided that he never knows himself" (Graves 1960, vol. 1, 286). The prophecy imposes the direct opposite of the oldest philosophical dictum "Know thyself!" There is a part of non-knowledge, an essential ignorance, which appears as the condition of a long and happy life, or, simply, of life—a part of fundamental loss that one has to incur. Narcissus will come to know himself, he will prefer the philosophical maxim to the prophet's warning, and that knowledge will be fateful for him. The legend foreshadows the essential part of a loss implied already in the minimal narcissistic mechanism presented by the mirror phase.

To put it simply: when I recognize myself in the mirror, it is already too late. There is a split: I cannot recognize myself and at the same time be one with myself. With the recognition, I have already lost what one could call the "self-being," the immediate coincidence with myself in my being and *jouissance*.[10] The rejoicing in the mirror image, the pleasure and the self-indulgence, had already to be paid for. The mirror double immediately introduces the dimension of castration—the doubling itself, already in its minimal form, implies castration: "This invention of doubling as a preservation against extinction has its counterpart in the language of dreams, which is fond of representing castration by a doubling or a multiplication of a genital symbol" (*Pelican Freud Library*, vol. 14, 356–57; cf. also *Pelican Freud Library*, vol. 4, 474).

The multiplicity of snakes on Medusa's head, to take another example of Freud's, is there to dissimulate the lack; the One, the Unique is missing. So the doubling, in the simplest way, entails the loss of that uniqueness that one could enjoy in one's self-being—only at the price of being neither an ego nor a subject. By the doubling, one becomes cut off from a part, the most valuable part, of one's being, the immediate self-being of *jouissance*. This is what Lacan will later add to his early theory of the mirror phase: the "object *a*" is precisely that part of the loss that one cannot see in the mirror, the part of the subject that has no mirror reflection, the nonspecular. The mirror in the most elementary way already implies the split between the Imaginary and the Real: one can only have access to imaginary reality, the world one can recognize oneself in and familiarize oneself with, on the condition of the loss, the "falling out" of the object *a*. It is this loss of the object *a* that opens the reality henceforward seen as "objective" reality, the possibility of subject-object relations, but since its loss is the condition of any knowledge of "objective" reality, it cannot itself become an object of knowledge.

We can see now what the trouble is with the double: the double is that mirror image in which the object *a* is included. It gains its own being, the Imaginary starts to coincide with the Real, provoking a shattering anxiety. The double is the same as me—*plus the object a,* that invisible part of being added to my image. Lacan uses the gaze as the best presentation of that missing object: in the mirror, one can see one's eyes, but not the gaze that is that lost part. But imagine that one could see one's mirror image close its eyes, or wink: that would make the object as the gaze appear in the mirror. This is what happens in the theme of the doubles. The anxiety that the double produces is the surest sign of the appearance of the object. (This can be also brought about in the opposite way, by the disappearance of one's mirror image, technically dubbed "negative autoscopia," as in Maupassant's *Le Horla* and a number of other stories.) Here, the Lacanian account of anxiety sharply differs from most other theories: it is not produced by a lack or a loss or an incertitude, it is not the anxiety of losing something (the firm support, one's bearings, etc.); quite the contrary, it is the anxiety of gaining something too much, of too close a presence of the object. What one loses with anxiety is precisely the loss—the loss that made it possible to deal with a coherent reality. "The anxiety is the lack of that support of the lack," says Lacan; the lack lacks, and this brings about the uncanny (cf. Blumel 1980, 49).

The inclusion of the object also entails the emergence of that lost part of *jouissance*. The double is always the figure of *jouissance:* on the one hand, he is somebody who enjoys at the subject's expense. He commits acts that one wouldn't dare to commit, indulges in one's repressed desires, but so that the blame falls on the subject. On the other hand, he is not simply someone who enjoys, but essentially a figure that commands the *jouissance*. It seems, though, that the double is a "disturber of love,"[11] he typically springs up at the moment when one is about to touch, or to kiss, the girl of one's dreams, when the subject comes close to the realization of his wishes, when he is on the brink of, finally, attaining the full enjoyment, the completion of the sexual relation. But if the double emerges as the spoiler, the obstructor, the situation has to be read in reverse: its significance lies in the choice of the object. I prefer to choose the double, the one who detains the object and who can provide *jouissance* and being, rather than that beautiful girl who can only give me pleasure. Only the alter ego can offer the true *jouissance,* which I am not willing to give up in favor of pleasure. The magnificent young girl is, rather, the obstacle in my privileged relation to myself, she is the real spoiler in this game, the spoiler of narcissism, so one has to get rid of her (and the double takes care of that) in order to join my real partner, my double. He detains that lost object that no woman can substitute. But of course joining one's *jouissance,* regaining one's "primordial" being, is lethal. The subject can only attain it by his death.

The appearance of the object in reality doesn't make it an object of possible "objective" knowledge. As a rule, it appears only to the subject, others don't see it and therefore don't understand the subject's peculiar activities. It cannot become a part of the accepted intersubjective space. It is the privileged private object accessible only to the subject, his incorporated self-being.

The double, detaining the object, also immediately introduces the death drive. The original function of the double (as the shadow and the mirror image) was "an insurance against the destruction of the ego, an 'energetic denial of the power of death' . . . and probably the 'immortal soul' was the first 'double' of the body" (*Pelican Freud Library,* vol. 14, 356). Yet what was designed as a defense against death, as a protection of narcissism—one's mortality is that *ananke* that most immediately contradicts and limits the narcissistic wholeness—turns into its harbinger: when the double appears, one's time is up. One could say, precisely as the protection against the "real" death, it inaugurates the dimension of the Real; as the defense against the biological death it introduces the death drive, that is, the drive in its fundamental sense. The double is the initial repetition, the first repetition of the same, but also what keeps repeating itself, emerging in the same place (one of the Lacanian definitions of the Real), springing up at the most awkward times, both as an irruption of the unexpected and with clockwork precision, totally unpredictable and predictable in one.

The love for the double is the extreme form of love, where love turns into its opposite and becomes lethal. On the one hand, one is not prepared to give up one's narcissism, and the double is the protection against love—love as the choice of the object, as the demand to give up one's narcissistic wholeness and contentment to the other. On the other hand, this love for the double can be maintained only by death, thus circumscribing the point where narcissism turns into death drive. The primordial object of *jouissance,* lost by recognition, is thus restored, the Real did "really" return the gaze, there was no blindness in this love, but the appearance of the gaze had nothing salutary in it, it was the death warrant. This extreme situation embodies "true love," a love too true to be bearable (not till death do us part, but till death do us unite), and the subject's protestations that he would give anything to be rid of the double cannot disguise the opposite: that he would give up anything but the double. The fatal relation to the double is both true love and the opposite of love. The object comes to effectively fill the lack, but this announces no radiant future. So love may well be seen as an extension of narcissism, but it is also at the same time a protection against it—protection against its lethal side. The object of love is put into a contradictory position where it must maintain the lack in the same time as filling it, it must protect against *jouissance* at the same time as aiming at it.

The narcissistic aspect of love can only be maintained in the form of an annihilation of narcissism, it takes the form of its opposite, the total submission to the Other. It masks the nature of subjectivity at stake, concealing it not behind the illusion of an autonomous subject as a *causa sui,* but quite the contrary, by offering one's being to the Other, by offering one's own particularity in response to the external contingency. The rest of the Real demands the offering of that rest in the subject, *the object within the subject,* and with that gesture, the rest is dealt with and the Other is sustained. The opacity of the Other is made transparent by love; the lawless becomes the lawful.

With the double, recognition immediately produced anxiety; it was a moment of sheer horror, and the subject then apparently did everything to fight the double, to get rid of the intruder in order to pursue his happiness. He refused to submit—but he was inexorably forced to submit in the very act of ultimate aggression, in killing the double. It was not the forced choice of embracing the sign of the Other as one's intimate being, quite the contrary—the subject took himself to be a free agent opposing his destiny, putting up the pretense of a free choice to the bitter end. So one can establish a point-by-point opposition with love, where, as we have seen, recognition produces the miracle of a new beginning, one freely submits to the Other and gives up the "freedom of choice," one does everything to join one's beloved, one is prepared to sacrifice any other concerns in service of love, one doesn't hesitate to disregard one's own well-being. But the implications of the two situations are reversed: in the first one, one does everything to join the double, against one's apparent wishes and proclamations; in the second one, one submits in order to protect oneself against the object, one pawns one's being to keep the object at a distance, one gives up one's freedom in order to be a subject. One renounces oneself in order to maintain oneself, along with the Other that one takes the support in, as in the courtly love that Lacan often takes up, willingly embracing all efforts and sacrifices only to keep the object at bay. One can even renounce love, in an ultimate gesture of sacrifice, in order to maintain love.

If love aims at the extimate—the intimate external kernel—it is also a protection against it, but a protection that is ambiguous and constantly failing. The other side of the extimate is the uncanny, the emergence of the object that brings about disintegration and that becomes lethal. In love, one pledges one's being as a protection against the other side of the object, one sustains the object with recognition and supreme sense. Not that the operation can be successful: it inevitably retains the ambiguity of what Lacan calls *hainamoration*, the inexorable tension between love and hate which makes the drama of love: "I love you, but, because inexplicably I love in you something more than yourself—the *objet petit a*—I mutilate you" (Lacan 1979, 263). If the beloved person detains the object, that can be a very perilous situation indeed.

If love makes the utmost to cover the object with recognition and sense, then analysis, as we shall see, uses love precisely to disentangle them.

The Love Machine

Let us now pursue another thread. If love comes from the Other, in that miraculous instant passage from external contingency to the intimate, if the inscrutable figure of destiny has to have its hand in it, if the inner decision can do nothing but endorse the choice already made, then love can also be artificially produced. There is something automatic, almost mechanical about falling in love, which can be used and abused.

This "artificial production of love" was a theme of great fascination in the time of the Enlightenment, suiting well the materialist and deterministic ideas of that age. One can think of numerous examples in Marivaux's comedies, which so frequently turn around the manipulation of love as a supposedly intimate choice. Or one can take the showcase example of Mozart's *Così fan tutte,* where a wager is made that two ladies deeply in love with their fiancés will change their minds, in the course of one day, and fall in love with new lovers, who happen to be their old lovers in disguise. Love doesn't finally triumphantly defeat all, but love is easily defeated. It takes very little to manipulate it: a speck of jealousy, a grain of doubt, a confession of love that is so difficult to resist, a portion of flattery, a fake sacrifice. There is something in love that is like a machine; it is not a set of unpredictable emotions: there is a mechanical predictability in its emergence that can be experimentally induced. Women, proverbially unstable and capricious, now appear to be the best embodiment of this mechanical character, exemplary machines, *les femmes machines,* puppets. If the new love of the two ladies was so easily provoked synthetically by simple devices, contingency and fate so easily counterfeited, then this second love casts long shadows over the original one, before the wager, when everybody seemed happy: it retroactively makes the first love just as artificial and arbitrary as the manufactured and contrived one; it strikes with contingency what in the beginning seemed "natural." One lover is as good as the other, equally dependent on arbitrary and haphazard accident—and this is the tricky problem that this extraordinary opera has to solve.[12]

Mozart's story is very much embedded in the Enlightenment fascination with automata. Behind the highly acclaimed autonomy there lurks an inanimate mechanism, the most sublime feelings can be produced by deterministic laws, they can be synthetically provoked. It can seem very paradoxical that the century that has so emphatically glorified freedom at the same time promoted automata—starting with Descartes's automata covered with hats and Pascal's automaton that unwittingly carries along the spirit, to La Mettrie's *L'Homme-machine* and Vaucanson, to mention just a few. The mechanical doll is a metaphor of, and a counterpoint to, autonomous subjectivity; autonomous self-determination and the automaton seem to go hand in hand. *Le mort saisit le vif*—this junction appears to condense the paradox of the Enlightenment view of subjectivity. And the most frequent and recurring criticism of *Così fan tutte* was precisely that its protagonists were mere puppets.

The inner relation between love and automaton obtained its last superb embodiment in Hoffmann's story "The Sandman" (we know the case Freud made of it) where this situation seems to be reversed. In the best-known episode, the automaton appears as the object of love. A young student, Nathaniel, falls madly in love with this beautiful girl who seems remarkably silent and reticent. It is true that she sings (as one can hear in Offenbach's *Tales of Hoffmann*, in the part based on this episode) and she dances (as one can see in Delibes's *Coppelia*), but in a very mechanical way, keeping her beat too accurately. Her vocabulary is rather limited: she only exclaims "Oh! oh!" from time to time and says "Good night, love!" at the end of their long conversations in which he is the only speaker. But this is sufficient to bring about the folly of love: "It is true that she says but a few words," remarks Nathaniel, "but those few words are like hieroglyphs of an inner world full of love and higher knowledge of the spiritual life which contemplates the eternal Beyond" (Hoffmann 1958, 403). "Oh you superior, deep soul! Only you, only you can truly understand me!" (404). A blank screen, empty eyes, and an "Oh!": it is enough to drive anybody crazy with love. But there is a strange reversal in this situation: the problem is not simply that Olympia turns out to be an automaton and thus placed in the uncanny area between the living and the dead; it is Nathaniel who strangely reacts in a mechanical way: his love for an automaton is itself automatic, his fiery feelings are mechanically produced.[13] It takes so little to set up that blank screen from which he only receives his own message. The question arises, who is the real automaton in the situation—the appearance of the automaton calls for an automatic response, it entails an automatic subjectivation.

Hoffmann's ironical twist, the social parody implied in the episode, highlights the role assigned to the woman: it is enough to be there, at the appropriate place, at the most to utter an "Oh!" at the appropriate time to produce that specter of Woman, the figure of the Other. The mechanical doll only highlights the mechanical character of love relations. Both the subject falling in love and the object can be reduced to an automaton: we have the perfect love machine.

To find another clear example, one can turn to Henry James. Many Jamesian plots turn around the relation between love and free choice, and the manipulation of love. A young girl, beautiful, rich, and intelligent, comes from America to Europe to take her time and fully enjoy the freedom of her choice of a husband. But it is precisely at her most free and autonomous that she is trapped: what she considered to be the sign of fate deciding about her marriage is revealed to be the result of a nasty intrigue. Her free choice was brought about artificially, and since she had made her decision in complete autonomy, it is only by persevering in it that she can be portrayed as a lady.

Another Jamesian example, taken at random: In the short story "Lord Beaupre" (1892), a young woman is persuaded to act as a kind of "fiancée of convenience" to a young lord during the time he needs to decide, at his leisure and in full freedom, about the choice of a wife. But this purely temporary measure of external convenience proves to be decisive for the young man, who has no other choice but to fall in love with his accidental companion (as her scheming mother had correctly foreseen). When the heroine's brother, indignant with the whole affair, confronts her mother, there is the following interesting piece of dialogue:

> "He's either in love with her or he isn't. If he is, let him make her a serious offer; if he isn't, let him leave her alone."
>
> Mrs. Gosselin [the mother] looked at her son with a kind of patient joy. "He's in love with her, but he doesn't know it."
>
> "He ought to know it, and if he's so idiotic I don't see that we ought to consider him."
>
> "Don't worry—he shall know it!" Mrs. Gosselin cried. (James 1975, 158–59)

"He's in love but he doesn't know it" could be read as the Jamesian version of Marx's "Sie wissen es nicht, aber sie tun es" [They don't know it, but they are doing it]. The unconscious involved in the matter takes the form of a purely external link—not something hidden deep in the dark corners of the hero's mind, but something seen by everybody (public proclamation of engagement). But since the young man didn't stand a chance, he was helplessly trapped in an automatism beyond his control, the girl finally refuses his proposal, firm in her conviction that the Other should be different from her mother.[14]

Falling in Love with the Analyst

But perhaps the paramount case that offers the key to the matter is the one discovered by psychoanalysis: the case of transference in the psychoanalytic cure. In 1915, Freud wrote his famous "Observations on Transference Love" (1958, vol. 12), analyzing that extraordinary love which is a kind of by-product of the analysis and which surprised Freud himself. It emerged as an artifact disturbing the smooth progress of the analytical cure, and for quite a long time its implications were not seen. This love of the patient for the analyst (in the beginnings, psychoanalysis had mostly to do with hysterical female patients) springs up with an astonishing, almost mechanical regularity from the analytical situation, regardless of the person of the analyst and that of the patient. It is a love artificially produced, only a function of the analytical situation, its infallible consequence, but nevertheless a true love, as Freud insists, in no way different from a "genuine" one, although experimentally induced. If it seems pathological, one should keep in mind that love itself is a highly pathological state. The only difference lies, at the most, in the utter predictability of its appearance in transference, not in its nature. Its structure is bared in a more obvious way as in its "normal" counterpart. It is here, in this laboratory situation, that this mechanism can be best studied in its pure form—psychoanalysis itself can be seen as ultimately the analysis of this mechanism.

The analytical situation is extremely simple: the patient, stretched on a couch, not seeing the analyst, is invited to tell freely whatever passes through his/her mind—the only rule in analysis is precisely this apparent absence of a rule, generally known as "the ground rule." Why should this elementary expedient, this external contiguity (not even by sight, a presence only surmised) ineluctably produce a relation of love? Yet one can be certain to find this love in every cure, a love that nobody called for and that can be highly embarrassing for the analyst. There are three possible outcomes, Freud says: interruption of the cure (but the patient would start another one and run into the same predicament there); marriage (which would be, as Freud puts it, a great success for the patient but a disaster for the cure; Fitzgerald's *Tender is the Night* is great literary evidence for this point); or a love affair (not exactly Freud's idea of analysis). If all three solutions are bad, the only thing that remains is to handle it—using it as a lever, as it were, of the cure, analyzing it as another formation of the unconscious, a pathology that the cure itself has produced. So the analysis, paradoxically, ultimately turns into analysis of a pathological state—transference—which it has itself created and which did not exist prior to the cure. Psychoanalysis can thus be seen as a device for artificial production of love, and at the same time an instrument to dissipate it.

It is remarkable, says Freud, that this transference love usually appears as a kind of resistance: it is usually at the moment when the analysis touches upon some particularly painful areas or subjects that the patient responds with love. Yet transference, from the outset, seemed the very opposite of resistance, it was what started off the analysis in the first place. The ground rule implied a promise that resistances can be lifted and the repressed could come to light. Given the absence of rules, the minimal mechanism of transference was embedded already in the very basic function of speech as addressed to the Other, the Other as an instance beyond all empirical interlocutors. This dimension puts in place the function of the analyst who is placed exactly in that special position of the Other beyond intersubjectivity. Transference necessarily arises from speech addressed to the Other, it is inscribed in the basic dimension of language. This is the function that Lacan subsequently called "the subject supposed to know." Transference thus initially appears as the opening of the unconscious—this is the aspect of transference by which the "ground rule" triggers off the flow of "free associations" and the ensuing process of remembering, repeating, and reconstructing the repressed. The Other to whom this flow of words is addressed is present as the figure of the analyst, as the supposed addressee of the messages of the unconscious, the symptoms, the dreams—the Other who is supposed to hold the key to their solution, to solve the enigmas posed by the unconscious, to decipher them, the "subject supposed to know" what they mean. It is this fundamental supposition that induces the patient into "free associations."

But then there is this other aspect of transference, the emergence of transference love, which spoils the game. It emerges as a halt of repetition, when the free flow is cut short, when the words fail, as a resistance, or, as Lacan puts it, as the *closing of the unconscious*. This halt that manifests itself as love brings forth a different dimension. Transference in this new and unexpected sense appears as an obstacle:

> What Freud shows us, from the outset, is that the transference is essentially resistant, *Übertragungswiderstand*. The transference is the means by which the communication of the unconscious is inter-

> rupted, by which the unconscious closes up again. Far from being the handing over of powers to the unconscious, the transference is, on the contrary, its closing up. (Lacan 1979, 130; cf. passim)

It is in this resistance, this closing of the unconscious, that transferential love is situated, *love as the opposite pole of the unconscious:*

> What emerges in the transference effect is opposed to revelation. Love intervenes . . . in its function as deception. Love, no doubt, is a transference effect, but it is its resistance side. We are linked together in awaiting this transference effect in order to be able to interpret, and at the same time, we know that it closes the subject off from the effect of our interpretation. (Lacan 1979, 253)[15]

So the "dialectics of transference" involves two different and opposed movements: one could say that transference opens the unconscious and closes it, it sets off free associations and it causes them to run out. Being the lever of analytical cure, it proves to be at the same time its major hindrance. It opens two perspectives, two different views on human condition: the infinite chain of signifiers, with the subject gliding along it in an unending process—each signifier only represents it for other signifiers, that is, represents it badly, since the very failure of a successful representation is what pushes this process of infinite metonymy and infinite repetition, with no final word, no ultimate signifier that could close or found it. But there is also a side that is "beyond words," the dimension of a mute presence, a silent being—the part initially presented by the silent and embarrassing presence of the analyst (who, just like Hoffmann's Olympia, utters at most an "Oh!" or perhaps a "Good night, love," turning him/herself into an automaton). The analyst is ultimately the one who stands in the way of the free flow and hinders the repetition of the signifier. With his massive presence, he puts himself in the place of the object that arrests the symbolic, something that cannot be symbolized and around which the symbolic revolves. He remains *"ein fremder Mensch,"* as Freud puts it, a stranger and a foreign body. It is this mute being that calls for the response of love on the part of the patient who offers him/herself as the object of the unfathomable desire of the Other. The unnameable object spoils the game of the free flow and repetition, and it is in this break, in this inert and unspeakable being, that the subject's *jouissance* can be situated. Where the signifier is arrested, one offers one's being, in this lack of words there is the silent being of the subject manifesting itself as love.[16]

So love emerges at the point of a lacking word, and one offers one's being to fill the lack, to sustain the Other, to seduce him. The miracle of transference love can display the panoply of effects known from world literature, it can appear to be the foundational moment transfiguring the whole of subject's being. But the outcome is quite different: *the Other doesn't return the gaze.* If the analyst necessarily produces love, then the paradox of his or her position, the ethical stance implied by it, is precisely not to respond to it, not to allow that the emergence of the object is covered by the emergence of sense and recognition. In love, the contingent and the senseless is miraculously transformed into the point of the highest sense, the realization of one's most intimate wishes, not something imposed and alien. But psychoanalysis, with its mechanism of transference, *makes love appear as a symptom,* it aims at the emergence of the object not covered by sense and recognition, of the object as alien. It is ultimately the process of baring the mechanism that produced that love, thus making it appear in its very contingency. Its conclusion is precisely the realization of the contingency of the object that has up to then covered "the lack in the Other," and thereby the crumbling of the Other that appears in its utter unfoundedness—hence Lacan's descriptions of that concluding moment as "the falling out of the object *a*" embodied in the analyst; or the maximum distance between the point "I" (the ego-ideal) and the *a* in the formula proposed in Seminar 11 (Lacan 1979, 273); or the "subjective destitution"; or the "crossing of the fundamental fantasy"; or, in his last phase, the "identification with the symptom." The analyst occupies the position of the rest; the contingent bit of the Real that was both the instigator of love and covered up by recognition and sense appears as such.[17]

Is this then the end of love? Is the whole point of psychoanalysis ultimately to cure us of this supreme predicament of human condition? Do we get rid of the object, given its contingency and its fall; do we get rid of the Other once we have seen its lack? And what would a "cured subject" be like—a cynic, a sage, a hermit, a rake, a misanthrope, a tyrant? Not at all. For if there are no prescriptions or advices that would follow from psychoanalysis, there is, nevertheless, maybe a final injunction of love: "Love your symptom as yourself!" For that alien extimate kernel that love has to deal with and which lies at the bottom of its paradoxes is the only precarious and evasive hold for the subject, and at the same time what makes its impossibility.

Notes

All translations have been done by the author, with the exception of those listed in the Works Cited.

1 This chapter freely uses some material previously published in my " 'I Shall Be with You on Your Wedding-Night': Lacan and the Uncanny," *October* 58 (Fall 1991), and in "Beyond Interpellation," *Qui parle* 6, no. 2 (Spring/Summer 1993).

2 "Even in its caprices the usage of language remains true to some kind of reality. Thus it gives the name of 'love' to a great many kinds of emotional relationship which we too group together theoretically as love; but then again it feels a doubt whether this love is real, true, actual love, and so hints at a whole scale of possibilities within the range of the phenomena of love. We shall have no difficulty in making the same discovery from our own observation" (Freud, *Pelican Freud Library,* vol. 12, 141).

3 One could say that the impossible choice of freedom is presented by psychosis. In an example given by J.-A. Miller (in his unpublished seminar "Extimité," 1985-86), a psychotic patient could say: "At a certain age, I was shown some people and I was told that those were my parents." The peculiarity of this statement lies in the external point of view from which it is made. For we are all in a position where we are merely told who our parents are, the parenthood being a fact of a verbal transmission, a testimony, a narration, and belief. But only a psychotic subject can maintain an "objective" distance to this fact, the freedom of disbelief and a choice, displaying thereby that some "fundamental signifier" (what Lacan calls "the Name of the Father") hasn't got hold of him, that it has been "foreclosed." He thus maintains an exterior relationship to the symbolic in general. But the price of this choice of freedom is the loss of subjectivity.

4 The point that the decision about love can never be freely and autonomously taken by the subject him/herself is illustrated in a very amusing way, e.g., in Somerset Maugham's short story, "A Marriage of Convenience": A marriage advertisement by an eligible bachelor is answered by thousands of letters. The poor man has to face the utter impossibility of a choice and has eventually to use another stratagem to make a decision—to put up at least some pretense of a choice made by fate, and even so, ends up only in a marriage of convenience.

5 For a more banal example one can take the lead song in Disney's version of *The Sleeping Beauty:* "I know you, I walked with you once upon a dream, / I know you, the gleam in your eyes is so familiar a gleam . . ."

6 Exhaustive studies by Otto Rank (1989 [1914]) and recently by Karl Miller (1985) have documented the very ample presence of this motive in literature (and elsewhere). The numerous examples range from Chamisso's Peter Schlemihl, Hoffmann,

the gothic novel, Andersen, Lenau, Goethe, Jean Paul, Hogg, Heine, Musset, Maupassant, Wilde, etc., to perhaps the most famous two, Poe's "William Wilson" and Dostoyevsky's Golyadkin.

7 The heroes of these stories are as a rule male. As it will appear later, the double is also a device to avoid a relationship with femininity and sexuality in general, to evade the choice of the object.

8 There is also the traditional "animistic" belief that what befalls the image will befall its owner—cf. the superstition, which is still alive, concerning broken mirrors; cf. also Heine: "There is nothing more uncanny than seeing one's face accidentally in a mirror by moonlight" (quoted by Rank 1989, 43)—since one sees the face of the dead. This explains also why ghosts, vampires, etc., don't cast shadows and don't have mirror reflections: they are themselves already shadows and reflections.

9 That is why trading one's image in a kind of "pact with the devil" or with some occult substitute always ends up badly: the devil knows the importance of the image that the subject overlooks. On the motive of the pact with the devil, cf. also "A Seventeenth-Century Demonological Neurosis," *Pelican Freud Library*, vol. 14, 392ff.

10 I do not think that *enjoyment, to enjoy* (as opposed to pleasure) are good English equivalents of *la jouissance, jouir* as used in psychoanalysis. It is very common in English to use the imperative form "Enjoy yourself!" and even the first person singular "I am enjoying myself," whereas in French, it is practically impossible to use the imperative "*Jouis!*" (the Lacanian imperative of the superego) or the first person singular "*Je jouis*" (unless under rather special circumstances where one is generally not inclined to say much). When used in a "technical" sense, I prefer to follow the practice of many English authors to retain the French word.

11 *Störer der Liebe,* says Freud in another context (*Pelican Freud Library,* vol. 14, 353).

12 For a more detailed analysis, cf. my "La femme-machine," *New Formations* 22 (Summer 1994): 43–54, in the special issue "Lacan and Love".

13 ". . . his senseless obsessive [*zwanghafte,* compulsory] love for Olympia," says Freud (*Pelican Freud Library,* vol. 14, 354).

14 The examples concerning falling in love are numerous; but a novel by Ruth Rendell, *The Tree of Hands* (1985), provides a good example of an artificially created love between a parent and a child: a mother finally accepts with all her love a substitute child for her dead son—on condition that the substitution was brought about through no intention or endeavor of hers. The decision had to be taken by the Other, which, yet again, happened to be her mother (but this time it worked, since it was not a scheming mother, but a crazy mother).

15 Cf. "Thus we can say that love is a demand—even though it remains unanswered—a demand addressing the being. . . . Love addresses that point of speech where the word fails" (Silvestre 1987, 301). The paper by Michel Silvestre on transference, "Le Transfert dans la direction de la cure," originally published in *Ornicar?* 30 (1984) and then included in his posthumous volume (Silvestre 1987), is the best account of transference in psychoanalysis that I know of.

16 Let me clarify two possible misunderstandings. First, there is nothing irrational or un-

graspable in this being beyond words, not something that would call for casting away language as insufficient or require some kind of immediate contact, a direct seizure of immediacy, etc. What is beyond language is the result of language itself, of the incidence of the symbolic. Secondly, what is beyond the signifier is not beyond reach — not something that one could not influence or work upon. Psychoanalysis is precisely the process designed to touch that being, that elusive object, and since it is the product of the impact of language, it can only be tackled through words (psychoanalysis being a "talking cure" from its very first occurrence on), and not by any other, supposedly more direct means (the hopes that the pharmaceutical industry is inclined to nourish).

17 I can only add that, in that experimentally produced pure form, we can touch upon something that could be called *love as an ideological mechanism*. Adorno has seen this surprisingly well: "That something is loved only because it exists — that follows from the obedience to the given, to the unavoidable; such obedience can be psychically brought about only through love. To accept what there is has become the strongest glue of the reality — instead of ideologies as specific, even theoretically justifying representations about being. The blind spot of the unquestionable acceptance of something existing which happens to be in its place is one of the invariants of the bourgeois society" (Adorno 1973, 222). There is, in this acceptance of the given as the intimate, a blind spot of ideological construction, a point beyond the signifier where the subject silently submits, responds to the Other by offering his/her being. It is a point that escapes the rational or faulty arguments that ideology presents, and also the analysis of its nodal points, floating signifiers, subject positions, open identities, etc. If there is an openness of every subject identity from the first point of view (the infinite chain without an ultimate foundation), then, from the second point of view, the being of the subject is limited, fixed, and inert in its *jouissance* — as a sort of ultimate foundation, but unable to found the signifying chain; there is no conjunction between the two. But to address the question how ideology tackles *jouissance* would require a much lengthier treatment. I can only refer to the work accomplished in this area by Slavoj Žižek (see Žižek 1989, 1992).

Works Cited

Adorno, Theodor W. 1973. *Einleitung in die Musiksoziologie*. In *Gesammelte Schriften*, vol. 14. Frankfurt: Suhrkamp.
Blumel, Eric. 1980. "L'Hallucination du double." *Analytica* 22:35–53.
Freud, Sigmund. 1972–86. *The Pelican Freud Library*. Ed. A. Richards. 15 vols. Harmondsworth: Penguin.
———. 1958. "Papers on Technique: Observations on Transference Love (Further Recommendations on the Technique of Psychoanalysis)." In *The Standard Edition*, vol. 12. Ed. James Strachey. London: Hogarth Press and Institute of Psycho-Analysis.
Graves, Robert. 1960. *The Greek Myths*. 2 vols. Harmondsworth: Penguin.
Hoffmann, E. T. A. 1958. *Poetische Werke*, vol. 2. Berlin: Aufbau-Verlag.
James, Henry. 1975. *Affairs of the Heart*. London: Pan Books.

Lacan, Jacques. 1979. *The Four Fundamental Concepts of Psycho-Analysis*. Ed. J.-A. Miller. Harmondsworth: Penguin.
Miller, Karl. 1985. *Doubles*. Oxford: Oxford UP.
Murdoch, Iris. 1975. *The Black Prince*. Harmondsworth: Penguin.
Poe, Edgar Allen. 1979. *Selected Writings*. Ed. D. Galloway. Harmondsworth: Penguin.
Rank, Otto. 1989. *The Double: A Psychoanalytic Study*. London: Karnac—Maresfield Library.
Rousset, Jean. 1984. *Leurs yeux se rencontrèrent*. Paris: Jose Corti.
Silvestre, Michel. 1987. *Demain la psychanalyse*. Paris: Navarin.
Wagner, Richard. 1977. *The Ring of the Nibelung*. Trans. A. Porter. New York: Norton.
Žižek, Slavoj. 1989. *The Sublime Object of Ideology*. London: Verso.
———. 1992. *Enjoy Your Symptom!* New York: Routledge.

6

On the Sexual Production of Western Subjectivity; or, Saint Augustine as a Social Democrat

Fredric Jameson

The issue of radical evil—particularly for those for whom evil is a theological concept, and worse yet, for those for whom the concept of evil is itself the root of all evil—needs to be sorted out into three distinct topics: the experience of guilt as the deeper accompaniment of human existence; the current ethical (and ideological) concern with limits and finitude; and finally the (equally current) anxiety about irrepressible violence, which it might be better to specify (if we really need to) as violence to the other, which is to say also, about the other as the occasion for violence. All of these topics are in these forms metaphysical, their boundless abstraction and timelessness needs to be closed back in by social and historical content, something that would clearly threaten to remove them from the philosophical domain altogether, were not the very fact of such philosophical abstraction itself a historical issue to be faced socially.

It is easy enough to see how concepts of otherness issue (as in Levinas) from the social and historical experience of ethnic minorities; it is a little more difficult to grasp (one of the themes of the following reflections) how the social equally exploits the initially meaningless fact of biological gender for its own purposes. Current anxieties about violence are however surely to be analyzed, not in terms of human nature, nor even of nihilism, so much as in relationship to the corrosive effects of late capitalism on all inherited social systems and on all forms of social legitimation, very much including its own. The realities of violence are not particularly controlled by a return to this or that anthropology, whether it posits the inherent aggressivity of some putative human nature or on the other hand this or that psychological repression or deviation of a "better" kind: if one wants to be constructivist about it, then it is preferable to affirm, with the Brecht of *Mann ist Mann,* that people can be turned into anything, and to take it from there.

Finitude, meanwhile, is an exceedingly suspicious category in the current anti-Utopian climate, where it is called upon, among other things, to reinforce market rhetoric and to encourage the renunciation of revolutionary politics and the collective project of social transformation, while co-opting the ecological discourse of the Promethean destruction of nature. But surely it would be just as Promethean to develop a correct collective exploitation of natural energies?

Guilt is however our primary theme here, for it seems inescapable in any comprehensively experienced human destiny and yet unacceptable in any theological formulation, which is to say in any formulation at all, since a nontheological conception of guilt has never seemed plausible. Heidegger tried to offer one, but had to fall back on the mere empirical fact of our feeling of guilt ("the call of conscience"), which then at once flips over dialectically into a thesis about the human condition as such. In Sartre, the fact of guilt remains, but is perhaps more satisfactorily secularized as the unjustifiability of our own (my own) existence: when the conductor asks for it, I have no ticket, even though everyone else seems to have one. But this still posits a conductor, and the requirement of justifiability as given in advance.

Nor is it satisfactory to derive guilt from some related yet independent phenomenon, such as sexuality, for that would amount to displacing the problem of substantialism and transferring the implication of some human "essence" from guilt itself to the sexual drive. What seems certain is that guilt has always been able to reinforce itself by leaning ("enclitically," as Freud might say) on sexuality, and the reverse also often seems to be true. In what follows, I want to see sexuality, not as an autonomous phenomenon, with some fundamental phenomenological meaning of its own, but rather as a phenomenon that must always mean something, even though the meaning is always constructed after the fact, and in the service of a host or system of other meanings; and which must always somehow conjoin with another, equally unstable and unpredetermined phenomenon, in order to take on the appearance of a fact as such. This is the sense in which, as with guilt, it would be vain to try to decide whether sexuality was evil or (much more rarely) good, but also to deplore the recurrence of such attempts at decision as are inherent in the very structure of this phenomenon, which must mean something even though it cannot, and which thus perpetually solicits judgment and ethical evaluation even where this last is impossible, thereby reinforcing ethics itself and lending it the content of its own lack.

St. Augustine offers a particularly privileged place in which to interrogate this process of construction. With him are traditionally associated two kinds of historical origination: the first is the invention of the modern autobiographical text; the second is a grim form of determinism and of the affirmation of the absolute sinfulness of human beings since the Fall, which is less often openly acknowledged to be the fundamental moment of the invention of "modern" or Western sexuality as well, as something both guilty and obsessive, and, we are told, radically different from the way sexuality has been lived and theorized in other cultures. The title of Augustine's autobiographical text, *Confessions* (which does not yet have its modern institutional sense here), suggests a link between these two inventions. Meanwhile, the contemporary theoretical concern with the autobiographical text on the one hand and the construction of the subject or subjectivity on the other—along with the postcontemporary *doxa* of the formative power of textuality itself, as though the autobiographical text could very well itself construct subjectivity as such—tend to encourage the introduction of Western subjectivity or the Western subject as a third term in this investigation, between the new discourse and the promotion of a new way of looking at sexuality that is also necessarily a new kind of sexuality in itself.

A reading of Peter Brown's biography, *Augustine of Hippo* (1967), however, suggests that Augustine was also original in yet another way from these: for in the hindsight of the great ideological struggles of the sixties and seventies we can now suddenly recognize in Brown's Augustine the quintessential political intellectual, and in particular the turncoat or apostate on the order of the American Trotskyists of the Cold War. Augustine was first a sympathizer of what we would today call the extreme or extraparliamentary Left (taking the pagans of his period to constitute something of an ideological Right). The Manichaeans (of which he was for a while one), indeed, practiced and preached an implacable secession from Roman (or as we would now say, bourgeois) society: their doctrine of the absolute evil of the body and sexuality constituted a practical and literal negation of that society, insofar as the cessation of sexual intercourse would clearly enough spell the end of the world as such. Augustine was tempted by this intransigence and absolutism, this implacable refusal to compromise with actually existing society, as that was organized around the family; and one may assume that he had sympathy with the Manichaean emphasis on sexuality, even though his own personal experience of sexuality was, so to speak, a positive one. What unites these opposing practical evaluations of sexuality, however, is the way in which sexuality becomes both the very center of life and its most fundamental concern. After that displacement and reorganization, it does not matter much whether you condemn or welcome it.

Augustine's official conversion to Christianity then brings a practical modification that eventually requires a theoretical revision: for his entry into the Church means a commitment to precisely that social fabric, including the family of the church believers, and the institution of marriage with its implications about sexuality, that the Manichaean ideology repudiated absolutely. Augustine now passes from an extreme left minority opposition to a position within the state itself and an adhesion to society as such (or at least to its Christian population). But in his case, the apostasy is not seen as a simple changeover of ideological allegiances, but is most often presented to us as an "evolution" or "development" in his own thought. This is because—although, as is so often the case with ex-communists, the Manichaeans now become the principal ideological enemy, and are understood to pose the most fundamental danger to the Church as such—his reply to them takes the form of absorbing and preempting some of their own program, co-opting the antisexuality impulses for the benefit of the Church. Augustinism, the doctrine of absolute determinism and also of the sexual nature of the Fall, will square this circle and constitute the very special ideological invention of this particular late Roman intellectual.

What is less clear from this account (which relies on Peter Brown's biography) is the symbolic meaning and significance of the sexual motif itself, and the social basis for its ideological centrality. This is something that Brown's new work, *The Body and Society* (1988), now luminously clarifies, as we shall see in what follows, which may also be considered an extended book review. But several questions remain.

One has to do with the way the conceptual inventions and solutions of a mere intellectual can be understood as modifying the entire culture and life practices of a population (not to speak of contaminating the inheritance of innumerable generations of what we now sometimes call "the West"). The recourse to "genius" or intellectual or philosophical brilliance is an idealistic convention that has nothing illuminating to offer social history. On the other hand, any general theory about such influence will be speculative, even though one is always necessary as a conceptual and methodological starting point.

The other question has to do with the constitution of the intellectual as such. It is immediately obvious, even confining ourselves to the West, that Augustine's intellectual landscape, Greek as well as Roman, swarms already with all the flora and fauna of what we call intellectuals today; and that he can scarcely be thought to be a pioneer in that sense. But Augustine's ideological mission, and the uncanny resemblance of his discursive struggles to those within the Left in modern times, makes it tempting to explore the possibility that as an ideological turncoat and defector, locked in a fundamental struggle within an ideology or worldview itself locked in struggle with an older one, Augustine pioneered some of the features of the modern intellectual that may not have been in evidence in the life practices of the Stoa, for example, or of the Babylonian priesthood or the Chinese mandarin elite. For to the structure of his ideological mission must also be added that this period generally is the one in which the Catholic priesthood, by way of the institution of celibacy, has begun socially to differentiate itself from the laity: it knows competition from the various monastic traditions (which are not yet orders exactly), and at the same time has begun since Constantine to be associated with state power, so that its doctrinal debates are also immediately bureaucratic ones. For all these reasons, then, Augustine's trajectory is likely to be suggestive and enlightening to us today, and endows Brown's new history with an additional kind of interest.

It should be added that it also places in perspective the various contemporary efforts, such as Foucault's abortive one, to produce a "history of sexuality"; and with this topic we return to the fundamental question at issue here, namely what sexuality may be thought to be that so many people have conceived of writing histories of it. If a narrative can be organized around sexuality as such, in other words, whether "sexuality" is a kind of actant or agent, or on the other hand a result, situation, dilemma, nonetheless in both cases it must be constituted as *something,* as a kind of object, in order for its metamorphoses to be thus tracked. This is, I think, something rather different from what Foucault had in mind when he formed the project of showing the emergence of a (modern? Western?) concept of sexuality (*History of Sexuality* 1980) that corresponded to a newly sexualized subjectivity: unfortunately, what remains of his attempt is a brilliant demonstration of the breakdown of the Greek or classical sexual practices, followed by a very traditional idealistic account of the "influence" of Christianity on the emergent new ones. In older histories of ideas, from Hegel on into the modern history of science, ideas and concepts, which have their bottom line in religion considered as a cultural formation, are always the ultimately determining instances, something Foucault avoided in his other histories by nimble footwork and prestidigitation, but which is here only too painfully evident.

What seems, rather, to have been influential in these final volumes of Foucault's life work is the ideological motif whereby *repression* is definitively (and rather perversely) consigned to the infernal region reserved for outworn and idealistic *doxa;* but also a prophetic new theme in which Foucault unexpectedly reinvents at least one constructivist variety of ethics—*le souci de soi,* probably modeled on Greenblatt's *self-fashioning*—in which the counterclaims of radicals and traditionalists today, queer theory on the one hand and the revival of the older philosophical disciplines (very much including ethics and political theory) on the other, have seemed to enjoy a miraculous reconciliation.

Foucault's abortive trilogy, however, does not overtly claim to make a statement about modern sexuality, nor even to offer phenomenological materials for its eventual history, which demands that we be able to separate the concept of sexuality from some unnamed yet unavoidable reality (whether one wishes to call it an instinct in Freud's very rigorous sense or not) that can be conceptualized and theoretically positioned in a great variety of ways, from relatively more *naturwüchsige* conventions, where it is an activity among others, to a charged and valorized centrality in which everything of significance in life must pass in one way or another through its circuits. Meanwhile, the culturally constructed value accorded to sexuality can also be borrowed and invested in the construction of other kinds of values, such as political symbolism or class consciousness (as for example, when nineteenth-century workers, or twentieth-century racial minorities, are considered to be sexually other in an association with the bestial or the animalic). Yet clearly enough these two kinds of constructions, that of the "meaning" of sexuality in and of itself and that of its symbolic role in other social realms of ideology and practice, are closely associated and interdependent. Meanwhile, this view also presupposes a point of departure for which, either "ontologically" or in reality, sexuality has no pregiven significance, even though something corresponding to it is always present in human reality and always imperiously demands interpretation or the construction of that significance. In other words, on this view, not even Freud is "right" exactly, however much we are inclined to choose Freud as our own contemporary construction of sexuality, and however much his own doctrine of instinct as unbound representations may correspond to the entry point adopted here.

Yet Freud gave us the crucial clue, when speaking of that prescient dream analysis of an obscure tribe of Indians, who had discovered that all dreams had sexual meanings . . . except for the sexually explicit dreams themselves, which meant something else! Is it possible, by the same token, that sexuality as an overt theme always bears an ideological message of a secondary kind that concerns anything but sexuality? At any rate, I take it that something like this is what also marks Peter Brown's starting point in *The Body and Society* when, evoking the classical context, he tries to demystify our stereotypes of Roman licentiousness (as does Foucault) by insisting strongly on the way in which, for the ancients, sexuality was a space in which a master demonstrated his fitness to rule (to rule either household or empire) by exercising restraint and discipline over his own physical inclinations.

This pagan code of sexual behavior and moderation will continue to be that of moderate Christians later on, from Paul himself (Brown 1988, 51) to Clement (134-35) and long after. However, the point about the analysis of any ideology — and the various doctrines relating to sexuality will be seen to be so many ideologies, or, if you prefer, components of distinct ideologies — is that its symbolic significance is not given in itself, intrinsically, like a belief whose positive content may be evaluated on its own merits, but lies very precisely in its reactive character, and can only be deciphered in terms of what it opposes or resists, seeks to displace or to modify. Seen from this perspective, sexual doctrines take on non-sexual social meanings: indeed, we will see that these meanings, which officially turn on the matter of "salvation," in fact all rehearse dilemmas about the form of society itself. We will thus be led to argue, against Weber, that religion is a figural form whereby Utopian issues are fought out (in the absence of "scientific" or secular political codes)—in contradistinction to Weber's notion that religions essentially manage the fear of death, which ends up privileging an existential and indeed a metaphysical conception of human nature as the bottom line for sociology. But the foundation of sociology should surely be the social itself, and the sociality of such drives and impulses, not some non- or antisocial human experience on which the social (in this case religion as a collective institution) is supposedly founded.

The crucial historico-philosophical issue at stake in the analysis of early Christian sexuality lies in the historiographic dilemma presented by periodization generally, namely that of the break, the radical discontinuity, or alternatively the continuity and deeper identity to be established between any two periods. Is Christian sexuality—which is to say our own, modern sexuality, with its burden of sin and guilt, its obsessive nature, its omnipresence and enforcement of notions of the unclean—is Christian sexuality radically different from the practices of ancient Rome and thus of the classical world in general? Or in other words, since, as we have seen, Christian sexuality is a figure for contemporary "Western" but now worldwide "Americanized" sexuality, is a sexuality radically different from our own conceivable, whether in the past or in the future?

Foucault's was the most revealing struggle with this unanswerable narrative dilemma: unanswerable in several ways, since on the one hand the positing of continuity or break is a methodological decision in the void that precedes all interpretation of the record and the evidence (and makes the latter's interpretation possible for the first time); but unanswerable also since, to deprive sexuality of this omnipresent modern power and meaning by positing it as radically other and different is to assign it a secondary or marginal position in human life and therefore to make it into something very different from what we call "sexuality." Foucault understood this very well, and therefore sometimes described his project as the history of the emergence or the invention of "sexuality" as such (in the way in which others will also speak of the invention of "homosexuality"): but this way of speaking about it then tends fatally to thrust the now foregrounded construct "sexuality" into the realm of the history of ideas, where it has become a kind of concept, rather than an ambiguous reality both distinct from and at one with the idea or the interpretation that a culture makes of it and then lives in its practices.

More than that: Foucault's temperamental inclination to what he grandly baptized transgression makes for a good deal of arbitrariness in these deliberately depersonalized pages, where he seems to have realized that he was drawing much more closely to his own personal experiences than ever before, and where his reputation now threatened to make any statement on such dangerous terrain into a kind of program or personal manifesto—something not really defused by reflexivity, as when he claims here to be dealing with the emergence of ethics as well. He need not have been wrong about that (although the ethical extends back into the classical materials he had to deal with), but to say so does not prevent this ostensible history from looking like a new ethics in our own climate of reaction, as I have already observed.

Arbitrariness and perversity, however (as opposed to perversion), here mean something as predictable and inveterate as the refusal of what is taken to be current doxa: thus, Foucault opposed the humane bourgeois philanthropic psychiatry of the early nineteenth century in favor of spatial segregation (and even capital execution, as in the famous pages on Damiens); he ruled out the dominant modern concept of "repression" and hermeneutics generally, which proved none too easy to do without, when it came to his own attempt to evoke resistance in a carceral world in which the latter seemed unthinkable. Here, in his late volumes, it is an inevitable reflex that he should at once repudiate the conventional notion that Christianity brings with it a wholly new and repressive attitude toward a sexuality that in classical times was either serene or orgiastic and Neronian (depending on one's stereotype).

Foucault will therefore at once insist that the repressive—the inclination to master the sexual impulses and to valorize abstinence and control—was no less present in classical antiquity. He thereby creates a supplementary problem for himself, since his theme—the historical originality of Christian sexuality—thereby risks disappearing altogether, and since his very project of chronicling the "emergence" of something called sexuality demands the form of a break and a discontinuity that it is ironic and unaccustomed to witness him here renouncing (even though, or perhaps because, he had himself become something of the very theoretical and master philosopher of the break as such and of the historiographic discontinuity).

Brown solves this problem better than Foucault, but perhaps because he is not working at the same historico-philosophical distance, at the same level of grand abstraction, as his master: the latter's project of distancing and defamiliarizing sexuality, indeed, still took the form of doing something new with this unitary named concept and experience; whereas Brown can shatter it (to use Foucauldian rhetoric), and divide it up into a multiplicity of ideological practices that no longer seem appropriately housed under the generality that in Foucault still bears their name.

In particular, Brown's solution is more persuasive, when it comes to the very first moment in the differentiation of pagan and Christian sexuality. Paganism meant the affirmation of mastery, over the self, the Empire, and the family and the woman: so far so good, and Foucault and Brown are at one in this account, which explains why a certain mastery over one's sexual impulses will also here be part of the arsenal of classical masculinity. But Brown's topic is not merely sexuality, it is asceticism and abstinence as such, a far more thoroughgoing repression of the body than anything to be found either in Marcus Aurelius or in the classically oriented Christians of the day, such as Clement of Alexandria. Thus, however propitious ascetic attitudes may find the relative sexual sobriety of the classical pagan ideal, another supplementary interpretation is needed for this new step, which is very far from being a simple intensification of the older practices.

Sociologists of small group formation—which very much includes the emergence of sects in the early stages of a world religion—have observed the functional presence of characteristic forms of content that both affirm solidarity with the new small group and in effect "burn the bridges" to the old society and old institutions (Gerlach and Hine 1970, quoted in Michael A. Williams's *The Immovable Race* [1985, 190]). It is clear that total abstinence and continence constitutes just such a content, whereby the dust of the old, fallen society, of "Babylon," is shaken off the feet and at the same time the practitioner is marked as radically different and as unsociable, as someone beyond the pale. It seems indeed that during the second and third centuries after Christ, the Roman world was riddled with just such patterns of secession, its cities filled with people who opt out in one way or another and leave the social institutions, some of them believing that the end of the world is approaching.

This plausible explanation of the form of the behavior of certain believers in the early Christian period does not, however, fully account for its content; and in particular, for the symbolic choice of sexuality as a realm in which such a statement of secession can best be made. Looked at in this way and from the standpoint of this kind of question, Roman or classical attitudes toward sexuality do not seem particularly relevant: that Roman mastery or restraint includes a specifically medical ideology, a belief in the debilitating influence of sexual intercourse and its capacity to drain the subject of power ("The fiery body was a fragile reservoir from which vital energy might leak away. Its fires had to be carefully banked up if they were to last. Frequent sexual activity was frowned upon" [Brown 1988, 18]), does not particularly prepare the terrain for the extremes of Christian renunciation in this period, which seem to have wholly different motivations (save in classically minded thinkers like Clement). Indeed, Foucault, who most strongly predicates his analysis of classical sexuality on just such notions of power and mastery (so that the essential contradiction in such an ideology is unsurprisingly to be found not in heterosexual practice, but in the problem of the submission of the partner of the same sex, who ought in principle to be a mirror image of such mastery), is led to identify the disintegration of the classical system in the new and more equal status of women in late Roman society, which clearly poses a threat to the operation of the classical sexual system as a whole. But how to explain this new status of women (if it is to be given the value of a cause)? The most obvious solution that proposes itself is that of Simone de Beauvoir, for whom the juridical status of women determines their social role; yet the heightened juridical status of women in Roman society (as opposed to Greece or Oriental societies) surely preceded Christianity and ought to have been operative in the earlier period.

Brown's explanations, more satisfying, return to the dynamics of small groups and emergent sects. In one, external sense, of course (the one that links sexuality with procreation), to abstain from sexuality is more than symbolically to bring about the end of the "present age" and of the world itself; such abstinence amounts to more than a sign or mark of difference—it is itself a powerful and active weapon in the literal and physical undermining of society as such; and Brown's pages are haunted by a science-fictional vision, an anticipation of some dark ages, in which countryside is deserted and the city falls silent, as in his remarks on John Chrysostom (at a later period and a rather different, post-apocalyptic context):

> John elevated the Christian household so as to eclipse the ancient city. He refused to see Antioch as a traditional civic community, bound together by a common civic patriotism, expressed by the shared rhythms of collective festivity. He made no secret of the fact that he wished the theater, the hippodrome, even the busy agora, to fall silent forever. The Antioch of his dearest hopes was to be no more than a conglomeration of believing households, joined by a common meeting-place within the spacious courtyards of the Great Church. He wished the doors of the Christian house to swing to, shutting out the murmur of a late classical metropolis. To him, the public life of Antioch was a "Devil's garbage tip," piled high outside the simple walls of Christian houses. (Brown 1988, 313)

How much the more intense is such radical secession, which saps the fabric of the ancient social system, in a period in which the end of the world is felt to be imminent and there is no longer any point in the preservation of even "Christian households" or marriages and families! Here radical abstinence is both an expression of the hope of the millennium and an act designed to bring it about.

Still, this is only one of the levels of significance of chastity taken as a symbolic act in its own right (and a relatively external one, which has more to do with the consequences of sexuality than with its inner essence). A further meaning returns us to the dynamics of ideology as a move in a cultural struggle between groups: this one has to do with Roman asceticism, but in quite the reverse of the approach that sought for continuities between such classical sobriety and the even more pronounced repudiation of the body in certain Christianities. For on the new view, it is precisely this general similarity or family likeness between the two sexual ideologies that demands some more radical differentiation, at least on the part of the extreme Christian sects. It is in order to affirm the break with classical Stoicism, in order to endow the new practices with what today is called a sense of "identity," that the Christian groups push forms of classical restraint so far that their effects are reversed, and what was to lend the household and the family something of the dignity of the Empire itself now undermines both and threatens to extinguish them: self-control no longer has the same kinds of associations and connotations when it aims at the achievement of radical self-mutilation and the utter obliteration of "natural" and inevitably recurrent impulses.

Yet we observe here a textbook example of the forms that ideological struggle with the class enemy tends to take: an appropriation of the other's privileged thematic space, a radical reversal of its meanings and oppositions, a process whereby a preexisting symbolic act is inverted.

But it is not only from and against the pagans that these early Christians must symbolically and ideologically differentiate themselves: it is also against the Jews and against Judaism, from which their own religion springs. Indeed, Judaism seems to have exerted its own kind of fascination over the earliest converts: "[It] was pagan converts, and not the local Jews, who put pressure on Paul to adopt Jewish customs. They wished to become like Jews, rather than creatures condemned to ritual invisibility" (Brown 1988, 59). But this is the period of the diaspora, in which exiled Jewish communities must very strongly reorganize themselves around the emergent institution of the rabbi as social leader: "[W]ith the destruction of the Temple and the strengthening of the synagogue and the house of study, Judaism was fast on its way to becoming a religion of the book and of the sanctified, married household" (61). Under these circumstances and in this specific new historical context, there can be no question of a privileging of abstinence and renunciation for a Judaism that needs to flourish by way of large families and patriarchal order. Such abstinence, then, is for the early Christians doubly overdetermined: for in the new context, it can also mean radical differentiation from Judaism as well and from the new Jewish form of society. Sexual extremism then includes the bonus of this double differentiation, from pagans and Jews alike.

But now it becomes interesting to set this system in motion and to introduce historical time into its operation: for it transpires that there are rhythms and cycles, not to say fashions, in asceticism; and these cycles are strictly correlated with the political climate of the not-yet-converted Empire, and in particular with its systematic and gruesome campaigns of persecution against the Christian minorities. For in this period there exists a more potent way of making the world end, and a more vivid sign of ideological and group commitment, than sexual abstinence and renunciation; and that is martyrdom itself, which becomes periodically available to the faithful. "Thus, continence, though a marked feature of Christian prophecy, remained a secondary feature; it was a preoccupation that tended to rise to the fore in Christian literature at times when the prospect of violent death was less immediate" (Brown 1988, 69). Continence is thus a substitute for an unavailable martyrdom, in a situation in which you do not wish to wait for the state and its rigors but can take the initiative yourself. It is thus symbolic martyrdom and self-chosen immolation: and at the same time it furnishes a kind of individual test or trial whereby the believer's commitment can be challenged, with results that are finally as public as any capital execution. This symbolic substitution thus initiates the space of self-examination, which will be so crucial in the "construction of subjectivity," even though it here remains in rudimentary or virtual state.

For the realm of subjectivity is here occupied by a rather different (and still very exterior and objective) kind of phenomenon, namely the state of prophecy. It has an instrumental relationship to sexual abstinence in the sense in which, along with fasting and sleep deprivation, the latter places the body in a situation receptive to visions and prophetic efflatus: it is a cleansing process that enables the spiritual transfiguration of which prophecy is a sign. Yet this instrumental use of sexual asceticism stands in contradiction with the obsessive denial and violent repression that began to emerge in the use of continence as a reliable instrument for destroying the world itself, and which will become, after the end of the waiting period, the principal ideology of the sexually extreme sects.

We have thus here, in the early period, a number of levels of significance, or, if another terminology is preferred, several different types of libidinal investment that coexist with respect to the use of this particular ideological or fantasy apparatus that is the interpretation of chastity, or the interpretation of sexuality that gives rise to the desire called chastity.

These investments include a social or analogical pole, in the expectation of the imminent end of the world; and a moral or individual one in the purification of the self with a view toward prophecy. In class terms, the motif becomes a means of differentiating early Christians from pagans or Jews of the same period; while formally or narratively, the enforcement of continence takes the shape of a test and can also substitute for martyrdom in periods of calm and tolerance (I am tempted to say in "nonrevolutionary periods" as opposed to those in which public tumult around such issues is productively articulated).

But any synchronic analysis of an ideologeme such as this one is also a moment in a historical configuration that is subject to change; moreover, that change sometimes results from effects and achievements forthcoming within the system itself, and it is precisely this kind of unintended change that is most often called dialectical. Two of the crucial results of continence, for example, have to do with inheritance, for in these extreme situations of renunciation and chastity (and at least until the end of the world) there will be no heirs to whatever property the individual saints in question may still have. This issue, along with the damage to the institution of the family as such, will obviously constitute the fundamental objection (the word is perhaps too weak) of what we may call worldly or centrist Christians to this sexual or extrafamilial extremism.

On the other hand, the problem undergoes a dialectical inversion when it is a question of women's or widows' inheritance: that type of fortune, which tends to be appropriated by the Church itself, now determines a more positive evaluation of celibacy as far as women are concerned. Meanwhile—whatever the traditional juridical status of women in classical Rome and its effect on their social powers—the possession of such fortunes available to the Church, along with the new kind of equality with men that the practice of celibacy brings with it (Brown 1988, 145 ff., 150, 332), leads to fundamental changes in the social situation itself in which these practices evolve.

Now we need to look at some new meanings of sexuality, before confronting the problem "produced" by Foucault about the relationship between sexuality in its increasingly modern sense and the constitution of an (equally modern) subjectivity. From the positions already outlined—as the hope of an immediate end of the world (read: an impending revolution, Utopia) recedes—what may at least be called political sects if not outright parties begin to emerge, whose likeness to extreme left sectarianism in modern times I wish very much to stress. Like these last, such sexual sectarianism is based not merely on ideological commitment, not merely on a choice of Christianity (or revolution) as a collective solution, but also on a passionate and personal impatience for individual reward or fulfillment, for a present taste of future satisfactions: here the *pur et dur* militant lives morally in his own present and by way of his own practices what everyone will live in Paradise (compare the Western Maoist repudiation of Soviet bourgeois and corrupt lifeways, and the refusal of the extraparliamentary Left to join bourgeois governments or to participate in alliances within the system, to "govern" under fallen prerevolutionary conditions). Brown's analysis of these varied sects (complicated by the cultural differences articulated by geography: the extremism of Syrian Christianity in general, as opposed to that of Italy, Alexandria, or North Africa—all differentiated culturally from one another) is very relevant here indeed. It raises the question of intellectual inheritance, in the links groups like the Marcionites and the Encratites have with the older Gnostic philosophies; and also that of social determination, in the rise of Manichaeanism and its rivalry with orthodox Christianity in the West. It has been suggested (by analysts of Islam, I believe), that all these groups steer an uneasy ideological course between polytheism (toward which Manichaeanism would clearly tend) and the kind of insipid deism of the classical period (which is threatened most explicitly by Arianism). But at least some of the enthusiasm for these protopolitical movements will depend on the investment of energies they offer: for young activists with purist and dogmatic political obsessions, sexual extremism offers satisfactions and a sectarian following that would not be available by a conversion to the norms of an institutional Church after the fashion of Augustine. Sexuality here becomes the acid test of this kind of extreme commitment; the achievement of continence becomes a matter of immediate individual ("spiritual") gratification at the same time that it can stand as an equally immediate publicly verifiable sign of political commitment.

On the other hand, the new stabilization—the resumption of the boring old time of daily life and the social routine (what Gregory of Nyssa will call "tainted time," Brown 1988, 297)—opens up some rather different possibilities for continence, namely the ultimate emergence (over several centuries) of an institutional double standard in which celibacy can be practiced by the clergy (and needs to be, fulfilling other institutional requirements, in particular that of differentiating priests from the faithful generally) while the followers can continue to reproduce and live in families, under whatever strict codes for restraint and practices are devised in the new situation.

Before we get that far, however, we must observe the emergence of yet a third social and institutional possibility in the Desert Fathers themselves, a third possibility then projecting itself into the far future in the form of the orders, as those are distinguished from both clergy and laity alike. This is a specific exploration of the possibilities of continence in and for itself, in a situation in which, as Brown puts it, a "particular form of heroism, linked to a particular form of sexual renunciation—the preservation of a virgin state in the strict sense— . . . increasingly caught the imagination of all Christians" (1988, 159). The philosophical developments that run parallel to this, in Origen and then in Plotinus and neo-Platonism, tend not only to produce small study groups, rather than sects on the one hand or collective movements (or even institutions) on the other; but also to deflect the sexual emphases toward the grossness of the body in general, in such a way as to give the matter of food and eating, particularly the devouring of animal flesh, an equally central role (this subtheme itself merits attention, for later on, when these have acquired a more open social significance, eating will be recoded in terms of poverty, want, and famine, and new versions of Adam's fall will circulate, in which the apple will stand for greed "in a famine-filled world" [Brown 1988, 220]—or even more interestingly as "a hot lust for land" and for property [336]—as opposed to Augustine's definitive sexual reading of the first disobedience, in *On Marriage and Concupiscence*).

The desert now represents a new space beyond the "present age": neither city nor village, neither this world nor the next, a new kind of imaginary scene that then ends up restructuring the Imaginary itself:

> The myth of the desert was one of the most abiding creations of late antiquity. It was, above all, a myth of liberating precision. It delimited the towering presence of "the world", from which the Christian must be set free, by emphasizing a clear ecological frontier. It identified the process of disengagement from the world with

a move from one ecological zone to another, from the settled land of Egypt to the desert. It was a brutally clear boundary, already heavy with immemorial associations. (Brown 1988, 216)

This new space now opens up a positive term in which the opposition between worldliness and continence can develop: it puts an end to a situation in which a refusal of worldliness remains a mere will to negation within a single framework that can only be resisted by the image of its absolute coming to an end in apocalypse. The new space of the desert, nonworldly yet real, now puts an end to a dilemma that hitherto offered no solution "other than through drastic rituals that promised total transformation, through the formation of small, inward-looking groups of the redeemed; or . . . in third-century Syria, through adopting the disturbing rootlessness of the religious vagabond" (216).

Thus, the new space—now within the world, rather than outside it, or in the future—will eventually allow asceticism to be institutionalized (in various ways, as we shall see). Such institutionalization will obviously be judged as a compromise, a capitulation or a sellout by the "extreme left" groups of sexual absolutists. It will also allow the attitudes toward sexual renunciation to be slightly modified: Augustinism is here foreshadowed not merely by the "sharpened awareness of sexual fantasy . . . sexual desire (being) now treated as effectively coextensive with human nature" (Brown 1988, 230); but also in the practice of self-examination and introspection that result from the lifelong necessity for this heightened vigil, and for the tangible occasion of keeping track of sexual thoughts that are clearly stimulated by the very act of searching for them, thereby very much contributing to a "construction of subjectivity" in some new and modern sense, which at one and the same time goes hand in hand with the latter's institutionalization.

Yet the emergence, in the form of the desert, of a competing real space to that of the fallen social world itself also leads to novel evaluations and interpretations of sexuality that will develop in wholly new directions in the centuries to come. In particular the practice of collective confession ("The inner world must be turned inside out. Nothing must linger in it that could not be placed unhesitatingly before others" [231]), will now mark sexual experiences as the very locus of the private, the secret, the personal as such: "[T]he continuance of sexual dreams and emissions served to warn the monk ... of the presence within his heart of a more faceless lingering desire—the wish to possess experiences of his own" (231). We are well placed in the contemporary period, after a renewed examination of the construction of subjectivity and selfhood as a form of private property par excellence (William James), to grasp the historic originality of this first emergence of the private or personal realm, and its immediate coincidence with images of property. Such a figural connection will then almost at once in the same period allow a modulation in the meaning of abstinence, toward some new social solidarity with the poor, with those who have nothing. Continence can now become, not heroism or the election of the pure revolutionary group, but rather a form of social poverty. Indeed, the working out of a real social space from which to confront that of the world—and its resultant institutionalized double standards and compromises—not merely enables, but positively demands a new investment of signification in the practices of continence, which must now, as opposed to fallen sexual practices, mean something more articulated than a mere absolute or extremist blanket refusal.

So it is, for example, that in Gregory of Nyssa we find a well-nigh existential view of the function of fallen sexuality that is reminiscent of certain contemporary critiques of consumerism. For him, the passion for the world (which continence rebukes and overcomes) can be analyzed as an occultation of death and the death anxiety: "It was by the accumulation of wealth, by the retaining of power, above all, by marriage and the search for direct and palpable in the form of sons and daughters, with all the social arrangements which dynastic continuity implied for members of the upper classes, that human beings sought to remedy the discontinuities inflected on them by death" (Brown 1988, 301). Gregory's is thus already a reinterpretation of sin in terms of class; but only partially so. And this may also be the moment in which to repeat some reservations about Max Weber's supremely influential and pioneering sociology of religion in general: despite the rich variety of his typology, he is led in several places to the (perhaps sociologically impossible) definition of religion as having in general the social function of offering institutional consolation for death in suffering. (It should be noted that his studies of ascetic practices, unlike the ones here considered, do not go around behind the emergence of modern sexuality and raise the issue of the meaning and historical originality of this last.) But this way of positioning the ultimate need for religion outside the divers historical manifestations of the social results, as does Gregory's analogous (but perhaps more subtle) viewpoint, in an ambiguously existential reading. Suffering is a social phenomenon, which is susceptible to class analysis; death is an absolute or existential matter, which transcends the historical altogether. Thus an emphasis on this last will lead out of sociology and history into something that is after all in the strictest sense the domain of religion itself (which was, however, the phenomenon to be interpreted). An emphasis on suffering as a social phenomenon, however, permits a determination in terms of historical and cultural variables.

Thus the tradition itself tends to take two distinct forms. On the one hand, and as it were in preparation for the Augustinian climax, Gregory's subtle analyses of human or "tainted" time offer rich existential documents: "The present human experience of time was an experience of 'tainted' time. It was a factious time, created within the self by unrelieved anxieties. It showed itself in the form of a perpetual, unquiet 'extension' of the soul into an unknown and threatening future. For Gregory, the clock whose tick measured off most inexorably and most audibly the passing of tainted time was the clock of marriage. He saw human time as made up of so many consecutive attempts to block out the sight of the grave" (297). This is virtually the Heideggerian *Sorge* (or existential "care") *avant la lettre,* and offers new hermeneutic instructions for decrypting the movements of subjectivity, the paradox being that such forms of close interpretive attention also end up *producing* the very "subjectivity" they are supposed to measure and analyze.

On the other hand, we have new kinds of demotic readings of the Fall in terms of property itself, most notably in terms of food: "It was widely believed, in Egypt as elsewhere, that the first sin of Adam and Eve had been not a sexual act, but rather one of ravenous greed. . . . In this view of the Fall, greed and, in a famine-ridden world, greed's blatant social overtones—avarice and dominance—quite overshadowed sexuality" (Brown 1988, 220). And later, in the sixth century, the author of *The Book of Degrees* believed that "Adam had fallen because he had looked around him in Paradise with a hot lust for the land. He wished to possess its rich soil. He had wished, through property, to replace God as creator. He had set about creating economic wealth by labor, and had wished to pile up the physical wealth of progeny by intercourse" (336). This powerful counterinterpretation, so modern in its reading of sexuality in terms of categories of property and economic production, is clearly out-trumped and finally vanquished by the triumphant hegemonic thought of Augustine, for whom sexuality becomes the mode of explanation rather than the thing to be explained, and in whose canonical works subjectivity as such displaces the social and the economic.

It is an ideological triumph that must surely be accounted for by the social victory of the Church and the requirements of its new institutionalization. (Thus, Ambrose will invent Mariolatry as a way of justifying the centrality of the theme of virginity in the later ideological developments.) In general, however, what confronts any institutionalized political body—whether the Catholic Church or the Communist Party—is the requirement of making a large place for all those ordinary humans who are not saints and cannot live by extremes and absolutes, and also of ideologically expelling those groups whose extremism and absolutism risk alienating this or that fundamental component of their larger social and class compromise. The sexual extremists, on the one hand, and these newly emergent spokesmen for the poor on the other, are both excellent examples of the kinds of tendencies any centrist power structure will necessarily have to fend off and if necessary excommunicate.

But such strategic necessities are not mere matters of power or politicking; they require ingenious and original ideological solutions, of which, for this period, it is Augustine who is the supreme figure. It is widely understood that Augustine is the virtual inventor (and "only begetter") of that unique sexual puritanism that distinguishes Christianity from the other religions; this doubtful achievement, along with the gloomy fatalisms of Augustinian predestination (equally an original conceptual achievement of this fertile ideologue), have led it to be supposed, in the stereotypicality of the popular mind, that Augustine must necessarily be counted among the radicals.

Nothing is, however, further from the truth: if he comes to seem the very epitome of the modern intellectual as such, this is because of the way in which Augustine is called upon to invent the practices of the intellectual for the first time (owing to the triumph of the Church) associated with state power. (He is the first, in the attack on Donatist heresy, to call down the forces of institutional violence and physical repression upon his ideological enemies, whom the state literally wipes out.) But to grasp Augustine as a political intellectual (rather than as a philosopher or theologian, or a "writer") is to grasp him as a kind of centrist or compromiser, and thereby to understand the functionality of his doctrine in a more satisfactory way than seems offered by the history of ideas or of *Weltanschauungen*. For from this perspective, it is the very radical or extremist appearance of that doctrine that enables practical compromises to take place.

That radical appearance, of course, he is able to derive from his Manichaean formation, which trains him in the deployment of a whole rhetoric of the evils and sinfulness of physicality. What needs to be repudiated, in the Manichaean perspective, is the threat to trinitarian monotheism posed by this worldview's vision of the eternal struggle between good and evil, between the spirit and the flesh, with its undesirable Utopian implication that the triumph of the spirit is somehow conceivable (in a Gnostic scenario): for such Utopian perspectives always lead to political activism and to political extremes. Augustine, however, will come to represent the newly emergent status quo of the institutional Church, and the fundamental thrust of his ideological polemics — against all kinds of adversaries, who differ as greatly among themselves as the Manichaeans do from the Pelasgians, or the Arians from the Donatists — remains throughout the repression of extrainstitutional political activism.

The Manichaean tradition will allow Augustine to single out the terrain of the fallen body itself as a field of ideological struggle. His originality is to have seen that the stark opposition between the condemnation of the flesh in Gnosticism and Manichaeanism and its affirmation as God's creation (later: the Pelagians and Julian) could be cut across and resolved in a new way by the foregrounding of sexuality as such, that is to say, in contemporary terminology, by its very production or construction as a new kind of phenomenon: "[T]he indirect and momentous result of Augustine's emphasis on the psychological momentum behind the sexual drive was to destroy the neat compartments with which Christians of an earlier age had tended to contain the anxieties raised by the sexual components of the human person" (Brown 1988, 418–19). The term "psychological" must also be retained: for it is the link between sexuality and "psychology" or subjectivity that is very centrally "part of the solution" here: so that the necessity of confronting ideological enemies whose positions are in themselves essentially contradictory will lead to a novel solution that opens up a novel kind of space: as opposed to that of the end of the world in the early centuries, that of a new inner world or subjectivity that is also a kind of absence of the world (even though it leaves this last virtually intact).

For Augustine must on the one hand oppose the Donatists, who stand for the notion of a perfectible community of the true faithful or elect: even if this is no longer as in earlier centuries the extremist ideology of the sectarian small group, as Brown argues (*Augustine of Hippo*, 218-19), it still threatens the very vocation of the Church as a mediatory institution in a necessarily imperfect world: yet it is precisely to that vocation that Augustine is committed. He must therefore argue for necessary imperfection on the level of human collectivities.

Yet the conventional ideological countermove to this one is also fraught with ideological peril and must equally be resisted: that consists, clearly enough, in repositioning perfectibility in the individual, a solution which the Pelasgians will propose. But this leads to a different kind of extremism and Utopianism, and threatens to undermine the institutional Church in a different but no less alarming way, by awakening a thirst for the purely individual extreme solution. Sexuality can now also solve this problem, by way of its unique constitution by Augustine as that privileged space in which the Fall is detectable and the corruption of the Will alone visible. For sexuality—quite literally, by way of involuntary erection and equally involuntary impotence (416-17)—can always be appealed to demonstrate that our will is corrupt and necessarily and constitutively imperfect.

Paradoxically, this allows Augustine to assert—both with and against Pelasgian optimism—that the body before the Fall, including prelapsarian sexuality, was essentially good, since it was God's creation: the Gnostic and Manichaean temptation to spiritual mysticism is thereby at once excluded. Meanwhile the fallen Will also explains why Donatist conceptions of a perfected community are also vain, and therefore why, on both individual and collective planes, an institution like the Church is required to supplement human frailty.

The price to be paid for this remarkable solution is a twofold one: on the one hand, now sexuality will exist in and of itself and not as the mere sign of something else (432-33): and this is what is meant by its "production" or "constitution," its autonomization. For in earlier periods sexuality is always allegorical of the cosmos in one way or another (and in ways wildly differing among themselves): it does not exist contingently in its own right, but is always pressed into service as a symbolic expression of other, more autonomous, metaphysical themes. But the thematics of the Fall and of Will do not function in this way in Augustine: rather, these last come themselves to be symbolic expressions of the new entity called sexuality: "[I]n Augustine's mind, sexuality served only one, strictly delimited purpose: it spoke, with terrible precision, of one single, decisive event within the soul. It echoed in the body the unalterable consequence of mankind's first sin. It was down that single, narrow, and profound shaft that Augustine now looked, to the very origins of human frailty" (422). Paradoxically, this seeming extremism of an obsessive focus on the new sexuality as such then allows Augustine to revert to the worldly tolerance of late Roman or pagan restraint and compromise in sexual practices, particularly for the married (426). Thus, as so often in the ideological realm, the extremist rhetoric masks a practical consent to the status quo.

Along with sexuality, however, there comes into being that other new thing, which has been signaled by the very language of the private or of subjectivity as such. For the other price to be paid, or if you prefer the other name for this particular price to be paid, is the opening up of an inward space in which contradictions that cannot be resolved in practical reality can somehow be conjured: the space of a new inwardness, which the existence of sexuality as a permanent threat will also bring into being. For the kind of self-examination that began to be organized by the Desert Fathers will here shed the ambiguities that invest it when it is a question for locating doubtfully identified sins, and will now offer a foolproof area for the organization of a check that always infallibly brings into being the very object it is supposed to search for. To look for sexual temptations is tantamount to creating or producing them, to awakening them there even where they did not previously appear. Sexuality now allows the practice of a permanent self-examination, which itself also predicates the permanent existence of that new thing called the Self, of which Augustine is notoriously the inventor. Sexuality guarantees the omnipresence of a fallen Will that can equally permanently be addressed by attention to a verifiable yet inward self, all the while in the outer social world the double standard of Church and laity, congregation and the monastic orders, is set in place. In this deeper and more fundamental, in all senses more original and originary, "subjective turn," we can find verified the conviction everywhere present in modern political culture that preoccupation with the subjective necessarily withdraws creative energies from the social and from praxis and ends up ratifying the status quo of a fallen and corrupt "present age."

The modern intellectual is constituted at precisely this point, with the mission equally precisely to constitute the Self as such, as an ideological solution. On the other hand, it is also from this same perspective that we may look back at the sorry history of sexual politics and sexual extremism, as these are acted out in the various forms of an ideal of continence or radical abstinence. The story of sexuality as a semiautonomous instance raises the seemingly Foucauldian question of what things would be like once sexuality (like humanism and "man") again disappeared (and indeed the question of whether it is exactly this that we have in mind today as we approach such questions historically). But it also raises the question of the intellectual as such and sharpens the dilemma whose intolerable alternatives take the form of the compromise of the turncoat and the apostate on the one hand (whose first momentous figure is Augustine himself) and of the absolute or purist politics of the extremist sects on the other.

Works Cited

Augustine. 1992. *Confessions.* 3 vols. Ed. James J. O'Donnell. Oxford: Clarendon Press.
Brown, Peter. 1967. *Augustine of Hippo.* Berkeley: University of California Press.
———. 1988. *The Body and Society: Men, Women, and Sexual Renunciation in Early Christianity.* New York: Columbia University Press.
Foucault, Michel. 1980. *The History of Sexuality.* 3 vols. Trans. Robert Hurley. New York: Vintage.
Gerlach, Luther P., and Virginia H. Hine. 1970. *People, Power, Change: Movements of Social Transformation.* Indianapolis: Bobbs-Merrill.
Williams, Michael A. 1985. *The Immovable Race: A Gnostic Designation and the Theme of Stability in Late Antiquity.* Leiden: E. J. Brill.

7

I Can't Love You Unless I Give You Up

Renata Salecl

Love for oneself knows only one barrier—love for others, love for objects.
—Sigmund Freud, *Group Psychology and the Analysis of the Ego*

One of the greatest illusions of love is that prohibition and social codes prevent its realization.[1] The illusionary character of this proposition is unveiled in every "self-help" manual: the advice persons desperately in love usually get is to establish artificial barriers, prohibitions, and make themselves temporarily inaccessible in order to provoke their love object to return love. Or, as Freud said: "Some obstacle is necessary to swell the tide of the libido to its heights; and in all periods of history, wherever natural barriers in the way of satisfaction have not sufficed, mankind has erected conventional ones in order to be able to enjoy love."[2] What is the nature of these barriers? What is the role of institutions, rituals, and social codes in relation to the subject's innermost passions, their love? And why does the subject persist in loving a person who has no intention of returning love?

I will try to answer these questions by taking the example, first, of two novels, Kazuo Ishiguro's *The Remains of the Day* and Edith Wharton's *The Age of Innocence*, and, second, a short story by Edith Wharton, "The Muse's Tragedy." While the latter deals with a woman using the love of a man to organize the symbolic space that would provide her with an identity and confirm her as an object of love, the two novels deal with the opposite problem, of love supposedly prevented by society's symbolic power structure. Let me first focus on the novels, which offer an aesthetic presentation of what Louis Althusser named ideological state apparatuses (ISAs), "a certain number of realities which present themselves to the immediate observer in the form of distinct and specialist institutions," and are primarily part of the private domain, like families, some schools, churches, political parties, cultural ventures, and so on.[3] In the two novels, it is precisely two of the most important ISAs, the family and "society," in the sense of codified social norms and the hierarchy of social relations, that dominate the private life of the protagonists: their love affairs are supposedly restrained by the influence of the oppressive ISAs that organize their lives.

The Age of Innocence is set in the extremely hierarchical New York high society of the nineteenth century, where every social act or movement is codified, and where there is a constant struggle not to misinterpret the unwritten rules and become an outcast. The extent of the codification in this society is visible from the way people organize their public and private lives: from the type of china they use at dinner parties, the way they dress, the location of their houses, the respect they pay to the people higher on the social ladder, and so forth. *The Remains of the Day* is also set in highly hierarchical English aristocratic society just before and after the Second World War. The central role is played by the highest of servants—the butler. This is also a society of unwritten codes, in which every part of life is fully organized. And the butler is the one upon whom the perfection and maintenance of this order depends. As Stevens in *The Remains of the Day* points out, the butler, by doing his service in the most dignified and perfectionist manner, contributes significantly to the major historical events his master is involved with. Stevens is the prototype of an "ideological servant": he never questions his role in the machinery, he never opposes his boss even when he makes obvious mistakes, that is, he does not think but obeys.

Both novels imply that there is something suppressed or hidden behind this ideological machinery—passions of the individuals engaged in rituals, their secret "true" loves. The film versions of the two novels especially stress this hidden terrain "beneath" the institution, the "real" emotions behind the fake, public ones. The main trauma of *The Age of Innocence* is thus the impossibility of love between Newland Archer, a young aristocrat, and Countess Ellen Olenska, an eccentric woman whose behavior is very much under the scrutiny of New York society.

Newland, who is engaged to be married to a "proper" society woman, tacitly gives up any hope of fulfilling his desire for Ellen but instead becomes a devoted husband as demanded by society's rules. In *The Remains of the Day* the story hinges on the unspoken passion between the butler, Stevens, and the housekeeper, Miss Kenton, both of whom are so obedient to the social codes that they will not let their feelings out and thus find some personal happiness. In short, both novels reveal the oppressiveness of the institutions in which their protagonists live, and which prevent them from finding love. The question is, however, whether it is really the institution that prevents love. Is it not actually the institution that, in a paradoxical way, produces love?

The Remains of the Day

The Remains of the Day is the story of a butler, Stevens, who has spent his whole life serving in the house of Lord Darlington. In his old age, Stevens takes a trip to visit the housekeeper, Miss Kenton, who had worked in the house twenty years earlier, with a view to convincing her to return to serve in the house. During this trip, Stevens writes a diary in which he remembers his relationship with Miss Kenton and the life in the house in the turmoiled times before the Second World War. These memories of Stevens are primarily a tribute to the principles of dignity and moral integrity that define a perfect servant wholly devoted to his master. The subtlety of the novel lies in the fact that emotions are never expressed: although Stevens and Miss Kenton care about each other in more than a professional way, they never admit this to each other. Even at the end, when they finally meet after all these years and when there is no actual barrier to their relationship, nothing happens between them. Ritual stays intact and emotions never fully come out—why not?

One interpretation of Stevens's behavior, of his complete repression of emotions, is that he is, in some way, nonhuman. This is exemplified in his attitude toward his father's death: even when his father is dying, it is more important for Stevens to perform his service in an impeccable way than to reveal his emotions. Such a humanist interpretation, of course, misses the point of the novel. To understand the logic of the novel, one should proceed in the opposite direction: rather than try to discern the repressed passions that do not emerge because of the rigidity of the social system and because of the butler's all-too-impeccable service, it would be better to begin by taking the ritual and institution seriously and then determine the place that love has in it.

How should one understand the title of the novel? A number of explanations are hinted at in the novel. First, "the remains of the day" might simply be the memories that Stevens records in his diary every evening of his journey. The second answer could be that both protagonists of the novel are already in their late years, so the "remains" are the few years they still have left. However, if we take the analogy between remains of the day and the Freudian "days residues," a more interesting explanation can be given. In Freud's theory of dreams, "days residues" are the events, the residues of the previous day, that acquire a new meaning in dreams because of the unconscious structure in which they get embedded. By reading Stevens's memories with the help of this Freudian concept, it can be said that the remains of the day concern primarily the memory of his relationship with Miss Kenton. In the memories that Steven cherishes most, he and Miss Kenton used to meet every evening in their private quarters for cocoa and discuss the events of the day. These meetings are "the remains of the day" which function as residues that he cannot incorporate in his perfectionist construction of an obsessive style of life. Stevens's relationship with Miss Kenton is therefore the residue around which his unconscious braids, the residue that forces him to confront his desire.

Lacan characterizes the obsessive person as one who installs himself in the place of the Other, from where he then acts in such a way that he prevents any risk of encountering his desire. That is why he invents a number of rituals, self-imposed rules, and organizes his life in a compulsive way. The obsessive person also constantly delays decisions in order to escape risk and to avoid the uncertainty that pertains to the desire of the Other, the symbolic other as well as the concrete other, the opposite sex.

Stevens never admits to himself that he is taking the trip because he wishes to meet Miss Kenton. He finds an excuse for the trip in the lack of the servants in the house and in the possibility that he might solve his staff plan by convincing Miss Kenton to return to the house:

> You may be amazed that such an obvious shortcoming to a staff plan should have continued to escape my notice, but then you will agree that such is often the way with matters one has given abid-

ing thought to over a period of time; one is not struck by the truth until prompted quite accidentally by some external event. So it was in this instance; that is to say my receiving the letter from Miss Kenton, containing as it did, along with its long, rather unrevealing passages, an unmistakable nostalgia for Darlington Hall, and—I am quite sure of this—distinct hints of her desire to return here, oblige me to see my staff plan afresh. Only then did it strike me that there was indeed a role that a further staff member could crucially play here; that it was, in fact, this very shortage that had been at the heart of all my recent troubles. And the more I considered it, the more obvious it became that Miss Kenton, with her great affection for this house, with her exemplary professionalism—the sort almost impossible to find nowadays—was just the factor needed to enable me to complete a fully satisfactory staff plan for Darlington Hall.[4]

This passage is the most profound example of obsessional discourse. To understand Stevens's "real" desire, we have to turn each sentence upside down. The obsessive's speech always suggests meaning that desperately tries to cover his desire, or, more precisely, the obsessive speaks and thinks compulsively only to avoid his desire. When Stevens speaks about the need to solve the staff problem, or when he detects in Miss Kenton's letter a wish to return to Darlington Hall, he creates excuses that would prevent him from recognizing his own desire. Stevens deposits his desire into the Other: he presents it as the desire of Miss Kenton. The obsessive thus substitutes thought for action and believes that the events in the real are determined by what he thinks. But this omnipotence of thought is linked with a fundamental impotence: "His actions are impotent because he is incapable of engaging himself in an action where he will be recognized by other people."[5] Freud observed that with the obsessive the thought process itself becomes sexualized, "for the pleasure which is normally attached to the content of thought becomes shifted onto the act of thinking itself, and the satisfaction derived from reaching the conclusion of a line of thought is experienced as a sexual satisfaction."[6] Stevens thus gets sexual satisfaction from the plan how to solve the staff problem by taking the trip to visit Miss Kenton, not out of thoughts about Miss Kenton herself.

When Stevens informs his master about his plan to visit Miss Kenton, the master mockingly comments that he did not expect his butler to be still interested in women at his age. This remark touches the core of Stevens's desire, and he immediately has to organize a ritual to contradict its implication. His conclusion is that Darlington expects Stevens to exchange banter as part of his professional service. Stevens, of course, fails in this task, so he tries to learn the art of witticism: "I have devised a simple exercise which I try to perform at least once a day; whenever an odd moment presents itself, I attempt to formulate three witticisms based on my immediate surroundings at that moment."[7] This is a difficult task because it presents the danger of encountering his desire. Stevens knows the danger witticism brings with it, the fact that its effects are uncontrollable, which means a real horror for an obsessive: "By the very nature of a witticism, one is given very little time to assess its various possible repercussions before one is called to give voice to it, and one gravely risks uttering all manner of unsuitable things if one has not first acquired the necessary skill and experience."[8]

This avoidance of desire is linked to the profession of butler. The high principles of serving as a butler take, for Stevens, the form of his ego-ideal. The most important among them is "dignity," which concerns the "butler's ability not to abandon the professional being he inhabits."[9] While the lesser butler easily abandons his professional being for the private one, the great butler never does this, regardless of the situation: "A butler of any quality must be seen to *inhabit* his role, utterly and fully; he cannot be seen casting it aside one moment simply to don it again the next as though it were nothing more as a pantomime costume."[10] The butler thus has to put duty in the first place. Jacques-Alain Miller defined the noble as the master who sacrifices his desire to the ego-ideal. The ego-ideal is the place in the symbolic with which the subject identifies. It is the place from which the subject observes him- or herself in the way he or she would like to be seen. For Stevens this point is that of the principles or code of the butler's service, or, more precisely, dignity. When the subject sacrifices his or her desire to the Ideal, when he or she completely subordinates him- or herself to symbolic identity and takes on some symbolic mask, it is in this mask that one can discern his desire. So when Stevens totally devotes himself to his profession, gives up his private life, and renounces any sexual contact with women, when he, therefore, unites himself with the Ideal, it is in this Ideal, in this social mask of decency that his desire reveals itself. The Ideal that has the meaning of adopting the figure of the Other is also the other of the subject's desire: the traits of the masks of decency, professionalism, and asexuality that form the Ideal are thus co-relative to Stevens's desire. For example, his intended, active ignorance of women can be read as the desire for a woman: "What the subject dissimulates and the means by which he dissimulates, is also the very form of its disclosure."[11]

There is nothing behind the mask: it is in the mask, in the veil that seemingly covers the essence of the subject, that we have to search for this essence. In the case of Stevens there is no "beyond," no suppressed world of passions hidden behind his mask of proper Englishness.[12] It is useless to search in Stevens for some hidden love that could not come out because of the rigid ritual he engaged himself in—all of his love is in the rituals. Inasmuch as it can be said that he loves Miss Kenton, he loves her from the perspective of submission to the codes of their profession. Miss Kenton is also a very competent servant, but what actually attracts Stevens to her is her periodical hysterical resistance to the rituals when she suddenly questions the codes but then again subordinates herself to them.

For that reason, it would be a mistake to depict Stevens as the only culprit for the nonrealization of the love affair. It is a naive conclusion that Miss Kenton would realize her love toward Stevens if only he had been different, more human. Miss Kenton is an example of the hysteric restrained by her paradoxical desire. On the one hand she wants Stevens to change, to reveal his love for her, but, on the other hand, she loves him only for what he actually is—a functionary who tries by all available means to avoid his desire. If Stevens changed, one could predict that Miss Kenton might quickly abandon him and despise him, in the same way she despises her husband.

Miss Kenton develops her first hysterical reaction when a young maid informs her that she is going to marry a fellow servant. The reaction of Miss Kenton to this news is very emotional, since she herself identifies with the young maid in her wish to find love. Even the young servants realize what Miss Kenton would like to happen between her and Stevens. The next hysterical gesture is Miss Kenton's announcement of her intention to marry Mr. Benn. By this act, as she admits at the end of the novel, Miss Kenton intended to provoke a reaction from Stevens.

The hysteric always deals with the question: "What will happen to him if he loses me?" The paradox of the hysteric's desire is that she wants to have a master, the Other, that she herself can control.

Paradoxically, it could thus be said that it is Miss Kenton who actually functions as the support of the institution. She is the *desire* of the institution. This is obvious from her relationship with her husband. When her husband abandons the institution she despises him. She herself cannot endure being outside the institution. At the end she returns to the institution of the family, although giving reasons outside herself—the husband, their daughter. Nonetheless, this is her true desire.

The Age of Innocence

At first sight, *The Age of Innocence* appears to be a novel of unfulfilled romantic love, of the desperate longing of two people deeply in love (Newland Archer and Ellen Olenska), who are unable to pursue their happiness because of the rigid society in which they live. Newland is a conformist, a decent member of New York high society, engaged to be married to May, one of the most eligible girls of this same society. By encountering eccentric Ellen and falling in love with her, Newland discovers that there might be something "outside" the societal codes to which he so dutifully relates. This outside is presumably the world of pure passions, a world where love reigns unconditionally.

The external constraints of society's codes and the fact that both lovers are married, produce the conditions for romantic love to develop. Newland himself admits that the image of Ellen in his memory is stronger than the "real" Ellen. Ellen thus has a special value precisely as a thing that is absent, inaccessible, as the object of Newland's constant longings. That is why he does not even intend to realize his relationship with her in any sexual form. During one of their emotional encounters, he says:

> Don't be afraid: you needn't squeeze yourself back into your corner like that. A stolen kiss isn't what I want. Look: I'm not even trying to touch the sleeve of your jacket. Don't suppose that I don't understand your reasons for not wanting to let this feeling between us dwindle into an ordinary hole-and-corner love-affair. I couldn't have spoken like this yesterday, because when we've been apart,

and I'm looking forward to seeing you, every thought is burnt up in a great flame. But then you come; and you're so much more than I remembered, and what I want of you is so much more than an hour or two every now and then, with wastes of thirsty waiting between, that I can sit perfectly still beside you, like this, with that other vision in my mind, just quietly trusting to it to come true.[13]

For romantic love to emerge, one thus does not need the real person present, what is necessary is the existence of the image. Lacan first defines love in terms of a narcissistic relationship of the subject: what is at work in falling in love is the recognition of the narcissistic image that forms the substance of the ideal ego. When we fall in love, we position the person who is the object of our love in the place of the ideal ego. We love this object because of the perfection that we have striven to reach for our own ego. However, it is not only that the subject loves in the other the image it would like to inhabit him- or herself. The subject simultaneously posits the object of his or her love in the place of the ego-ideal, from which the subject would like to see him- or herself in a likeable way. When we are in love, the love object placed in the ego-ideal enables us to perceive ourselves in a new way—compassionate, lovable, beautiful, decent, and so on. Because of the ideal invested in the person we love, we feel shame in front of her or him, or we try to fascinate this person.

However, to understand the mechanisms of love, one has to go beyond the Ideal. Lacan's famous definition of love is that the subject gives to the other what he or she does not have. This object is the traumatic *objet petit a*, the object cause of desire. Behind the narcissistic relationship toward the love object we encounter the Real, the traumatic object in ourselves, as well as in the other: "Analysis proves that love is in its essence narcissistic, and reveals the substance of the presumably—fallaciously—objectal as that which is in the desire its residue, i.e., its cause: the support of its dissatisfaction, even its impossibility."[14]

How does the subject relate to the object of his or her desire in romantic love? Newland wants to escape with Ellen to a place where they would be able freely to enjoy their love, where they would be "simply two human beings who love each other; and nothing else on earth will matter." Significantly, it is Newland—the conformist—who believes in the possibility of this place of fulfillment outside institutions, and it is Ellen, the nonconformist half-outcast, who dispels his illusions when she answers him by saying:

> "Oh, my dear—where is that country? Have you ever been there? . . . I know of so many who've tried to find it; and, believe me, they all got out by mistake at wayside stations; at places like Boulogne, or Pisa, or Monte-Carlo—and it wasn't at all different from the old world they'd left, but only rather smaller and dingier and more promiscuous. . . . Ah, believe me, it's a miserable little country!" . . .
>
> "Then what, exactly, is your plan for us?" he asked.
>
> "For us? But there is no us in that sense! We're near each other only if we stay far from each other. Then we can be ourselves. Otherwise we're only Newland Archer, the husband of Ellen Olenska's cousin, and Ellen Olenska, the cousin of Newland Archer's wife, trying to be happy behind the backs of the people who trust them."
>
> "Ah, I'm beyond that," he groaned.
>
> "No, you're not! You've never been beyond. And *I* have, and I know what it looks like there."[15]

It is only at the very end of the novel that this message—and thereby the truth of Newland's desire—is brought home to him. Lacan points out that "desire is formed as something . . . the demand means beyond whatever it is able to formulate."[16] On the level of *demand,* Newland's passion could be perceived as his wish to unite with Ellen; however, his *desire* is to renounce this unification: Newland submits himself to the social code in order to maintain Ellen as the inaccessible object that sets his desire in motion. This logic enables us to understand the ending of the novel when Newland, now widowed, during his trip to Paris decides not to see Ellen and thus finally gives up the realization of his great love. When Newland, sitting in front of Ellen's house, tries to imagine what goes on in the apartment, he contemplates:

> "It's more real to me here than if I went up," he suddenly heard himself say; and the fear lest that last shadow of reality should lose its edge kept him rooted to his seat as the minutes succeeded each other.
>
> He sat for a long time on the bench in the thickening dusk, his

eyes never turning from the balcony. At length a light shone through the windows, and a moment later a man-servant came out on the balcony, drew up the awnings, and closed the shutters.

At that, as if it had been the signal he waited for, Newland Archer got up slowly and walked back alone to his hotel.[17]

This last act is an ethical one, in the Lacanian sense of "not giving up on one's desire." All previous renunciations of the love affair between Newland and Ellen depended on an "ethics with the excuse." Thus we can read Ellen's statement, "I can't love you unless I give you up,"[18] as a declaration of romantic love and not as an ethical act: the love becomes romantic because of the suffering that pertains to it. Similarly, Newland's giving up on Ellen in his youth is still linked to the expectation of a "future" when he will stop lying to his wife and when the reality (of his love) will get a true form. Only the last renunciation has the meaning of an ethical act because there is no utilitarian demand any more. From a pragmatic point of view, this renunciation is stupid: Newland is celibate, the same goes for Ellen, he still loves her, presumably she is also far from indifferent to him, and even Newland's son wishes his father would finally find his great love. Not only are there no social obstacles to their relationship, on the contrary, it is the expectation of Newland's society that as a new widower he would find a new life companion.

Why did Newland decide not to see Ellen? The answer could be traced to "the fear lest that last shadow of reality should lose its edge." Our perception of reality is linked to the fact that something has to be excluded from it: the object as the point of the gaze. Every screen of reality includes a constitutive "stain," the trace of what had to be excluded from the field of reality in order that this field can acquire its consistency; this stain appears in the guise of a void Lacan names *objet petit a*. It is the point that I, the subject, cannot see: it eludes me insofar as it is the point from which the screen itself "returns the gaze," or watches me, that is, the point where the gaze itself is inscribed into the visual field of reality. For Newland, this object has to stay closed in the room in Paris, for his reality to retain consistency. That is why he can leave the scene, when the manservant closes the window. This gesture of closing the window is a sign for Newland: a sign that the object is securely excluded so that his reality may remain intact.

Throughout his life, Newland perceived his married life with May as a necessity to which he must submit because of society as well as the "innocence" and "purity" of his lovely wife. He thus obeyed society's codes and acted as was expected. At the very end of the novel, there is however another duty he encounters: the recognition that there is no "other country," that there is no "beyond" of the codes and rituals that suppressed him throughout his life.

The other person that was aware of there being no "beyond" is May. After May's death, Newland learns that she knew about his great love for Ellen. However, May responded to this fact in her "innocent" way: she never revealed her knowledge or made reproaches to Newland, but manipulated the situation with the help of society rules and codes. This recognition of the nonexistence of the "beyond" of the institutions is what May, paradoxically, has in common with Ellen.

The Big Other in Love

How does it happen that people subordinate themselves to the logic of the institution and obey all kinds of social rituals that are supposedly against their well-being? Althusser points out that individuals in their relation to other individuals function in the mode of transference.[19] Transference is thus the "stuff" of social relations. But what is transference other than a specific form of love? What then is the function of love as a social bond?

In his writings on psychoanalysis, Althusser refers to Stendhal's *The Red and the Black*. This novel is an esthetic discourse composed of a series of utterances, presented in a certain order. This discourse is the very existence of Julien Sorel and his "passions": Julien's passion in its affective violence does not precede the discourse; it is also not something uttered between the lines—his passion is the discourse itself: "The *constraints* which define this *discourse* are the very existence of this 'passion.'"[20] The same goes for the discourse of the unconscious: "the unconscious is structured as language" means that the unconscious is the constraints that are at work in this discourse, this constraint is the very existence of the unconscious—there is no unconscious hidden behind the discursive constraints that "express" themselves in the discourse.

The effect (of the unconscious, of "passions") is therefore not exterior to the mechanism that produces the effect: "The effect is nothing other than the discourse itself."²¹ For each discourse can be said to be defined by a system of specific constraints that function as the law of the language, and the effects of this discourse are the products of the constraints. In the case of the unconscious, the constraints that function in this discourse produce the libido as its effect; in the case of ideological discourse the constraints produce the effect of (mis)recognition.

Along the same lines, we can say that it is the constraint (of discourse, of the social symbolic structure) that actually produces love. This institution involves what Lacan names "the big Other." In his seminar on transference, Lacan pointed out the role that the "big Other" plays in love: "the divine place of the Other" confers a consecrated status on the relationship between subjects, as long as the fortune of the desire of the loved one inscribes itself in this divine place.²²

In Lacanian psychoanalysis, the Other is a symbolic structure in which the subject has always been embedded. This symbolic structure is not a positive social fact: it has a quasi-transcendental nature, it forms the very frame structuring our perception of reality; its status is normative, it is a world of symbolic rules and codes. As such, it also does not belong to the psychic level: it is a radically external, nonpsychological universe of symbolic codes regulating our psychic self-experience. It is a mistake either to internalize the "big Other" and reduce it to a psychological fact, or to externalize it and to reduce it to institutions in social reality. By doing this we miss the fact that language is in itself an institution to which the subject is submitted.

How is love connected to the "big Other"? There is no love outside speech: nonspeaking beings do not love. As La Rochefoucauld observed, people do not love if they do not speak about it. Love emerges out of speech as a demand that is not linked to any need. Love is a demand that constitutes itself as such only because the subject is the subject of the signifier.²³ As such the subject is split, barred, marked by a fundamental lack. And it is in this lack that one encounters the object cause of desire. This object has a paradoxical status: it is what the subject lacks, and at the same time what fills this lack. The enchantment of love is how the subject deals, on the one hand, with his or her own lack, and, on the other hand, with the lack in the loved one. As such, love does not call for an answer, although we usually think so: "From the times men write about love, it is clear that they survived far better the longer the beauty remained mute, the longer she did not answer at all—which provokes the thought that the discourse on love itself engenders a kind of enjoyment, that it makes the extreme limit at which speech becomes enjoyment, an enjoyment of the speech itself."[24]

The fact that love does not expect an answer can be understood as bearing witness to its imaginary, narcissistic character: any possible answer from the beloved object would undermine this narcissistic relationship, it would disturb the mirroring of the subject's ego in the beloved object. In the case of *The Remains of the Day,* for example, Miss Kenton does not expect Stevens's answer, she actually escapes from the possible answer. Her act of marriage is a kind of acting-out that tried to resolve the dilemma of her love for Stevens. Her intention was not to hear a confession of Stevens's love for her: for a hysteric, the world collapses if the master loses his sacred place and becomes human.

However, the perception of love as a narcissistic relation loses ground the moment we take into account that "love is a demand (although it remains without the answer) that addresses being . . . some being that is inaccessible as long as it does not answer. Love addresses that point in speech where the word fails. Confronted with this experience, the subject has two solutions at hand: the point at which he no longer has any words, he can either try to encircle or to stuff it with a stopper."[25] What love as a demand targets in the other is therefore the object in him or herself, the Real, the nonsymbolizable kernel around which the subject organizes his or her desire. What gives to the beloved his or her dignity, what leads the loving subject to the survalorization of the beloved, is the presence of the object in him or her:

> . . . by being overvalued, it [the object] has the task of saving the dignity of the subject, that is, of making something else out of us than a subject submitted to the endless sliding of the signifier. It makes of us something other from the subject of speech, and exactly this something other is unique, invaluable, irreplaceable, it is the true point at which we can finally mark what I have named the dignity of the subject.[26]

As we have already seen, there are two relations of the subject to this object. On the one hand, we can use the object as the stopper, which, by its fascinating and *éblouissant* presence, renders invisible the lack in the Other: such as is the case in the elevation of the object in romantic love. On the other hand, we can deal with the object in the terms of sublimation, of a circulation around the object that never touches its core. Sublimation is not a form of romantic love kept alive by the endless striving for the inaccessible love object. In sublimation, the subject confronts the horrifying dimension of the object, the object as *das Ding*, the traumatic foreign body in the symbolic structure. Sublimation circles around the object, it is driven by the fact that the object can never be reached because of its impossible, horrifying nature. Whereas romantic love strives to enjoy the Whole of the Other, of the partner, the true sublime love renounces, since it is well aware that we can "only enjoy a part of the body of the Other.... That is why we are limited in this to a little contact, to touch only the forearm or whatever else—ouch!"[27]

Such a sublimation is well exemplified in Jane Campion's film *The Piano*. What I have in mind here is not only the slow advance of the two lovers to the sexual act, their endless foreplay, in which the body of the other is accessible only part by part and never as a whole (the little piece of skin that can be reached through the hole in Holly Hunter's stocking, for example), but the contractual relationship that exists between the characters played by Harvey Keitel and Holly Hunter. The two make a deal under which she can earn back her piano by allowing Keitel to touch her. This contract is so specified that it even defines how many piano keys are worth a certain touch. The miracle is that out of this subordination to the sexual contract the most passionate and sublime love emerges.

A similar development is at work in Pedro Almodóvar's film *Átame* (*Tie Me Up, Tie Me Down*), in which the kidnapper ties the actress but never sexually abuses her: their daily ritual unexpectedly produces love—the actress falls in love with her kidnapper and even plans to marry him. Here, the partial discovery of the body of the loved one goes on through the act of tying: when the kidnapper carefully chooses the appropriate tie or when he buys masking tape that allows the actress to breathe, by doing this he part by part discovers her body. The kidnapper does not do what might be expected, he does not take the actress by force, he does not try to take her by "whole." Through the ritual of tying he remains all the time distanced and thus he inflames her desire for him.

This, then, is the supreme paradox of love and institution: the true sublime love can only emerge against the background of an external, contractual, symbolic exchange mediated by the institution. Love is not only the guise for the impossibility of relationship with other fellow beings, but the dissimulation that covers the subject's own radical lack. Freud's motto "love for oneself knows only one barrier—love for others, love for objects" can thus be paraphrased into "love for others knows only one barrier—love for oneself, love for the object in oneself."

"Never, Will I Stoop to Wanting Anything Else"

The way the subject deals with its own radical lack could also be the cause of its constant failure in love relationships. One encounters such a failure in a hysteric who desperately searches for the Other that would eternally love him or her and thus annihilate his or her radical lack.

As an example of this attitude, I will take Edith Wharton's story "The Muse's Tragedy." In this short story we encounter two unrealized love relationships, first between a famous poet, Vincent Rendle, and a married lady, Mrs. Anerton; and second, between Mrs. Anerton and a young writer, Lewis Danyers. Here is a summary of the story: Danyers is a great admirer of the late poet Vincent Rendle, about whose work he has written an excellent study. One of the most distinguished of Rendle's works is his "Sonnets to Silvia." As a widespread rumor has it, Silvia is actually Mrs. Anerton, with whom Rendle presumably had a secret love affair. Danyers has a strong desire to meet this woman who had been such an inspiration for the famous poet. Once, during a vacation in Italy, Danyers happens by chance to run into Mrs. Anerton, who is now widowed, living a lonely life. Through their long conversations about Rendle's poetry, Danyers and Mrs. Anerton quickly become close friends. At the end of the holidays, they decide to meet again in a month, ostensibly so that Danyers can start writing a book on Rendle with the help of Mrs. Anerton. However, this project is more an excuse for them to see each other again. The last part of the story consists of a long letter that Mrs. Anerton has written to Danyers and from which we discover that when they actually met in Venice, they spent a wonderful time, not once mentioning the dead poet. At the end of their stay, Danyers had asked Mrs. Anerton to marry him, and in this letter she explains why she cannot accept his offer. Mrs. Anerton confesses that contrary to the widespread belief, there was never anything but friendship between her and Rendle; she had never been Rendle's lover, although she had been very much in love with him. Since she never was Silvia, the object of

Rendle's love, she cannot accept Danyers's proposal; although she is very much taken by him, Danyers cannot take the place of the unattainable love object that Rendle was.

What is common to all the protagonists of the story is their love for poetry: they are either poets or close readers of poetry. But poetry also represents the object of love through its own elusive character. In a poem, rhythm and form capture that "something else" that makes a poem a work of art, an artistic object that is also an object in the Lacanian sense of the term: an object that has no price, an object that is at the same time both beautiful and horrifying and that sets in motion our desire. The object of love also shares with the art object a framed quality. Mrs. Anerton was, for example, described to Danyers as being like "one of those old prints where the lines have the value of color."[28] For Danyers the "Sonnets to Silvia" were the frame into which Mrs. Anerton was placed as the object of his desire long before he met her. Symptomatically, Mrs. Anerton becomes the object of Danyers's love in the first instance because he assumes that she was the great love of the famous poet. At work here is the Lacanian maxim that desire is always the desire of the Other.[29]

The first meaning of this maxim is that the subject desires the same thing as the Other, either in the sense of a concrete other human being or in the sense of the symbolic order. For Danyers, Rendle, the most admired poet of his time, was the Other in whom he invested his ego-ideal; thus Danyers became fascinated by the woman who was supposedly the object of Rendle's love. Notably, when Danyers "really" falls in love with Mrs. Anerton, the dead poet quickly becomes an intruder, since now Danyers himself wants to become the object of Mrs. Anerton's love. Here, one encounters the second meaning of the maxim "desire is the desire of the Other," which concerns the subject's question about what he or she is for the Other, that is, what kind of an object is the subject for the Other. It is significant that Danyers never questions whether he loves Mrs. Anerton as herself or only as Rendle's assumed mistress. When Danyers falls in love, the essential thing for him is what *he* represents in the eyes of Mrs. Anerton. That is why he is so flattered when she inquires about his work and encourages him to start writing.

> "You must write," she said, administering the most exquisite flattery that human lips could give.

Of course he meant to write—why not do something great in his turn? His best, at least; with the resolve, at the outset, that his should be *the* best. Nothing less seemed possible with that mandate in his ears. How she had divined him; lifted and disentangled his groping ambitions; laid the awakening touch on his spirit with her creative *Let there be light!*[30]

This quotation offers a perfect example of the Freudian description of love as a narcissistic relationship: the subject posits the object of his or her love in the place of the ego-ideal and then tries to appear before this object in the most lovable way, as the most admirable human being. This positing reflects the lover's desire that the beloved return love and thus subjectify him- or herself as a lover, too. Danyers is so fascinated by Mrs. Anerton's encouragement to write, since this encouragement proves to him that she sees in him that "something more"—the artistic genius, the object of her admiration, a possible love. Mrs. Anerton's urging him to write gives Danyers hope that the "something more" that he sees in her is something she acknowledges in him, too, and that, therefore, love is reciprocal. His enthusiasm is quickly shattered when Mrs. Anerton proposes to Danyers that he write a book on Rendle: with this proposal Danyers loses the place of the object of Mrs. Anerton's love, and becomes only the link to Mrs. Anerton's love for the dead poet. From the letter we can guess that this situation changes when they meet in Venice and that at that time Rendle's spirit ceased to haunt them, which encourages Danyers to ask Mrs. Anerton for her hand.

In Danyers's case, one can find a fairly simple scheme of love: a man becomes fascinated with his ideal, and when this ideal apparently returns love (when the spirit of the dead poet presumably leaves the stage), the realization of a love relationship in marriage seems the natural course of events. In the case of Mrs. Anerton, however, things are more complicated.

As for her relationship with Rendle it could be said that it was an intellectual friendship among equals. From her description of the relationship, it is clear that Rendle treated her as an intellectual partner, as a friend that knew a lot about poetry and as a person with whom he could have interesting conversations. As Mrs. Anerton says: "He was always quite honest and straightforward with me; he treated me as one man treats another; and yet at times I felt he *must* see that with me it was different. If he did see, he made no sign. Perhaps he never noticed—I am sure he never meant to be cruel. He had never made love to me; it was no fault of his if I wanted more than he could give me."[31] We also learn from Mrs. Anerton's letter to Danyers that the famous "Sonnets to Silvia" were written as a "cosmic philosophy" and not as a love poem: they were addressed to the Woman and not to a woman. After Rendle's death, when Mrs. Anerton edited a book of his letters, she slightly changed the letters that Rendle had addressed to her by marking them at certain points as if something had been left out, thus giving the impression to the reader that the more intimate parts were held back from publication. Although the "Sonnets to Silvia" were addressed to the nonexisting Woman, Mrs. Anerton did all she could to maintain the impression that in reality she was Silvia. Mrs. Anerton therefore identified with Woman. And the question is, What is the logic of such an identification?

From Lacanian theory it is well known that Woman does not exist. Lacan points out that no general notion of Woman can embrace all women. Woman is for men, as for women, barred, crossed, just as the "big Other" is also barred: Woman is radically unattainable, "what women never are by themselves, a woman that is mythologized as ideal, muse, etc."[32] The belief in Woman therefore is nothing other than an attempt to erase the bar that marks the subject and to negate the lack in the Other. That is why for Lacan, Woman is essentially a man's fantasy. This mythical woman, a muse or an ideal is by itself asexual. And the identification with this ideal presents an attempt to escape the split, the lack that pertains to the sexual difference.

Such a desperate attempt to identify with Woman arises in the transsexual's demand for a change of sex. As Catherine Millot[33] points out in her analysis of transsexualism, transsexual men usually identify with Woman (*la Femme*) when they demand the operation that would change their sex. With this demand, male transsexuals put the image of Woman in the place of the "Name of the Father" in an attempt to escape castration. A transsexual man tries to be more feminine than a woman, which is why he tries to embody "all women." In this attempt, the transsexual man falls prey to the male myth that presupposes the existence of Woman who is not submitted to castration. As someone that is not castrated, Woman serves the same function as the Freudian primordial father who, as the possessor of all the women, also possesses all enjoyment and thus blocks his sons' access to their enjoyment. Lacan points out that "Woman is one of the Names of the Father."[34] But as Millot says, in the case of the transsexual, Woman occupies the place of the Name of the Father. Here, as Jacques-Alain Miller emphasizes, one has to be careful to distinguish the Name of the Father from the Names of the Father: the first notion delineates the empty form of the law, the father as the symbolic function, while the plural of "the Name of the Father" means the Freudian primordial father, the father who is the full embodiment of authority and not the empty symbolic figure.[35] Woman therefore does not play the role of the empty symbolic father, but as one of the Names of the Father occupies the place of the primordial father. According to Catherine Millot, transsexuals do not present a case of psychosis even though the Name of the Father is missing, since "the transsexual symptom *strictu sensu* (conviction and the demand for transformation) corresponds to an attempt to palliate the absence of the Name of the Father. . . . The transsexual symptom appears to function as a substitution of the Name-of-the-Father inasmuch as the transsexual aims to incarnate Woman."[36] This symptom thus performs the paradoxical function of limiting the enjoyment of the subject. One encounters here the same logic at work as in the case of the psychotic who also finds a kind of solution to his or her problems by forming a delirium. Such a delirium or symptom allows some psychotics to posit a limit to enjoyment. Lacan argued that in the case of James Joyce, his writing was the symptom that replaced the missing function of the Name of the Father and thus prevented Joyce from falling into actual psychosis.[37] Likewise, in the case of transsexuals, their symptom (the demand to incarnate Woman) replaces the Name of the Father and thus also prevents psychosis.

What happens if a woman identifies with Woman? She also has two possibilities: psychosis and hysteria. In hysterical identification with Woman, the paternal function, the Name of the Father, is fully in place: however, the hysteric is traumatized by the split that pertains to her entry into language, and to escape this split, she tries to present herself as a phallic Woman.

As was pointed out in the case of *The Remains of the Day*, the hysteric is perturbed by the question "What am I for the Other?" The hysteric does not try to obtain the satisfaction of her desire through this question, but to question the desire of the Other, since for the hysteric, the problem is that she encounters her desire as Other. Thus the trauma of the hysteric evolves from the dilemma of what kind of an object is she without knowing it for the Other. The hysteric's question in regard to love is thus not "Do I love him?" but a narcissistic "Does he love me?" The narcissism of the subject that one encounters in hysteria is a fundamental narcissism that touches the very core of the subject's being. The hysteric's narcissism is linked to her desperate attempt for certainty: what she seeks is the Other that would grant her the identity. The hysteric's questions and appeals to the Other to give her answers as of who she is, what value she has, what object she is, are all attempts to overcome the constitutive split that marks the subject as the speaking being. The hysteric searches for the signifier that would give her unity, wholeness: "In the meantime, she becomes devoted to the cult of Woman . . . in the hope that this signifier will someday appear."[38]

Hysteria is also the way the subject deals with the impossibility of sexual rapport. The hysteric's symptoms are usually desperate attempts to deny this impossibility. In his scheme of the discourse of the hysteric, Lacan points out how the hysteric tries to overcome the impossibility of sexual rapport via the belief that the Other has knowledge about her (that the Other knows the truth about her object a); thus she holds a belief that such an Other exists and that it is flawless. The hysteric also demands that every man be the embodiment of such an Other, which forces her to constantly question the authority of her partner. "The hysteric, looking for an Other without lack, offers herself to him as phallicized object to make him complete, to install him as Other without flaw."[39] Through this desperate attempt, the hysteric hopes to become the only object of the desire of the Other, which would give her certainty as of her being.

How are we to understand this hysteric's attempt to embody the phallus? For Lacan, the phallus occupies the position of the third element that disrupts the symbiosis between subjects. In the relationship between the mother and the child, the father's phallus is what prevents the child from being all for the mother, that is, mother does not desire only her child (the child is not all for her) because of the phallus. What is crucial is that "the phallus forbids the child the satisfaction of his or her own desire, which is the desire to be the exclusive desire of the mother."[40] The phallus is a signifier of the desire of the Other and, as such, it is a signifier that is equivalent to the lack in the Other. For Lacan, the phallus marks the entry of the subject into language, since it introduces the child into symbolic castration: "Castration means first of all this—that the child's desire for the mother does not refer *to* her but *beyond* her, to an object, the phallus, whose status is first imaginary (the object presumed to satisfy her desire) and then symbolic (recognition that desire cannot be satisfied)."[41]

Of women who deal with the trauma of castration through their attempt to be the phallus, Lacan says: "Paradoxical as this formulation may seem, I am saying that it is in order to be the phallus, that is to say, the signifier of the desire of the Other, that a woman will reject an essential part of femininity, namely, all her attributes in the masquerade. It is for that which she is not that she wishes to be desired as well as loved."[42] Lacan took the term "masquerade" from Joan Riviere, for whom womanliness is a masquerade that is at the same time a dissimulation of a certain masculinity, a mask a woman puts on in order to incite man's desire, a mask that presents horror for men, since men suspect some hidden danger behind it. This masquerade for Lacan concerns the phallus, which is primarily a fraud, a semblance, nothing in itself, only a signifier of the lack as such—"the supreme signifier of an impossible identity."[43]

In the case of Mrs. Anerton, what is at stake in her love life is not so much her desiring an unattainable love object (Rendle) but her identifying with the object that is presumably desired by Rendle. She masquerades as a phallic Woman—Silvia, since it is Silvia who is the signifier of Rendle's desire. Silvia is the object of his desire that goes beyond any existing woman, which is why she can take on the role of the phallus. In this desperate attempt to be the object of Rendle's love, Mrs. Anerton had done everything to maintain the public impression that she was Silvia. But, although she desperately tried to identify with Woman, to be Silvia, Rendle's muse, she always knew that this project was doomed to failure. As she says in her letter to Danyers, at some moments she would almost believe that she was Silvia because of the rumors people were spreading, however, she knew this was not true: "Oh, there was no phase of folly I didn't go through. You can't imagine the excuses a woman will invent for a man's not telling her that he loves her. . . . But all the while, deep down, I knew he had never cared."[44] And because of this awareness, Mrs. Anerton was not a psychotic but a hysteric. She *would* be a psychotic had she never doubted that she *was* Silvia. In that case she would not have needed to encourage rumors about her being Rendle's love. However, because Mrs. Anerton did not truly identify herself as Silvia, she needed symbolic structures (rumors, the published letters that she herself edited, etc.) through which she could organize a whole fantasy scenario that would assure others, and through their belief assure herself, that she was Silvia.

Eric Laurent says that often one encounters women who, in the name of love "try to give all and be all"—and thus try to embody the nonexistent fantasy of Woman. When women recognize the impossibility of such an attitude they usually fall into the other extreme and start perceiving themselves as nothing. "The wrong solution given by female masochism is that the subject tries to reserve for herself the place in man's fantasy that would be all or nothing. This solution is wrong since the reality of woman's position for man is not to be all or nothing, but to be his Other."[45] To be all, to be "Woman that all men lack" is therefore a psychotic position. Woman in this case becomes "the Other of the Other," which is a psychotic position because it has no representation in the symbolic.[46]

The pathos of Mrs. Anerton is that she tried to get proof that she was not this "nothing," not someone unworthy of love, in her relationship with Danyers. As she admits in the letter, her original aim was to provoke Danyers's love to get reassurance about her own worth. However, she miscalculated the course of events to follow, since she herself started feeling for Danyers more than she intended. That her feelings for Danyers were more than cunning cordiality becomes clear from the end of her letter, when she worries whether Danyers was sincere in his feelings: did he intend only to play around with her; did he love her as Silvia or as herself? These are again hysteric's questions, through which Mrs. Anerton tries to get an answer as to what kind of an object she was for Danyers.

When the hysteric subject posits the question of her being, questioning what she is for the Other, the subject does not get an answer. The Other does not answer. Thus the subject tries to get proof outside words:

in acts, behavior, between the lines, and so on. As Colette Soler points out, it is essential for the subject that he or she is an interpreter. Since the Other cannot answer, the subject interprets: the subject invents the answer as to the Other's desire.[47] Mrs. Anerton admits to Danyers that there was one question that hounded her night and day, that became her obsession: "Why had he [Rendle] never loved me? Why had I been so much to him, and no more? Was I so ugly, so essentially unlovable, that though a man might cherish me as his mind's comrade, he could not care for me as a woman?"[48] Her experiment with Danyers was supposed to give her an answer as to who she was as a woman, as to her ability to be an object of love. However, as she says in the letter, she did not plan it all: "I liked you from the first—I was drawn to you (you must have seen that)—I wanted you to like me; it was not a mere psychological experiment."[49] That Mrs. Anerton cared for Danyers more than she initially intended is noticeable from her joy in recognizing how jealous Danyers was of her past. Further evidence of her interest in Danyers emerges when Mrs. Anerton explains why she did not reject him earlier during their stay in Venice: "I couldn't spoil that month—my one month. It was so good, for once in my life, to get away from literature."[50] Her desperate attempt to identify with Silvia accounted for the fact that in her past there was no love for Mrs. Anerton outside literature, but by meeting Danyers she got a glimpse of what a "true" love could be: when she and Danyers escaped the hounding of the dead poet, they opened a space for a genuine love to begin.

But why did Mrs. Anerton prevent this from happening? The answer is not that she still loved the dead poet and did not want to give up on her desire for him. From what Mrs. Anerton says in the letter, it could be concluded that her refusal of Danyers has something to do with how her relationship with him uncovered the falsehood of the story that she had created about her relationship with Rendle and her full, if not fatal, belief in that story. When Mrs. Anerton recognized the full scope of the illusion in which she had lived almost her whole life, her whole identity collapsed. As she speculates at the end of the letter, Danyers as a young man will probably quickly forget the pain that she had caused him, but her experiment will affect her far more deeply: "[I]t will hurt me horribly . . ., because it has shown me, for the first time, all that I have missed."[51] However, Mrs. Anerton's refusal of Danyers could also be understood as another hysterical gesture. Her refusal of love has to do with the impossibility of her desire. What she was primarily concerned with in both of her failed love relationships was what kind of an object she was for the Other, first for Rendle and then for Danyers. It was also in her relationship with Danyers that her primal concern evolved around her demand to be the object of his love. Danyers's actual falling in love with her would mean the fulfillment of her desire. However, this is what the hysteric cannot accept: her desire has to remain unsatisfied. But in this refusal, she presents her act as a help to Danyers. As she says in the letter, "Somebody must save you from marrying a disappointed woman. . . ."[52]

In giving up Danyers, does Mrs. Anerton act in a Socratic way by revealing the truth that she is not Silvia? Does she, in effect, admit to her lover, "There where you see something, I am nothing"? As Lacan stresses in his analysis of Plato's *Symposium*, Socrates refuses Alcibiade's courting and does not recognize himself as the loved one because "for [Socrates] there is nothing in himself worthy of love. His essence was that *ouden*, emptiness, hollowness. . . ."[53] Socrates' refusal to acknowledge himself as the loved one and to return love discloses the traumatic, empty nature of the object of love. As Lacan says, "[T]he Other whom we long for is anything other than love, it is something that literally causes the love to decay—I want to say, something that has the nature of object."[54] When Socrates refuses to be the object worthy of Alcibiades' desire, he uncovers how the object of love does not possess what the loving one expects.[55] Mrs. Anerton does not act in the Socratic tradition, since she still believes in that "something else" in her that should be worthy of love. That is why she can write: "It is just when a man begins to think that he understands a woman that he may be sure that he doesn't. It is because Vincent Rendle *didn't love me* that there is no hope for you. I never had what I wanted, and never, never, never, will I stoop to wanting anything else."[56]

How then are we to understand Mrs. Anerton's giving up on Danyers when, on the one hand, it is clear from her letter that she was truly happy with him, but, on the other hand, her nostalgia for her unrealized love with Rendle remains constant. Mrs. Anerton falls into the paradox of love when she expects from love something other than what is at work in it. A common question among loved women is, does the man love me because of myself or because of something else? In a film by Claude Chabrol, the hero, a millionaire, reverses the logic of this question by saying: "If only I were to find a woman who would love me only for my millions, not for myself!" However absurd it might sound, this reversed logic represents the true nature of love. The expectation that the other will love you because of yourself is some kind of a psychotic position: in this case the loved one takes him- or herself as the subject without lack. The truth about love is that the other has to love you because of something that is in you more than yourself.

Until their meeting in Venice, Danyers obviously loved Mrs. Anerton because she presumably was the object of the desire of the Other (Rendle). However, he did not recognize at all the moment he started to love her regardless of her relationship with Rendle. In Danyers's libidinal economy, his love for Mrs. Anerton was always the love for that "something more than herself." Mrs. Anerton, on the contrary, had an impossible demand: she wanted Danyers to love her both as what she was by herself and as something else, as Silvia, the phantasmatic muse. This impossible demand reflects the impossibility of the sexual relationship: for Mrs. Anerton, her relationship with Danyers collapsed when the image of Silvia faded and when the Other, Rendle, disappeared from her unity with Danyers. One could speculate that the relationship between Danyers and Mrs. Anerton might have been possible had she still presumed that Danyers loved her as Silvia. However, for Mrs. Anerton, she would really have had to have been Silvia (her love for Rendle would have had to be realized).

Mrs. Anerton came close to an understanding of what love is when she faked Rendle's published letters by inserting asterisks, to signify things left out that were never there in the first place. This lack, emptiness, is what the object of love is. However, her tragedy is that she wants this emptiness to be fulness and to have a name—Silvia. Mrs. Anerton therefore wants to be all, the full object of love, and when she realizes that she is not, she rejects love altogether and chooses nothingness. She cannot deal with the fact that she is lacking as a subject; since she could not accept love's phantasmatic nature, and since she did not realize her grandest love, Mrs. Anerton also gives up on her second chance for love.

Paradoxically this is the limit of love—that we see in the other what he or she does not have, and not him- or herself. Such is the very condition of love. The position of the hysterical subject is that he or she always guesses what is behind the curtain, that is why such a subject usually ends up by having nothing—by totally giving up on love.

The subjects in *The Age of Innocence* and *The Remains of the Day* needed the "big Other" (society's codes and institutions) to prevent their love from being realized, but Mrs. Anerton creates her own prohibitions by constantly seeking the way to be Woman, the muse[57] that would be the true object of the Other's desire. And by not recognizing the emptiness of this object, she gives up on love. While a poet longs for the object of his love, his muse, and creates around this impossible object a work of art, the muse must live in the realm of disavowal.

Notes

All English translations have been done by the author, with the exception of those cited in the notes.

1. An early version of the first part of this essay appeared as "Love: Providence or Despair" in *New Formations* (London: Lawrence and Wishart) 23 (1994).
2. Sigmund Freud, *Sexuality and the Psychology of Love,* trans. Joan Riviere (New York: Macmillan, 1963), 57.
3. Louis Althusser, *Lenin and Philosophy and Other Essays,* trans. Ben Brewster (London: Monthly Review Press, 1971), 136.
4. Kazuo Ishiguro, *The Remains of the Day* (London: Faber and Faber, 1989), 9–10.
5. Stuart Schneiderman, *Rat Man* (New York: New York UP, 1986), 35.
6. Sigmund Freud, *Standard Edition,* vol. 10, 245.
7. Ishiguro, *The Remains,* 131.
8. Ibid.
9. Ibid., 42.
10. Ibid., 169.
11. "Sur le Gide de Lacan," *La Cause freudienne* (Paris: Navarin/Seuil) 25 (1993): 37.
12. Significantly, Stevens points out that butlers only truly exist in England. In other countries they have only menservants: "Continentals are unable to be butlers because they are as a breed incapable of the emotional restraint which only the English race are capable of." Ishiguro, *The Remains,* 43.
13. Edith Wharton, *The Age of Innocence* (New York: Macmillan, 1986), 289.
14. Jacques Lacan, *Le Séminaire,* book 20: *Encore* (Paris: Éditions du Seuil, 1975), 12.
15. Wharton, *The Age,* 290, 291.
16. Jacques Lacan, *The Ethics of Psychoanalysis,* trans. Dennis Porter (1959–60; London: Routledge, 1992), 294.
17. Wharton, *The Age,* 362.
18. Ibid., 172.
19. Louis Althusser, *Écrits sur la psychanalyse: Freud et Lacan* (Paris: Stock/Imec, 1993), 176.
20. Ibid., 157.

21 Ibid., 158.
22 Cf. Jacques Lacan, *Le Séminaire,* book 8: *Le Transfert* (Paris: Éditions du Seuil, 1991).
23 Cf. Jacques Lacan, *Écrits: A Selection,* trans. Alan Sheridan (New York: Norton, 1977), 270.
24 Michel Silvestre, *Demain la psychanalyse* (Paris: Navarin Editeur, 1987), 300–301.
25 Ibid., 301.
26 Lacan, *Le Transfert,* 203.
27 Lacan, *Encore,* 26.
28 Edith Wharton, "The Muse's Tragedy," in *Souls Belated and Other Stories* (London: Everyman, 1991), 29.
29 Cf. Jacques Lacan, "The Subversion of the Subject and the Dialectic of Desire in the Freudian Unconscious," in *Écrits,* 312.
30 Wharton, "Muse's Tragedy," 35.
31 Ibid., 38.
32 Cf. Elizabeth Cowie, *To Represent Woman? The Representation of Sexual Difference in the Visual Media* (London: Macmillan, forthcoming).
33 See Catherine Millot, *Horsexe: Essay on Transsexuality,* trans. Kenneth Hylton (New York: Autonomedia, 1990).
34 Cf. Jacques Lacan, *Le Sinthome* (unpublished seminar, 1975/6).
35 Cf. Jacques-Alain Miller, *Ce qui fait insigne* (unpublished seminar, 1986/7).
36 Millot, *Horsexe,* 42.
37 Cf. Lacan, *Le Sinthome.*
38 Julien Quackleben et al., "Hysterical Discourse," in *Lacanian Theory of Discourse: Subject, Structure and Society,* ed. Mark Bracher, Marshal W. Alcorn, Ronald J. Corthell, and Francoise Massardier-Kenney (New York: New York UP, 1994), 131.
39 Ibid., 136.
40 Jacques Lacan, *Les Formations de l'inconscient* (unpublished seminar, 1957–58), quoted by Jacqueline Rose, "Introduction II," in *Jacques Lacan and the École Freudienne,* ed. Juliet Mitchell and Jacqueline Rose (London: Macmillan, 1982), 38.
41 Jacqueline Rose, "Introduction II," in *Jacques Lacan and the École Freudienne,* 38.
42 Jacques Lacan, *Écrits,* 290.
43 Stephen Heath, "Joan Riviere and the Masquerade," in *Formations of Fantasy,* ed. Victor Burgin, James Donald, and Cora Kaplan (London: Methuen, 1986), 58.
44 Wharton, "Muse's Tragedy," 38.
45 Eric Laurent, "Positions féminines de l'être," in *La Cause Freudienne,* no. 24 (Paris: Navarin/Seuil 1993), 108.
46 Ibid., p. 109.
47 See Colette Soler, "The Real Aims of the Analytic Act," in *Lacanian Ink,* no. 5 (New York: Wooster Press, 1992), 53–60. It is the fantasy that gives the subject the answer to the question of desire. What is crucial is that the fantasy is the invention of the subject and not of the Other. Lacan says that desire is the desire of the Other, which means that the subject always determines her desire in relation to the Other's desire: it is the presumed Other's desire that keeps the subject's desire in motion. But fan-

tasy is always fantasy of the subject, the Other does not form fantasies, since the Other does not exist.
48 Wharton, "Muse's Tragedy," 40.
49 Ibid., 41.
50 Ibid., 42.
51 Ibid.
52 Ibid.
53 Jacques Lacan, *Le Transfert*, 185. One can ask whether Socrates does not act in a similar way to the lady in courtly love when she also constantly refuses to return love. It can be said that both Socrates and the lady occupy the same place—both are objects of unfulfilled love. However, the function that they perform at this place is different. The lady is the master who constantly imposes on her admirer new duties and keeps him on a string by hinting that sometime in the future she might show him some mercy. Socrates, on the other hand, refuses the position of master. With his refusal Socrates points to the emptiness of the object of love, while the lady believes that there is in herself something worthy of love. That is why she puts herself in the position of the Master (S_1), from which she capriciously gives orders. Socrates opposes this attitude altogether and does not want to encourage false hope.
54 Ibid., 203.
55 Socrates's position is similar to that of the analyst, since both of them occupy the position of the object *a* and try to "keep that nothingness," emptiness, the traumatic and horrifying nature of the object. Putting oneself in the position of the object accounts for the fact that the subject is not represented by any signifier—what we have here, is therefore the subject as pure emptiness. The analyst is not a Master whom the analysand would identify with and who would impose duties on the subject. By occupying the place of the object, the analyst enables the subject to find the truth about his or her desire.
56 Wharton, "Muse's Tragedy," 36.
57 Mrs. Anerton wanted to be—but in reality wasn't—Rendle's muse. It can be said that as the object of Danyers's fascination, she was his muse all the time. The muse's tragedy was therefore that she was a muse for the wrong poet.

Slavoj Žižek

8
"There Is No Sexual Relationship"

One of the enigmas of Richard Wagner's *Ring* concerns the motif usually designated as that of "renunciation": this motif is first heard in scene 1 of *Das Rheingold,* when, answering Alberich's query, Woglinde discloses that "nur wer der Minne Macht versagt [only the one who renounces the power of love]" can take possession of the gold; the "renunciation" motif is then repeated approximately twenty times, most noticeably toward the end of act 1 of *Die Walküre,* at the moment of the most triumphant assertion of love between Siegmund and Sieglinde—just prior to his pulling out the sword from the tree trunk, Siegmund sings it: "Heiligster Minne höchste Noth [Holiest love's deepest need]".[1] Why, then, does the same motif stand first for the renunciation of love, then for its most intense assertion? Claude Lévi-Strauss[2] provided the hitherto most consistent answer. According to his reading, the central problem of the *Ring* is the constitutive imbalance of the (social) exchange. Wotan—the very "god of contracts" supposed to safeguard exchanges—again and again engages in attempts to break the self-imposed bond of his own rules and to get "something for nothing"; in contrast to him, Alberich is more honest: he exchanges something (love) for something else (power), thereby obeying the fundamental symbolic law according to which "you can't have it all," that is, you can have what you possess only on the basis of a previous renunciation. The problem with Siegmund, Wotan's offspring, is that, like his father, he again "wants it all," power (the sword) *and* love, refusing to enter the circle of social exchange. Insofar as exchange (of women) is grounded in the prohibition of incest, it is quite logical that Siegmund and Sieglinde form an incestuous couple—and the motif of renunciation is here to remind us that this incestuous combination of power and love must end in a catastrophe.

This Lévi-Straussian analysis must be supplemented by a self-referential twist: the choice of power doesn't involve only the loss of love (and vice versa), it also leads to the truncation or outright loss of power itself. The outcome of Alberich's choice of power is that he ends up as a powerless dwarf: the lesson of his downfall is that in order to have power, we have to limit its exercise, to acknowledge our subordination to some higher power that invests us with a limited amount of power. The outright choice of love is even more suicidal: in order for the love to survive, one has to resist yielding to its immediate urge and to subordinate it to the necessities of social exchange via the prohibition of incest. In short, the impediment that prevents the full realization of love is internal, so the solution to the enigma of the motif of renunciation is to treat the two lines as two fragments of the complete sentence that was distorted by the "dreamwork," that is, rendered unreadable by being split into two—the solution is to reconstitute the complete proposition: "Love's deepest need is to renounce its own power." The ultimate proof of a true (absolute, "incestuous") love is that the lovers split, renounce the full consummation of their relationship—if the lovers were to remain together, they would either die or turn into an ordinary everyday bourgeois couple—"I can't love you unless I give you up," to quote Edith Wharton. From a certain perspective, Wagner's entire opus is nothing but a variation on this theme: from *The Flying Dutchman* to the *Ring*, fulfillment goes awry and can be achieved only in death. For that reason, Nietzsche was right in conceiving *Meistersinger* as complementary to *Tristan:* if one is to survive in the everyday world of social reality, one has to renounce the absolute claim of love, which is precisely what Hans Sachs does, thereby enabling the only semblance of a *happy end* in Wagner. By adding to this list *Parsifal*, one obtains three versions of redemption, which follow the logic of the Kierkegaardian triad of the aesthetic, the ethical, and the religious. *Tristan* gives body to the aesthetic solution: refusing to compromise one's desire, one goes to the end and willingly embraces death. *Meistersinger* counters it with the ethical solution: true redemption resides not in following the immortal passion to its self-destructive conclusion; one should rather learn to overcome it via creative sublimation and to return, in a mood of wise resignation, to the "daily" life of symbolic obligations. In *Parsifal*, finally, the passion can no longer be overcome via its reintegration to society in which it survives in a gentrified form: one has to deny it thoroughly.

The mention of Kierkegaard was by no means accidental: it was precisely Kierkegaard who provided the hitherto most elaborated account of why "love's deepest need is to renounce its own power." In all three Kierkegaardian "stages," aesthetic, ethical, and religious, the same sacrificial gesture is at work, each time in a different "power/potential" (in Schelling's sense of the term). The religious sacrifice is a matter of course (suffice it to recall Abraham's readiness to sacrifice Isaac, Kierkegaard's supreme example), so we should concentrate on the renunciation that pertains to the "ethical" and the "aesthetic."

The ethical stage is defined by the sacrifice of the immediate consumption of life, of our yielding to the fleeting moment, in the name of some higher universal norm. In the domain of erotics, one of the most refined examples of this renunciation is provided by Mozart's *Così fan tutte*. If Mozart's *Don Giovanni* embodies the aesthetic (as developed by Kierkegaard himself in his detailed analysis of the opera in *Either/Or*), the lesson of *Così fan tutte* is ethical—why? The point of *Così* is that the love that unites the two couples at the beginning of the opera is no less "artificial," mechanically brought about, than the second falling in love of the sisters with the exchanged partners dressed up as Albanian officers that results from the manipulations of the philosopher Alfonso— in both cases, we are dealing with a mechanism that the subjects follow in a blind, puppet-like way. Therein consists the Hegelian "negation of negation": first, we perceive the "artificial" love, the product of Alfonso's manipulations, as opposed to the initial "authentic" love; then, all of a sudden, we become aware that there is actually no difference between the two—the original love is no less "artificial" than the second. So, since one love counts as much as the other, the couples can return to their initial marital arrangement. This is what Hegel has in mind when he claims that, in the course of a dialectical process, the immediate starting point proves itself to be something already mediated, that is, its own self-negation: in the end, we ascertain that we always already were what we wanted to become, the only difference being that this "always already" changes its modality from in-itself into for-itself.[3] Ethical is in this sense the domain of repetition *qua* symbolic: if, in the aesthetic, one endeavors to capture the moment in its uniqueness, in the ethical a thing only becomes what it is through its repetition.[4]

In the aesthetic stage, the seducer works on an innocent girl whom he considers worthy of his efforts, but at a crucial moment, just prior to his triumph, that is, when for all practical purposes her surrender is already won and the fruits of his labor have only to be reaped, he has not only to renounce the realization of the sexual act but, over and above, to induce *her* to drop him (by putting on the mask of a despicable person and thus arousing her disgust).[5] Why this renunciation? The realization of the process of seduction in the sexual act renders visible the goal the seducer was striving at in all its transience and vulgarity, so the only way to avoid this horror of radical "desublimation" is to stop short of it, thereby keeping awake the dream of what *might have* happened—by losing his love in time, the seducer gains her for eternity.[6] One must be careful here not to miss the point: the "desublimation" one tries to avoid by renouncing the act does *not* reside in the experience of how realization always falls short of the ideal we were striving for, that is, of the gap that forever separates the ideal from its realization; in it, it is rather the ideal itself that loses its power, that changes into repugnant slime—the ideal is, as it were, undermined "from within," when we approach it too closely, it changes into its opposite.[7]

In all three "stages," the same gesture of sacrifice is at work in a different "power/potential": what shifts from the one to the other is the locus of impossibility. That is to say, one is tempted to claim that the triad aesthetic-ethical-religious provides the matrix for the three versions of the impossibility of sexual relationship. What one would expect here is that, with the "progression" (or rather leap) from one to the next stage, the pressure of prohibition and/or impossibility gets stronger: in the aesthetic, one is free to "seize the day," to yield to enjoyment without any restraints; in the ethical, enjoyment is admitted, but on condition that it remains within the confines of the Law (marriage), that is, in an aseptic, "gentrified" form that suspends its fatal charm; in the religious, finally, there is no enjoyment, just the most radical, "irrational" renunciation for which we get nothing in return (Abraham's readiness to sacrifice Isaac). However, this clear picture of progressive renunciation immediately gets blurred by the uncanny resemblance, noticed by many a sagacious commentator, between Abraham's sacrifice of Isaac (which, of course, belongs to the religious) and Kierkegaard's own renunciation to Regina (which belongs to the aesthetic dialectics of seduction). On a closer look, one can thus ascertain that, contrary to our expectations, the prohibition (or rather inhibition) *loosens* with the leap from one to the next stage: in the aesthetic, the object is completely lost, beyond our reach, due to the inherent instability of this level (in the very gesture of our trying to lay our hands on the fleeting moment of pleasure, it slips between our fingers); in the ethical, enjoyment is already rendered possible in a stable, regular form via the mediation of the Law; and, finally, in the religious . . . what is the religious mode of erotics, if its aesthetic mode is seduction and its ethical mode marriage? Is it at all meaningful to speak of a religious mode of erotics in the precise Kierkegaardian sense of the term? The point of Lacan is that this, precisely, is the role of *courtly love:* the lady in courtly love suspends the ethical level of universal symbolic obligations and bombards us with totally arbitrary ordeals in a way that is homologous to the religious suspension of the ethical; her ordeals are on a par with God's ordering Abraham to slaughter his son Isaac. And, contrary to first appearance, that sacrifice reaches here its apogee, it is only here that, finally, we confront the Other *qua* Thing that gives body to the excess of enjoyment over mere pleasure. If an aesthetical endeavor to seize the full moment ends in fiasco and utter loss, paradoxically, religious renunciation, the elevation of the lady into an untouchable and unattainable object, leads to the trance of enjoyment that transgresses the limits of Law.

And is not this extreme point at which radical ascetic renunciation paradoxically coincides with the most intense erotic fulfillment the very topic of Wagner's *Tristan?* One can also see why Nietzsche was right in claiming that *Parsifal* is Wagner's most decadent work and the antithesis to *Tristan*. In *Parsifal,* normal, everyday life totally disappears as a point of reference—what remains is the opposition between hysterically overexcited chromatism and asexual purity, the ultimate denial of passion.[8] *Parsifal* thus offers a kind of spectral decomposition of *Tristan:* in it, the immortal longing of the two lovers, sexualized and simultaneously spiritualized to extremes, is decomposed into its two constituents, sexual chromatic excitation and the spiritual purity beyond the cycle of life. Amfortas and Parsifal, the suffering king who cannot die and the innocent "pure fool" beyond desire, are the two ingredients that, when brought together, give us Tristan.

We can see, now, how we are to interpret Wagner: the "meaning" of *Tristan* becomes visible when we establish the connection between it and the two other music dramas (in short, when we apply to it the structural interpretation of myths elaborated by Lévi-Strauss, himself a great Wagnerian).[9] What really matters is not the pseudo-problem of which of the three solutions reflects Wagner's "true" position (did he really believe in the redemptive power of the orgasmic *Liebestod*? did he resign himself to the necessity of returning to the everyday world of symbolic obligations?), but the formal matrix that generates these three versions of redemption. What effectively defines Wagner's position is this underlying problematic, the unstable relationship between the "ethical" universe of social-symbolic obligations ("contracts"), the overwhelming sexual passion that threatens to dissolve social links (the "aesthetic"), and the spiritualized self-denial of the will (the "religious"). Each of the three operas is an attempt to compress this triangle into the opposition between two elements: between the spiritualized sexual passion and the sociosymbolic universe in *Tristan,* between sexual passion and the spiritual sublimation of socialized art in *Meistersinger,* between sexualized life and pure ascetic spiritualism in *Parsifal.* Each of these three solutions relies on a specific musical mode which predominates in it: the chromaticism of *Tristan,* the choral aspect of *Meistersinger,* the contrast between chromaticism and static diatonics of *Parsifal.*

In *Parsifal,* "love's deepest need" to renounce its own power thus finds its ultimate formulation: sexual passion itself contains a secret longing for its radical self-denial, which only brings peace and redemption. This self-impediment inherent to the dynamics of love transpires in the deadlock of hysteria, this modern phenomenon par excellence, and it was, again, already Nietzsche who claimed that the problems Wagner presents on the stage are "all of them problems of hysterics—the convulsive nature of his affects, his overexcited sensibility, his taste that required ever stronger spices, his instability which he dressed up as principles."[10] The first move in interpreting Wagner's hysteria should be therefore to "translate Wagner into reality, into the modern—let us be even crueler—into the bourgeois":[11] "All of Wagner's heroines, without exception, as soon as they are stripped of their heroic skin, become almost indistinguishable from Madame Bovary!"[12] This experience is known to every perceptive spectator of Wagner: is the dance of the Flower Maidens in act 2 of *Parsifal* not a cabaret performance from a high-class nineteenth-century brothel? Is act 2 of *The Twilight of the Gods* not a bourgeois farce on the deceived housewife and the humiliated, impotent husband? If Flaubert was able to dress up his poor lower-middle class heroine as Salammbo and transpose her into the mythical space of Carthage, one should be also able to discern in Fricka the jealous high-society lady, in Brünhilde a rebellious adolescent daughter of a wealthy merchant, in Hagen a proto-Fascist populist.... What we are dealing with here is not merely the reduction of Wagner's mythical universe to a distorted expression of bourgeois everyday life: if it is to function normally, this everyday life itself needs its mythic support, like the Italian men who (according to a popular racist and sexist myth) want, during the sexual act, the woman to whisper into their ears obscenities about what she was doing with another man or men—only by the help of this mythic support can they perform as the proverbial good lovers in reality; *mutatis mutandis,* the same goes for German bourgeois—only if they hear whispers that they are actually Wotans and Siegfrieds can they lead their power struggles and cheat on their wives.... Wasn't it already Marx who pointed out that the Frenchmen were able to carry out the revolution only by way of perceiving themselves as old Romans establishing their republic?

Flaubert, however, made a crucial step further. That is to say, why was *Madame Bovary* dragged to court? Not, as it is usually claimed, because it portrays the irresistible charm of adultery and thus undermines the fundamentals of bourgeois sexual morality. *Madame Bovary* rather *inverts* the standard formula of the popular novel in which the adulterous lovers are at the end punished for their transgressive enjoyment: in this kind of novel, of course, the final punishment (mortal illness, exclusion from society) only enhances the fatal attraction of the adulterous affair, at the same time allowing the reader to indulge in this attraction without penalty. What is so profoundly disturbing and depressing about

Madame Bovary is that it takes away from us even this last refuge—it depicts adultery in all its misery, as a false escape, an inherent moment of the dull and gray bourgeois universe. This is the reason why *Madame Bovary* had to be brought to trial: it deprives the bourgeois individual of the last hope that an escape is possible from the constraints of meaningless everyday life. A passionate extramarital liaison not only does not pose a threat to the conjugal love, it rather functions as a kind of inherent transgression that provides the direct phantasmatic support to the conjugal link and thus participates in what it purports to subvert. It is this very belief that, outside the constraints of marriage, in the adulterous transgression, we can really obtain "that," the full satisfaction, which is questioned by the hysterical attitude: hysteria involves the apprehension that the "real thing" behind the mask of social etiquette is itself void, a mere mirage.

If there is a feature that serves as the clear index of modernism—from Strindberg to Kafka, from Munch to Schoenberg's *Erwartung*—it is the emergence of the figure of the hysterical woman, which stands for the radical disharmony in the relationship between the two sexes. Wagner doesn't yet venture this step into hysteria: the problem with him is not his hysteria, but rather that he is not hysterical *enough*—although his dramas provide all possible variations of how "love can go wrong," all this takes place against the phantasmatic background of the redemptive power of full sexual relationship—the very catastrophic outcome of the stage action seems to assert *per negationem* the belief in the redemptive power of sexual love. And my aim is to use the Wagnerian phantasm of sexual relationship as the framework to interpret both aspects of his artistic revolution, musical as well as political.

Concerning the political, the debate usually centers on the change in the ending of *The Twilight of the Gods*: from Feuerbach to Schopenhauer, from the revolutionary assertion of new humanity delivered from the oppressive rule of gods and finally free to enjoy love, to the reactionary resignation and disavowal of the very will to life—in a paradigmatic case of ideological mystification, Wagner inflates the defeat of the revolution and his betrayal of the revolutionary ideals into the end of the world itself. . . . However, on a closer look, it soon becomes clear that the true state of things rather resembles the good, old Soviet joke on

Rabinovitch: Did he really win a car in the lottery? In principle, yes, only it wasn't a car but a bicycle; besides, he didn't win it, it was stolen from him. . . . So the standard explanation for the changed ending of *The Twilight of the Gods* is also in principle true, only that the ending we actually have is closer to the original one (people, common mortals, do survive and just stare as mute witnesses at the cosmic catastrophe of the gods); furthermore, the early revolutionary Wagner is definitely more proto-Fascist than the late one—his "revolution" looks rather like the restitution of the organic unity of the people who, led by the prince, have swept away the rule of money embodied in Jews. . . .

The true problem lies elsewhere. In his *Ring,* Wagner addresses the fundamental ethicopolitical question of German idealism: how is it possible to unite love and Law? In contrast to German idealists whose political vision involved the hope of a reconciliation between the assertion of authentic intersubjective bond of love and the demands of the objective social order of contracts and laws, Wagner is no longer prone to accept this solution. His apprehension articulates itself in the opposition between Wotan and Alberich, between contractual, symbolic authority and the spectral, invisible Master: Wotan is a figure of symbolic authority, he is the "god of contracts," his will is bound by the Word, by the symbolic pact (the giant Fasolt tells him, "What you are, / you are through contracts only"),[13] whereas Alberich is an all-powerful (because invisible) agent not bound by any law:

> Nibelungs all,
> bow down to Alberich!
> He is everywhere,
> watching you! . . .
> You must work for him,
> though you cannot see him!
> When you don't think he's there,
> You'd better expect him!
> You're subject to him for ever! [14]

Wagner's crucial insight is, of course, that this opposition is inherent to Wotan himself: the very gesture of establishing the rule of law contains the seeds of its ruin—why? Wagner is here guided by a perception that was given different theoretical articulations by Marx, Lacan, and Derrida: equivalent exchange is a deceptive mirage—what it conceals is the very excess on which it is grounded. The domain of contracts, of giving and receiving something in return, is sustained by a paradoxical gesture that provides in its very capacity of withholding—a kind of generative lack, a withdrawal that opens up space, a lack which acts as a surplus. This gesture can be conceptualized as the Derridean gift, the primordial *Yes!* of our openness to dissemination, or as the primordial loss, the Lacanian "symbolic castration." (In Wagner's mythical space, this violent gesture of grounding the domain of legal exchange is depicted as Wotan's tearing out of the World Ash-Tree, from which he then cuts his spear and inscribes on it runes containing the laws; this act is followed by a whole series of similar gestures: Alberich's snatching the gold, Siegmund's pulling out the sword. . . .) Wagner is thus well aware that the very balance of exchange is grounded on the disturbance of the primordial balance, on a traumatic loss, an "out-of-joint," which opens up the space of social exchange. However, at this crucial point, the critique of exchange becomes ambivalent: it either endeavors to assert the primordial *Yes!*, the irreducible excess of the openness toward the Otherness that cannot be restricted to the field of balanced exchange, of its "closed economy"; or it aims at restoring the primordial balance prior to this excessive gesture. Wagner's rejection of (the society of) exchange, which is the basis of his anti-Semitism, amounts to an attempt to regain the prelapsarian balance. Nowhere is this more obvious than in his sexual politics, which asserts the incestuous link against the exogamic exchange of women: Sieglinde and Siegmund, the "good" incestuous couple, against Sieglinde and Hunding, the "bad" couple based on exchange; Brünnhilde and Siegfried against two further couples based on exchange (Brünnhilde and Günther, Gutrune and Siegfried) . . .

In dealing with Wagner's anti-Semitism, we should always bear in mind that the opposition of German true spirit versus the Jewish principle is not the original one: there is a third term, modernity, the reign of exchange, of the dissolution of organic links, of modern industry and individuality—the theme of exchange and contracts is *the* central theme of the *Ring*. Wagner's attitude toward modernity is not simply negative but much more ambiguous: he wants to enjoy its fruits, while avoiding its disintegrative effects—in short, Wagner wants to have his cake and eat it. For that reason, he needs a Jew: so that, first, modernity—this abstract, impersonal process — is given a human face, is identified with concrete, palpable features; then, in a second move, by rejecting the Jew who gives body to all that is desintegrated in modernity, we can retain its fruits. In short, anti-Semitism does not stand for antimodernism as such, but for an attempt to combine modernity with social corporatism, which is characteristic of conservative revolutionaries. So, since the rule of Law, the society of "contracts," is founded on an act of illegitimate violence, Law not only has to betray love but also has to violate its own highest principles: "The purpose of their [the gods'] higher world order is moral consciousness: but they are tainted by the very injustice they hunt down; from the depths of Nibelheim [where Alberich lives] the consciousness of their guilt echoes back threateningly."[15]

Aware of this impasse, Wotan concocts the figure of the hero not bound by any symbolic bond and thereby free to deliver the fallen universe of contracts. This aspect of Wagner is to be located within the great ideologico-political crisis of the late nineteenth century that turns around the malfunctioning of "investiture," of assuming and performing the paternal mandate of symbolic authority. This crisis found its most aggravated expression in the fate of Daniel Paul Schreber whose memoirs were analyzed by Freud: Schreber fell into psychotic delirium at the very moment when he was to assume the position of a judge, that is, a function of public symbolic authority: he was not able to come to terms with this stain of obscenity as the integral part of the functioning of symbolic authority.[16] The crisis thus erupts when the obscene, enjoyful underside of paternal authority becomes visible — and is not Alberich the paradigmatic case of the obscene ludic father on account of whom Schreber failed in his investiture? The most disturbing scene of the entire *Ring*, the "mother of all Wagnerian scenes," Wagner at his best, is probably the dialogue between Alberich and Hagen at the beginning of the act 2 of *The Twilight of the Gods*: Wagner put a tremendous amount of work in it and considered it one of his greatest achievements. According to Wagner's own stage indications, throughout this scene, Hagen must act as if asleep: Alberich is not effectively there, as a part of everyday reality, he is rather an "undead" who appears as Hagen's *Alptraum*, nightmare or, literally, "elf dream" (another occasion that would fully justify the procedure of staging part of the action as the delirious delusion of one of the stage persons). We all know the classical Freudian dream in which the dead son appears to his father, addressing him with a horrifying reproach "Father, can't you see I'm burning?" What we have in this scene from *The Twilight of the Gods* is a *father* appearing to his son, addressing him with "My son, can't you see I'm burning?" burning with an obscene enjoyment underlying his overwhelming passion to take revenge. When confronted with such a figure, a humiliated, ludic, tragicomical dwarf of a father, what can the subject do but assume an attitude of shuddering coldness, which contrasts clearly with father's overexcited agitation—it is here, in the figure of Hagen, that we have to look for the genesis of the so-called totalitarian subject. That is to say, far from involving a "repressive" symbolic authority, the "totalitarian" subject, rather, emerges as a reaction to the paternal authority gone awry, run amok: a humiliated father, a father transformed into the obscene figure of ludic enjoyment, is the *symptom* of the "totalitarian" subject.

How, then, are we to resolve this deadlock of legal power that participates at what it officially prohibits, that is, at illegitimate violence? The deadlock of property that is in itself, in its very notion, a theft, of contract that is in itself a fraud? It is the reference to sexual relationship that serves as the ultimate support for Wagner's political project: "The mediator between power and freedom, the redeemer without which power remains violence and freedom caprice, is therefore—love."[17] And: "Love in its fullest reality is only possible between the sexes: only as man and woman can we human beings truly love. Every other love is merely derived from this, arisen from it, connected with it, or artificially modelled on it."[18]

In order to grasp how Wagner is able to use sexual relationship as the paradigm for authentic political order, one has only to bear in mind the way, according to him, man and woman complement each other: Woman is the all-embracing unity, the ground that bears man, yet precisely as such she has, in her positive, empirical existence, to be subordinated to the "formative power" of man. For that reason, the elevation of and subordination to the essential Woman goes hand in hand with the exploitation of and the domination over actual flesh-and-blood women. Suffice it to recall here Schelling's notion of the highest freedom as the state in which activity and passivity, being-active and being-acted-upon, harmoniously overlap. Schelling gives here a specific twist to the distinction between *Vernunft* and *Verstand,* reason and understanding, which plays a crucial role in German idealism: "*Vernunft* is nothing else than *Verstand* in its subordination to the highest, the soul."[19] *Verstand* is the intellect as active, as the power of active seizing and deciding by means of which one asserts himself as a fully autonomous subject; however, one reaches one's acme when one turns one's very subjectivity into the predicate of an ever higher power (in the mathematical sense of the term), that is, when one, as it were, yields to the Other, "depersonalizes" one's most intense activity and performs it as if some other, higher power is acting through him or her, using him or her as its medium—like an artist who, in the highest frenzy of creativity, experiences himself as a medium through which the impersonal spirit expresses itself. What is crucial is the explicit sexual connotation of this highest form of freedom: feminization (adoption of a passive attitude toward the transcendent absolute) serves as the inherent support of masculine assertion. It is therefore clearly wrong to interpret the Wagnerian elevation of the feminine as a protest against the male universe of contracts and brutal exercise of power, as the utopian vision of a new life beyond aggressive modern subjectivity: the reference to the eternal feminine toward which the male subject adopts a passive attitude is the ultimate metaphysical support of the worldly aggressive attitude—and, incidentally, the same goes for the contemporary New Age assertion of the (feminine) Goddess.

The political use of this notion is thus easy to grasp: in an authentic political order, the prince (*der Fürst*) to whom Wagner refers even in his revolutionary period as the one to head the revolution, is to behave toward his people like the man to his feminine ground: his very subordination to the transcendent notion of the people (the fact that he adopts a feminine attitude toward the people and merely serves it, brings forth its deepest interests) legitimizes him in acting as the "formative power" and exerting full authority over empirically existing, actual people. It is this organic, sexualized relationship between the prince and his people that the modern society of egotistic mechanical links and profit-oriented contracts threatens to disrupt. . . . The same notion of harmonious sexual relationship also serves as the ultimate phantasmatic support of the notion of "music drama." Wagner described music as a means to an end in drama, and drama as a "musical deed made visible": how are we to resolve this paradox of drama as a function of music and music

"No Sexual Relationship" 221

a function of drama? Wagner resorts again to the matrix of sexual relationship: music is Woman made fecund by the male word, so that the subordination of music to word equals the subordination of the background to the figure, of woman to man. On that account, music is doubly inscribed. It is the Schopenhauerian "Thing," the direct vibration of our true inner life, the ground which "embraces drama in itself," since the latter is merely its external, phenomenal manifestation. However, Wagner is as far as possible from any notion of absolute music—drama is the "formative motive" of music, so that music in its positive, determinate existence has to serve as a means to render present the dramatic stage action, it can actualize, self-realize, itself only as the musical envelope of the stage action.[20]

What danger is Wagner trying to avoid by means of this sexualization of the relationship between drama and music? In his *Opera and Drama*, he himself provides the key: "[E]ach art tends toward an indefinite extension of its power . . . [T]his tendency leads it finally to its limit . . . [I]t would not know how to pass this limit without running the risk of losing itself in the incomprehensible, the bizarre, and the absurd." On that account, "each art demands, as soon as it reaches the limits of its power, to give a hand to the neighboring art."[21] This "refusal to transgress" is what is ultimately at stake in the project of *Gesamtkunstwerk*: each art

> is ordered by a sort of law of the "passage to the limit": but if it tries to move beyond this limit, and this will be exactly the enterprise of modern art (Wagner sees things very clearly), it is threatened with absurdity and inanity.
>
> The dialectical confrontation of the individual arts in the "total work of art" is consequently a means of containing excess and safeguarding meaning.[22]

This Wagnerian "conservative revolution," which unites music and drama in the *Gesamtkunstwerk* in order to prevent the two elements to follow their inherent logic and thus step over the threshold of true modernism, is at work as far as Hollywood, where the most daring atonal music is fully acceptable insofar as it accompanies a scene of madness or violence, that is, insofar as it serves to illustrate some clearly defined psychological state or realist action. This mention of Hollywood is by no means accidental, since Wagner's music is intimately related to it.

222 Žižek

What I have in mind here are not so much John Williams's scores for the big-budget science fiction and fantasy films of the seventies and eighties, which provide merely a series of pseudo-Wagnerian effects, but rather the so-called Hollywood classicism, which exerted its hegemony from mid-thirties till mid-fifties (in the films of Max Steiner, Franz Waxman, Miklos Rosza, etc.). This "Hollywood classicism" is characterized by the following main features:

–the invisibility of the apparatus that produces music, that is, the displacement of the music into an imaginary "invisible pit" correlative to the Wagnerian "hidden orchestra": the music that accompanies the screen action emanates from a kind of atemporal nonlocalized present;

–emotions translated by music (as in Wagner, not only direct emotional reactions of the persons on the screen but also emotional undercurrents these persons are not aware of—music can announce the birth of fatal love in what the future lovers experience as an insignificant, passing encounter . . .);

–"narrative cueing": the unending melody with its leitmotifs accentuates narration and provides for its continuity and unity.[23]

My hypothesis is that Hollywood classicism was an attempt to resolve a deadlock that was similar to that of the pre-Wagnerian opera. Exemplary is here the credits sequence of Fritz Lang's *Testament des Dr. Mabuse*, in which the noisy, spectacular music gradually changes into the rhythmic buzz of vibrating machines—a passage reminiscent of the music accompanying Wotan's and Loge's descent into Niebelheim in *Rheingold*, with its intermingling of the rhythmic beat of the instruments and the sound of hammering. The late twenties and early thirties thus provide a series of attempts to "inscribe music into the movement of life—of the collective, physical life—and, simultaneously, to extract from reality its own latent symphony,"[24] predominantly in the form of the so-called symphony of the city, of the celebration of industrious city life, with its incessant buzzing of the machines and the noise of the human crowd, which are elevated into the direct presentation of the fundamental rhythm of the metaphysical life itself. (This "rhythm of life itself" returns much later, in the guise of the obscene-uncanny pulsation of the life substance, in some of the films of David Lynch [*Blue Velvet, Dune, Elephant Man*].)

There is, however, one element that resists inclusion into this "symphony of life": *speech,* not a song or a poetic declamation but precisely speech in its capacity as "natural" conversation. In order to accommodate this element, the rhythmic continuum of noise and music gradually withdraws into the background, so that cinema is more and more centered on speech accompanied by an unending melody that provides its emotional and/or mythical context. What takes place is the shift of accent from a dynamic, assertive, clearly articulated rhythm to a lyrical chromatism of unending melody that serves as the elusive complex background to the naturalized speech and action. The price for the naturalization of the action on the screen is thus the displacement of the mythical dimension onto the antinaturalist lyricism of the musical score: the musical score is clearly subordinated to the "naturalist" screen action, illustrating and accompanying it, yet precisely as such, it "denaturalizes" it, serves as the means of its stylization, confers on it its mythical dimension. Music is thus simultaneously *more* present (ideally the spectator is submerged in it all the time, relying on it for the proper emotional attitude toward the screen action) and *less* present (the spectator's attention is not focused on the musical score, music just provides the invisible emotional, mythical, etc., frame for what goes on on the screen). Is all this not strictly homologous to the way the Wagnerian orchestral melody "weaves the immense background to the events from reminiscences and fleeting allusions"? So

> the orchestral store of mythic motives—those of the ring, Valhalla, Erda, the gods' downfall, contracts and the curse—connects the events now taking place to their primeval premisses and origins. . . . If there is any danger of the divine myth fading in significance beside the heroic drama, because it does not take physical shape on the stage, the music restores it—and the overall context of the cycle— to its rightful dramatic place.[25]

As is well known, Flaubert's main stylistic device was the so-called *style indirect libre* in which propositions immediately "objectivize" the feelings and attitudes of the persons—and does Wagner's use of leitmotivs not amount to a kind of musical *style indirect libre?* The problem, of course, was that Wagner's attempt to synchronize music and poetry was doomed to fail: what we get instead of their organic harmony is a paradoxical double surplus. "Too much theater" (for the partisans of absolute music who bemoan the fact that Wagner effectively reduces music to an illustration or a psychological commentary of the stage action) seems to invert continually into "too much music" (which, as the all-present background, overflows everything, so that we, the spectators, are submerged in it). Both domains are furthermore split from within: music oscillates between timeless mythical monumentalism and modern "hystericity"; drama oscillates between traditional monumental heroism and relapses into bourgeois vulgarity. Either the heroic stage action lags behind and is belied by the chromatic modernity of the musical texture, or the stage action strikes us as modern-bourgeois, sometimes even bordering on naturalism, in contrast to the timeless-mythical monumentalism of the music. However, although one is therefore tempted to agree with Dahlhaus that the notion of music drama is a "metaphor for unresolved problems" rather than their solution, one should be quick to add that the above-mentioned inconsistencies and gaps in the realization of the concept of music drama in no way impinge on the artistic impact of Wagner's work but are precisely the most reliable index of its authenticity—nowhere is Wagner more authentic than when the chromatic musical texture renders manifest the "hysterical" foundation and background of the heroic stage action, or when the modern bourgeois features of the stage action reveal the concrete sociohistorical foundation of the music's mythical monumentalism: hysterical chromatism and mythical timelessness are unitary insofar as they present the two facets of the dissolution of everyday realism. As Adorno would have put it, the artistic truth of Wagner resides in the very contradictions brought about by the realization of his project.

This noncontemporaneity of music and words (the dramatic plot) designates the way the impossibility of sexual relationship is inscribed into the very notion of the music drama. Nietzsche was the first to discern this crack in the edifice of the music drama when he emphasized how, in Wagner, music loses its autonomous structure and is turned into a means to render and accentuate melodramatic stage action: "Wagner was *not* a musician by instinct. He showed this by abandoning all lawfulness and ... all style in music in order to turn it into what he required, theatrical rhetoric, a means of expression, of underscoring gestures, of suggestion, of the psychologically picturesque."[26] The unmelodic chromaticism of the Wagnerian music, its lack of a firmly erected inner structure, intoxicates, hypnotizes, seduces, excites our nerves, overwhelms us; its unique mixture of sentimentality and empty pomposity, of artificiality and brutality, reduces the public to the passive attitude of the feminine hysteric. The inherent obverse of this overexcited universe of hysteria is the longing for "redemption," for the pacification that, within this hysterical perspective, can only be imagined in the guise of a saintly, life-denying, asexual, aseptic-anemic figure—Christ, Parsifal. The hysterical search for shocking effects and the longing for eternal peace are thus strictly codependent: in modern decadence, the authentic *vita activa* dissolves into the empty shell of superficial excitations and the denial of the will, the stepping out of the cycle of life. It is the music of *Tristan* that gives the purest expression to the inherent link between hysterical chromaticism and the longing for death: chromaticism allows for no pacification, no dissolution of the tension, in social reality—only death, only the very annihilation of the life process, brings peace and redemption. In *Parsifal,* this tension is externalized into, on the one hand, Klingsor with his magic castle, a new edition of *Venusberg,* a decadent *paradis artificiel,* full of oriental perfumes, and, on the other hand, Parsifal himself, the apathetic saint who shares with his hysterical counterpart oversensitivity and an inability to endure the passions and struggles of real life. The immobility of space exempted from the flow of time, the refuge in the self-enclosed Grail community, which stands for Wagner's negation of modernity and its discontents, is a modernist myth par excellence and as such is no less modernist than overexcited chromaticism. As has been pointed out already by Adorno, what is so modern about *Parsifal* is not only the chromaticism of Kundry and Amfortas's suffering, but also the static diatonics of the Grail community that endeavors to negate it.

The very form of *Parsifal* (musical as well as dramatic) thus belies its ideological project of androgynous reconciliation: its two spheres, Klingsor's castle and the temple of the Grail—or, musically: chromaticism and diatonics—remain side by side in their irreconcilable opposition. The universe of *Parsifal* is "incestuous" to extremes precisely insofar as it involves the refusal of any exchange between its two spheres: Kundry, the element circulating between the two, has to drop dead at the end. Klingsor's castle stands for the asocial excess of incestuous enjoyment; the temple of the Grail, its sterile counterpoint, is no less asocial in its incestuous rejection of any mingling with the Otherness. The two domains are thus opposed as surplus and lack: luxuriant, putrefying abundance versus ascetic purity. No wonder Wagner entertained the notion that the Montsegur castle, the mysterious seat of Cathars, was the possible location of the temple of the Grail: according to Cathars, sexuality as such should be abandoned since all sexual intercourse is incestuous. The disappearance of "normal" secular social life in *Parsifal* is therefore unavoidable: society is based on (linguistic, sexual, economic) exchange. In *Parsifal*, surplus and lack remain side by side, they are not united on the base of the paradoxical gesture that provides in its very withholding. This disappearance of the domain of (social) exchange bears witness to the dimension of psychosis: *Parsifal* stages a psychotic resolution of the deadlock of hysteria. For that reason, far from signaling castration, Parsifal's renunciation of the sexual urge stands for its most forceful denial: Parsifal rejects the loss involved in the act of man's opening up to the other-woman.

One is tempted to evoke here a painfully comic scene from Terry Gilliam's *Brazil:* in a high-class restaurant, the waiter recommends to his customers the best offers from the daily menu ("Today, our tournedo is really special!" etc.), yet what the customers get on making their choice is a dazzling color photo of the meal on a stand above the plate, and on the plate itself, a loathsome excremental paste-like lump. One encounters in *Parsifal* the same dissolution of "reality" into the substanceless, shadowy image (the phantasmagoria of Klingsor's castle) and the excremental remainder of the real. In Lacan's formula of symbolic castration (*–phi*), enjoyment (written as *phi*) is permitted, provided it has been furnished with a minus sign, that is, "castrated," domesticated-phallicized, caught in the frame of the paternal metaphor. Jacques-Alain Miller developed the possibility for the two elements of this formula, – and *phi*, that is, the gesture of symbolic negation and the substance of enjoyment, to fall apart and go their separate ways, so that we obtain, on the one side, the pure –, the symbolic deprived of the last vestiges of enjoyment, and, on the other side, *phi*, an enjoyment that freely ranges outside the domain of the symbolic. The price we have to pay, of course, is that this enjoyment loses its relaxed, satisfying, "healthy" character—there is always something putrid and damp that sticks to it. Suffice to recall Lenin's famous description of the "spiritual state" of Russia in the years following the breakdown of the 1905 revolution: an upsurge of mystical pure spirituality, of violent denial of anything bodily and carnal, accompanied by an obsession with "damp," "unnatural" forms of sexuality (pornography, sexual perversions . . .). One can see how Lenin is here unexpectedly close to Nietzsche's critique of the Wagnerian decadence.

What Nietzsche detects in Wagner is the *fin de siècle* couple of *le maître et l'hystérique:* Wagner is the Charcot of music, the "master of hypnotic tricks," who dominates his feminized public. Instead of the authentic Master who exuberates the naive, unmediated will to life, we obtain an impostor desperately striving to seduce the public with his bag of cheap tricks. Isn't therefore the place at which the position of Wagner himself is inscribed into his work that of the maimed obscene ludic father, author of phantasmagorias, Klingsor in *Parsifal* or Alberich in *Rheingold?* Therein resides the tension Wagner was unable to master: he is inscribed into his work in the very guise of what his work is striving to reject. However, Nietzsche's engagement with Wagner is more ambiguous than it may appear: it was already Thomas Mann who discerned in Nietzsche's most sarcastic denigration of Wagner a "panegyric with inverted signs." Nietzsche's de-Germanization of Wagner, his rejection of the bombastic "state composer" aspect of Wagner, his reading of Wagner as one of the French decadents, his perspicacious perception that the true strength of Wagner resides in his "miniaturism," in his rummaging about hysterical details and excitations—all this prefigures the main feature of the French appropriation of German culture, which is clearly discernible even in Derrida's reading of Heidegger (his implicit rejection of the "great" themes of the destiny of being, of the modern epoch of technique, etc., and the "miniaturist" concentration on the "micropractice" of reading).

Nietzsche's last written text, finished at Christmas 1888, a few days before his final mental collapse, is *Nietzsche contra Wagner,* a collection of passages from his older writings destined to prove that Nietzsche's sudden violent rejection of Wagner is not inspired by sudden malice, but presents a logical outcome of his entire work. And it is as if Nietzsche stumbled here, as if he wasn't able to delimit himself clearly from the neurosis called Wagner—what we encounter here is the old topic of *cogito and madness.* Modern philosophy in its entirety can be read as a desperate endeavor to draw a clear line that separates the transcendental philosopher from the madman (Descartes: how do I know I'm not hallucinating reality? Kant: how to delimit metaphysical speculation from Swedenborgian hallucinatory rambling? etc.). Along the same lines, Nietzsche's problem is, how do I know I'm not just another Wagnerian, another victim of hysterical hallucinations? It is as if Wagner was Nietzsche's symptom: the element Nietzsche desperately needed in order for his thought to retain its minimal coherence by way of projecting into it all that he found so despicable in himself—the attempt to cut off all links with Wagner thus necessarily ended in his final breakdown.

Why, then, did Nietzsche's delimitation fail? It would be easy, all too easy, to focus on the clearly sexualized character of Nietzsche's scorn for Wagner: Nietzsche perceives in Wagner the lack of an erect, assertive, firm male attitude—instead of the clearly structured rhythmic and melodic edifice, his music indulges in the "feminized" attitude of passively submerging into the shapeless ocean of feeling. . . . This femininity scorned by Nietzsche is the "eternal Feminine," the phantasmatic support of the actual subordination of women; paradoxically, Nietzsche's scorn for Wagner's "feminization" of music is thus much closer to feminism than the Wagnerian elevation of woman as man's redeemer. So the failure of Nietzsche's delimitation from Wagner is not the failure of the male subject's attempt to delimitate himself from the feminine. The problem with Nietzsche's rejection of Wagner's hysteria resides elsewhere. Contrary to the deceptive appearance according to which Nietzsche and Freud share here a common ground (they both seem to conceive hysteria as resulting from the suppression of the healthy life substance by an anemic moralism), it is *Freud contra Nietzsche* that is appropriate here: for Freud, hysteria is not based on the decadent denial of life power; the hysterical subject is rather a kind of *symptom* of the Master—what he renders palpable is the primordial deadlock that pertains to the dimension of subjectivity as such and which is concealed by the posture of the Master. Freud's name for this deadlock, for this authentic kernel of the hysterical theater that eludes Nietzsche's grasp and undermines from within *vita activa*, is *death drive*.

For Freud, the death drive is not merely a decadent reactive formation—a secondary self-denial of the originally assertive will to power, the weakness of the will, its escape from life, disguised as heroism—

but the innermost radical possibility of a human being. When one says "death drive and Wagner," the first association is, of course, Schopenhauer, Wagner's principal reference for the redemptive quality of the longing for death. Our thesis, however, is that the way the longing for death effectively functions within Wagner's universe is much closer to the Freudian notion of "death drive." The death drive is not to be confused with the "Nirvana principle," the striving to escape the life cycle of generation and corruption and to achieve the ultimate equilibrium, the release from tensions: what the death drive strives to annihilate is not this biological cycle of generation and corruption, but rather the symbolic order, the order of the symbolic pact that regulates social exchange and sustains debts, honors, obligations.[27] The death drive is thus to be conceived against the background of the opposition between "day" and "night" as it is formulated in *Tristan:* the opposition between the "daily" social life of symbolic obligations, honors, contracts, debts, and its "nightly" obverse, an immortal, indestructible passion that threatens to dissolve this network of symbolic obligations. One should bear in mind how sensitive Wagner was to the borderline that separates the realm of the symbolic from what is excluded from it: the deadly passion defines itself against the everyday public universe of symbolic obligations. Therein resides the effect of the love potion in *Tristan:* it is in its capacity of the "drink of death" that it acts as the "drink of love"—the two lovers mistake it for the drink of death and, thinking that they are now on the brink of death, delivered from ordinary social obligations, feel free to acknowledge their passion. This immortal passion does not stand for biological life beyond the sociosymbolic universe: in it, carnal passion and pure spirituality paradoxically coincide. That is, we are dealing with a kind of "denaturalization" of the natural instinct that inflates it into an immortal passion raised to the level of the absolute, so that no actual, real object can ever fully satisfy it.

More precisely, there is a dimension of life that the death drive wills to annihilate, but this dimension is not the simple biological life; it has rather to be located in the uncanny domain that Lacan called "between the two deaths." In order to elucidate this notion, let us recall the other big enigma of the *Ring:* since the gold—the ring—is finally returned to Rhine, why do the gods nonetheless perish? We are obviously dealing with *two* deaths: a biologically necessary demise and a "second death," the fact that the subject died in peace, with his accounts settled, with no symbolic debt haunting his memory. Wagner himself changed the text concerning this crucial point: in the first version of Erda's warning in the final scene of *Rheingold*, the gods will perish if the gold is not returned to the Rhine, whereas in the final version, they will perish anyway, the point is merely that prior to their demise, the gold should be returned to the Rhine, so that they will die properly and avoid the "irretrievable dark perdition." . . . What we encounter in this uncanny space between the two deaths is the palpitation of a life substance that cannot ever perish, like Amfortas's wound in *Parsifal*. Suffice it to recall Leni Riefenstahl who, in her unending search for the ultimate life substance, focused her attention first on the Nazis, then on an African tribe whose male members allegedly display true masculine vitality, and finally on deep-sea animals—as if it was only here, in this fascinating crawling of primitive life forms, that she finally encountered her true object. This underwater life seems indestructible like Leni herself: what we fear when we are following reports on how, well into her nineties, she is engaged in diving in order to make a documentary on deep-sea life, is that she will never die—our unconscious fantasy is definitely that she is immortal. . . . It is crucial to conceive the notion of death drive against the background of this "second death," as the will to abolish the indestructible palpitation of life beyond death (of the Dutchman, of Kundry and Amfortas), not as the will to negate the immediate biological life cycle. After Parsifal succeeds in annihilating the "pathological" sexual urge in himself, this precisely opens up his eyes for the innocent charm of the immediate natural life cycle (the magic of Good Friday). So, back to Wotan, who wants to shed his guilt in order to die properly, in peace, and thus to avoid the fate of an undead monster who, unable to find peace even in death, haunts common mortals—this is what Brünnhilde has in mind when, at the very end of *The Twilight of the Gods,* after returning the ring to the Rhinemaidens, she says: "Rest, rest now, you god!" [Ruhe, ruhe, du Gott!]

This notion of the "second death" enables us to locate properly Wagner's claim that Wotan raises to the tragic height of willing his own downfall: "This is everything we have to learn from the history of mankind: to will the inevitable and to carry it out oneself."[28] Wagner's precise formulation is to be taken literally, in all its paradoxicality—if something is already in itself inevitable, why should we then actively will it and work toward its occurrence, one might ask? This paradox, central to the symbolic order, is the obverse of the paradox of prohibiting something impossible (incest, for example), which can be discerned in Wittgenstein's famous "What one cannot speak about, thereof one should be silent"—if it is in any case impossible to say anything about it, why add the superfluous prohibition? The fear that one would nevertheless say something about it is strictly homologous to the fear that what is necessary will not occur without our active assistance. The ultimate proof that we are not dealing here with futile logical games is the existential predicament of predestination: the ideological reference that sustained the extraordinary explosion of activity in early capitalism was the Protestant notion of predestination. That is to say, contrary to the common notion according to which, if everything is decided in advance, why bother at all, it was the very awareness that their fate is already sealed up that propelled the subjects into frantic activity. The same goes for Stalinism: the most intense mobilization of the society's productive effort was sustained by the awareness that the people are merely realizing inexorable historical necessity....

At a different level, Brecht gave a poignant expression to this predicament in his "learning plays," exemplarily in *Jasager* in which the young boy is asked to accord freely with what will in any case be his fate (to be thrown into the valley). As his teacher explains to him, it is customary to ask the victim if he agrees with his fate, but it is also customary for the victim to say yes.... All these examples are far from exceptional: every belonging to a society involves a paradoxical point at which the subject is ordered to embrace freely, as the result of his choice, what is anyway imposed on him (we all *must* love our country, our parents), that is, at a certain point, every one of us is ordered to choose freely what is imposed on her or him.[29] Our point, however, is that all these paradoxes can only occur within the space of symbolization: the gap that exists in the demand to embrace freely the inevitable can only be the gap that forever separates an event in the immediacy of its raw reality from its inscription into the symbolic network—to embrace freely an imposed state of things simply means to integrate this state of things into one's symbolic universe. In this precise sense, the gesture of willing freely one's own death signals the readiness to come to terms with one's death also on the symbolic level, to abandon the mirage of symbolic immortality.

This paradox of "willing (choosing freely) what is necessary," of pretending (maintaining the appearance) that there is a free choice although effectively there isn't one, is closely connected to the splitting of the law into the ego-ideal (the public written law) and superego (the obscene unwritten secret law). Since, at the level of ego-ideal, the subject wants the semblance of a free choice, the superego injunction has to be delivered "between the lines." The superego articulates the paradoxical injunction of what the subject, its addressee, has to choose freely; as such, this injunction has to remain invisible to the public eye if the Power is to remain operative. In short, what the subject effectively wants is a command in the guise of freedom, of a free choice: he wants to obey, but simultaneously to maintain the semblance of freedom and thus to save his face. If the command is delivered directly, bypassing the semblance of freedom, the ensuing public humiliation hurts the subject and can induce him to rebel; if there is no order discernible in the Master's discourse, this lack of a command is experienced as suffocating and gives rise to the demand for a new Master capable of providing a clear injunction.

We can see, now, how the notion of freely choosing what is anyway inevitable is strictly codependent with the notion of an empty symbolic gesture, a gesture—an offer—that is meant to be rejected: the one is the obverse of the other, that is, what the empty gesture offers is the possibility to choose the impossible, that which inevitably will *not* happen (in Brecht's case, the expedition turning around with the sick boy instead of getting rid of him by way of throwing him into the valley). Another exemplary case of such an empty gesture is found in John Irving's *A Prayer for Owen Meany*: after the little boy Owen accidentally kills John's—his best friend's, the narrator's—mother, he is, of course, terribly upset, so, to show how sorry he is, he discreetly delivers to John a gift of his complete collection of color photos of baseball stars, his most precious possession; however, Dan, John's delicate stepfather, tells him that the proper thing to do is to return the gift. What we have here is symbolic exchange at its purest: a gesture made to be rejected; the point, the "magic" of symbolic exchange, is that, although at the end we are where we were at the beginning, the overall result of the operation is not zero but a distinct gain for both parties, a pact of solidarity. And is not something similar part of our everyday mores? When, after being engaged in a fierce competition for a job promotion with my closest friend, I win, the proper thing to do is to offer to retract, so that he will get the promotion, and the proper thing for him to do is to reject my offer—this way, perhaps, our friendship can be saved.[30] In short, far from standing for an empty romantic hyperbole, Wagner's notion of freely embracing the inevitable points toward a feature constitutive of the symbolic order.

However, Wotan's gesture of willing his own destruction in order to shed his guilt and Tristan and Isolde embracing their disappearance into the abyss of nothingness as the climactic fulfillment of their love, these two exemplary cases of the Wagnerian death drive, are to be supplemented by a third one, that of Brünnhilde, this "suffering, self-sacrificing woman" who "becomes at last the true, conscious redeemer."[31] She also wills her annihilation, but not as a desperate means to compensate for her guilt—she wills it as an act of love destined to redeem the beloved man, or, as Wagner himself put it in a letter to Liszt: "The love of a tender woman has made me happy; she dared to throw herself into a sea of suffering and agony so that she should be able to say to me 'I love you!' No one who does not know all her tenderness can judge how much she had to suffer. We were spared nothing—but as a consequence I am redeemed and she is blessedly happy because she is aware of it."[32] Once again, we should descend here from the mythic heights into the everyday bourgeois reality: woman is aware of the fact that, by means of her suffering which remains invisible to the public eye, of her renunciation for the beloved man and/or her renunciation to him (the two are always dialectically interconnected, since, in the phantasmatic logic of the Western ideology of love, it is for the sake of her man that the woman must renounce him), she rendered possible man's redemption, his public social triumph—like la Traviata who abandons her lover and thus enables his reintegration into the social order; like the young wife in Edith Wharton's *The Age of Innocence* who knows of her husband's secret adulterous passion, but feigns ignorance in order to save their marriage. Examples are here innumerable, and one is tempted to claim that—like Eurydice who, by sacrificing herself, that is, by intentionally provoking Orpheus into turning his gaze toward her and thus sending her back to Hades, delivers his creativity and sets him free to pursue his poetic mission—Elsa also intentionally asks the fateful question and thereby delivers Lohengrin, whose true desire, of course, is to remain the lone artist sublimating his suffering into his creativity. We can see here the link between the death drive and creative sublimation, which provides the coordinates for the gesture of feminine self-sacrifice, this constant object of Wagner's dreams: by way of giving up her partner, the woman effectively redeems him, that is, compels him to take the path of creative sublimation and work the raw stuff of the failed real sexual encounter into the myth of absolute love.[33] What one should do is, therefore, read Wagner's *Tristan* the way Goethe explained his *Werther:* by way of writing the book, the young Goethe symbolically acted out his infatuation and brought it to its logical conclusion (suicide); this way, he relieved himself of the unbearable tension and was able to return to his everyday existence. The work of art acts here as the phantasmatic supplement: its enactment of the fully consummated sexual relationship supports the compromise we make in our actual social life—in *Tristan,* Wagner erected a monument to Mathilde Wesendonck and to his immortal love for her, so that, in reality, he was able to get over his infatuation and return to normal bourgeois life.[34]

The conclusion to be drawn is not that the death drive is merely a mask in the guise of which the male Master mystifies his political betrayal or his male chauvinist attitude toward women: it simultaneously points toward the traumatic kernel of the real, which underlies the pompous ideological mask of guilt or of feminine sacrifice. The extent to which, in today's social theory, the motif of sacrifice is automatically translated into that of scapegoating is deeply suspicious: the Other into whom we project our own disavowed, repressed content is sacrificed, so that, through the destruction of the Other, we purify ourselves. However, the true enigma of the sacrifice does not reside in the magic efficiency of scapegoating, of sacrificing a substitute other, but rather in the readiness of the subject effectively to sacrifice *himself/herself* for the cause. This disturbing fact that somebody is ready to put at stake everything, including his life, is what makes the so-called fundamentalist fanaticism so shocking in the eyes of our late-capitalist sensitivity used to reason in the categories of utilitarian calculus: one desperately endeavors to "explain it away" by providing some kind of psychopathological or sociopathological account of it (collective madness, the strange workings of a mind that hasn't yet progressed to the Western notions of rational choice and individual freedom, etc.). It is as if the good, old Hegelian dialectics of master and slave is repeated here, with the West behaving like the slave who dares not embrace fully the radical negativity and put everything at stake. In this sense, every ideology relies on some kernel of the real (the readiness to make the ultimate sacrifice, the fear of death), which cannot be interpreted away as the outcome of ideological manipulation, of the "false consciousness" due to the social situation of the subject. *Mutatis mutandis*, it is homologous with sexual relationship: its fulfillment is not impossible because political and social circumstances forbid it; the impossibility is rather inherent, it comes first, and the "externalization" of the real of this inherent impediment into a secondary obstacle ("social repression") serves to maintain the phantasm that, without these obstacles, the object would have been accessible. What Freud called the "death drive" is the impediment inherent to the drive that forever prevents its fulfillment, and, perhaps, the primordial gesture of ideology is not only that of elevating a limitation grounded in concrete historical circumstances into an a priori of human existence, but also that of explaining away a structural impediment as the result of unfortunate concrete circumstances.

A critique of ideology has thus to proceed in two moves. First, of course, it has to follow Jameson's well-known injunction "Historicize!" and to discern in an apparently universal unchangeable limitation the ideological "reification" and absolutization of a certain contingent historical constellation—what presents itself as a "metaphysical" longing for death can have its roots in the foreboding of the ruling class that its days are running out; what presents itself as an eternal condition of love (the inherent necessity to renounce its fulfillment) can well be grounded in the contingent historical conditions of the bourgeois patriarchal symbolic economy within which love is allocated to the domain of "private" as opposed to the "public"; and so on. The second move then, in a kind of reflective turn, compels us to conceive this explanatory reference to concrete historical circumstances itself as a "false," ideological attempt to circumvent the traumatic kernel of the real (the death drive, the nonexistence of sexual relationship), to explain it away and thus render invisible its structural necessity. Apropos of Wagner, a critical analysis of the Wagnerian longing for redemption in death has thus to avoid two pitfalls: it isn't enough to refuse to take at its face value the ideological coating of the sacrificial gesture and to discern in the metaphysical will to self-destruction displayed by Wotan and Brünnhilde an overblown mystified expression of contingent historical circumstances; at a more radical level, one should at the same time demarcate the contours of the kernel of the real, of the "death drive," which sustains the will to destruction in its specific ideological coating.

The lesson of all this for the staging of Wagner is clear. The three basic modes of staging Wagner broadly correspond to the triad of realism, modernism, and postmodernism: traditional "realistic historicism" (old Teutonic heroes with helmets and swords); the ascetic modernism of the "New Bayreuth" of the fifties (the "reduction to bare essentials," to the ahistorical existential dilemmas: indeterminate time and place; lights and shadows instead of solid sets; singers in plain costumes who look more like Greek sculptures than Nordic gods); postmodernism, deliberately inconsistent bricolage (the violent intrusion of the real of history: Nazi uniforms, gods in tuxedos, hysterical hallucinations staged as such, Klingsor's castle as the kingdom of technological cyberpunk...). It is crucial to perceive the logic of the succession of these three modes: by means of its emptying of the stage, of its violent erasure of the realist-historicist lumber, modernism opens up the field for the intrusion of the historical real. The aim of these postmodern stagings is thus to "traverse the (Wagnerian) fantasy" by way of rendering visible the crack in the phantasmatic unity of the Wagnerian project in all its main dimensions, sexual and artistic as well as political: the asymmetry that undermines the phantasmatic frame of sexual relationship; the noncontemporaneity of drama and music; the hollowness of the political project. This is what is at stake in seemingly "arbitrary" encroachments upon Wagner's narrative, which serve as a kind of trademark of postmodernist stagings: at the end of *Lohengrin,* not only does Elsa not die but she is even reconciled with Ortrud; at the end of *Parsifal,* not only does Kundry not die but women are allowed into the temple of the Grail....

These stagings that intervene in the plot and change it are ironical, not cynical: the point of Ponelle's changed ending of *Tristan* is not simply to ridicule Wagner's assertion of *Liebestod* and to propose a more mundane solution (Isolde is actually a good housewife who, after a brief fling, returns to her husband, with Tristan reduced to a credulous sucker); the true magic resides in the fact that the passion embodied in music miraculously survives even the most cruel mockery of the staging—in the gap between the passion rendered by music and the ridicule of what goes on on the stage, the truth is on the side of music.

Exemplary is here the procedure of resubjectivization by means of which a part of the stage action is presented as the delirious delusion of one of the stage persons (Isolde's arrival and her ecstatic death at the end of *Tristan* as the hallucination of the dying Tristan: the appearance of the Dutchman as Senta's hallucination). This resubjectivization, the very opposite of the standard Jungian (mis)reading of Wagner, which reduces the "external" action to an allegory of the hero's inner process of libidinal maturation,[35] merely brings to its logical conclusion what is already present in Wagner himself: in his music dramas, persons onstage often appear as a kind of realized hallucination of the hero or, rather, of the heroine: the Dutchman seems to step out from his portrait as the result of Senta's fascinated stare; Elsa seems to conjure up Lohengrin by the mere intensity of her vision. Even the "real" place of action is often presented as a phantasmagoria that crumbles to dust the moment the hero breaks its spell (Venusberg, Klingsor's castle).[36] This procedure, which breaks up the continuum of stage reality by way of projecting the gap that separates phantasm from reality back onto reality itself, renders manifest the phantasmatic character of the Wagnerian redemptive denouement: no, Isolde doesn't expire in the orgasmic trance, her *Liebestod* is merely the dying Tristan's delusion, while she returns to her husband, cured of her infatuation. In other words, we are dealing here with an interpretive gesture that brings to the light of the day a crack in Wagner's original itself, with a gesture that relies on the presupposition that it is already Wagner's artistic practice that gives a lie to his ideological project. In his famous staging of *Tannhäuser,* Goetz Friedrich had the roles of Elisabeth and Venus, self-sacrificing redemptrice and the voluptuous temptress, sung for the first time by the same singer. Is, however, this interpretive intervention not fully justified? For, thirty years after *Tannhäuser,* Wagner succeeded in resolving the artistic deadlock of *Parsifal* only when he suddenly apprehended that "the fabulous, savage messenger of the Grail has to be one and the same creature as the seductress in the second act," as he himself put it in a letter to Mathilde Wesendonck from 1860. Such strong interventions are by definition risky, there is no guarantee they will succeed, they are always undertaken in the mode of *futur antérieur,* as a gesture that, perhaps, by way of changing our perception of the work, will itself create the conditions which will make it legitimate. Risky as they are, however, there is no alternative to such iconoclastic procedures.

This Wagnerian reference remains crucial even today, at a time when the process Freud tried to encapsulate in the title of his article "On the Universal Tendency to Debasement in the Sphere of Love" seems to be approaching its climax. Two recent films, Kieslowski's *Short Film on Love* and Sautet's *A Heart in Winter*, endeavor to counter this "tendency to debasement" by rendering a male gesture of rejection, of refusal to engage in sexual commerce; however, as we shall see, the scope of the two gestures is almost exactly opposed.

There is an unexpected formal homology between the two central instalments (5 and 6) of Kieslowski's *Decalogue*, *A Short Film on Killing* and *A Short Film on Love*: in both case, we are dealing with a failed metaphoric reversal-substitution. The second act, instead of accomplishing a successful "sublation" [*Aufhebung*] of the first act (by way of compensating for its damage and reestablishing the lost balance), actually makes things worse by ending up as a *repetition* of the first act. In *Killing*, a young unemployed man commits the brutal and meaningless murder of a taxi driver; the second part then renders in painful detail the trial and the execution of the murderer. This rendering of the machinery of law at work is so disturbing because it registers the *failure of the "metaphor of Law,"* that is, of the metaphoric substitution of the punishment for the crime: the punishment is not experienced as just retribution that undoes the harm brought about by the crime, but rather as its uncanny repetition—the act of punishment is somehow tainted by an additional obscenity that makes it a travesty, an obscene repetition of the original crime in the guise of law. *A Short Film on Love* is also a film about a failed metaphoric substitution, the substitution (of the beloved for the loving one) that, according to Lacan, defines love. From his bedroom in a large, dreary, concrete apartment block, Tomek, a young postal clerk, each evening and night peeps on Maria Magdalena [*sic*], a mature, sexually attractive, and promiscuous woman who lives in the same block, across from Tomek's backyard. His activity is not limited to passively observing her sexual prowess in dealing with her numerous lovers; step by step, he intervenes in her life, sending her false notices of money orders so that she will come to his window in the post office, calling plumbers to her apartment in the middle of her lovemaking, and so on. When, finally, he gathers courage, contacts her and discloses that he is the source of her recent nuisances, her curiosity is aroused. She entices him into a humiliating sexual game that ends in his attempted suicide. After his return from hospital, their respective roles are reversed: stirred by her guilt, she "stretches out her hand," constantly observes his window from her apartment, endeavors frantically to attract his attention in order to make him come to her again and to offer him her apologies, whereas he now ignores her. In short, the metaphor of love fails: when the beloved object turns into the loving one, she is no longer loved.

A closer analysis renders visible a fundamental ambiguity that pertains to this film, an ambiguity that becomes fully visible in the crucial difference between the two versions of the *Short Film on Love*, the original sixty-minute television version and the ninety-minute version for release in movie theaters. The longer version ends up in a kind of Catholic reconciliation and compassion (with Maria sitting by Tomek's bed, silently holding his hand, the implication of it being that a kind of spiritual contact has taken place between the two, beyond the self-destructive dialectic of sexuality), whereas in the television version, their encounter remains failed, nonsynchronized. In this precise sense, *A Short Film on Love* is the stage of a "class struggle" in art, the battleground of the two lines, the irreconciled "materialist" and the spiritualist "idealist," in dealing with the fundamental deadlock of love. When, upon their becoming acquainted, Maria asks Tomek what he effectively wants from her, a mere kiss, a little tenderness, or a full sexual act, his resolute answer is "nothing." This "nothing," of course, is the unmistakable index of true love: Tomek is not to be satisfied with any positive content or act (going to bed with him, for example) by means of which Maria could reciprocate his love. What he wants her to offer in return is the very "nothingness" in her, what is "in her more than herself"—not something that she possesses but precisely what she does *not* have, the return of love itself. In response to his unconditional demand of love, Maria arouses him by offering her sexual services to him, so that, inexperienced as he is, he reaches orgasm before intercourse proper takes place, and then, triumphantly, tells him: "Now you see, this is all love is really about! Go and wash yourself in the bathroom!" This gesture of offering herself, her body, to him, effectively amounts to an act of utter rejection and/or humiliation: what she accomplished therewith is radical desublimation, that is, she renders palpable the gap that separates the void of the Thing from the physiological functioning of sexual intercourse. This humiliation, this experience of the gap between the "nothingness" of the true object of love and the desublimated bodily sexual mechanism, is more than he can stand: utterly ashamed, he runs out of her apartment and cuts his veins. What follows thereupon is a shift of perspective from his to her point of view, so that, in a sense, his suicide *does* succeed, that is, he totally obliterates himself as the narrative point of view. And, as we already hinted, at this point, the two versions differ: the longer one takes a Catholic turn and suggests the possibility of a compassionate solidarity beyond carnal passions, of a spiritual communion that can fill out the void of the inherent impossibility of a sexual relationship, whereas in the shorter version, the deadlock remains unresolved.[37]

On a closer look, one is compelled to state that the crucial metaphoric substitution in *A Short Film on Love* actually runs contrary to the standard substitution by means of which the loved one changes into the loving one, that is, solves the impasse of not knowing what the other (the loving one) sees in him by returning love: the true enigma of the film is Tomek's change from the loving one into the object of Maria's love. So how does he succeed in substituting his position of the loving one with the position of the beloved? How does he capture Maria's desire? The answer, of course, resides in the very purity and absolute intensity of his love: he acts as the pure $\$$, the subject whose desire is so burning that it cannot be translated into any concrete demand—this very intensity, because of which his desire can only express itself in the guise of a refusal of any demand ("I want nothing from you"), is what makes him irresistible. This second metaphoric substitution is not simply symmetrical to the first one: their difference hinges on the opposition of "to have" and "to be." In the first case, we are in the dimension of *having* (the loved one doesn't know what he *has* in himself that makes him worthy of the other's love, so, in order to escape this deadlock, he returns love), whereas in the second case, the loving *is* (becomes) the beloved object on account of the sheer intensity of his love.[38]

What one has to reject here is the notion that Tomek's love for Maria is authentic and pure, spiritual, elevated above vulgar sensuality, whereas Maria, disturbed by this purity, intends to humiliate him and later changes her attitude out of a feeling of guilt. It is, on the contrary, Tomek's love that is fundamentally false, a narcissistic attitude of idealization whose necessary obverse is a barely conceived lethal dimension. That is to say, *A Short Film on Love* should be read against the background of *slasher* films, in which a man observes and harasses a woman who traumatizes him, finally attacking her with a knife: it is a kind of introverted *slasher* in which the man, instead of striking at the woman, deals a blow to himself.[39] The reason his love for Maria is not genuine does not reside in its "impure" character: the murderous burst of self-inflicted violence is the inherent obverse of its very "purity." This inauthenticity of his love is corroborated by his inability to undergo the experience of desublimation, of the splitting between the woman *qua* impossible-idealized Thing and the flesh-and-blood woman who offers herself to him, that is, by the way this experience sets in motion the murderous *passage a l'acte*: the measure of true love is precisely the capacity to withstand such a splitting. Maria's love for him, in contrast, is fully authentic: from the moment Tomek tells her he wants nothing from her, true love—which, as Lacan points out, is always a love returned—is here, and her humiliation of Tomek is merely a desperate attempt to disavow this fact.

Our second example, Claude Sautet's *A Heart in Winter* (*Un coeur en hiver*), a film on the deadlocks of love from the same period, tells the story of a love triangle with two high-class violin makers and Camille, a young, beautiful, and charismatic violin player. When Camille starts to live with one of them, she thereby perturbs the well-established routine of their professional relationship. Gradually, with the help of his ambiguous, active-passive cooperation, she falls in love with the other partner, Stephan; however, when, in a passionate outburst, she declares her love and offers herself to him, Stephan calmly explains to her that it's all a misunderstanding—maybe he was flirting a little with her, but he definitely does not love her. Stephan's character is rather enigmatic: the point is not that Camille isn't his true love, but rather that he simply feels no need for love—there is no place for love in his psychological universe. This incapacity to love accounts for the kind of inner peace and completion irradiated by his personality: unperturbed by any emotional turmoils, profoundly *apathetic,* he is able to devote himself fully to his craft. In other words, far from being a person whose mask of normal social functioning conceals madness, Stephan is a person who, although to an outside view he may appear "abnormal," possesses an inherent norm, measure, completeness. We are dealing here with a variation on the Lacanian motif of "non-all": what, in a way, makes him more "complete" and harmonious than "normal" people, that is, what makes him a person who, in a way, lacks nothing, is the very aspect that appears from the outside as his deficiency or even psychic mutilation. In other words, the trap one has to avoid in analyzing Sautet's film is the search for any kind of "psychological" background or foundation that would account for Stephan's incapacity to love: there is no need here for any "psychoanalytical" reference to sexual frustrations, childhood traumas, and so on. When, in the course of the film, Stephan himself evokes the possibility of such an explanation, he obviously indulges in an irony homologous to that of a neo-Nazi skinhead who is always quick to provide a sociopsychological explanation of his violence against foreigners. Stephan is an *empty* subject: beneath the surface of his acts there is no plenitude of "pathological" content, no secret desires and anxieties. One is tempted to draw a comparison between Stephan and Wagner's Parsifal: when, alone with Camille in his car, Stephan utters his final "Je ne vois aime pas," is he not a contemporary Parsifal who, by not giving way to the woman's advances, redeems her (enables her to pursue her artistic career)?[40]

We are thus already deep in the murky Wagnerian waters of the implacable antagonism between man's ethical "vocation," which commits him to the full deployment of his creative potential, and his (sexual) relationship with a woman: what a woman effectively wants from a man is the hidden kernel of his being, she feels envy and hatred toward the mysterious ingredient beyond her reach that accounts for his creative genius, so she wants to snatch it from him and destroy it. Even prior to *Parsifal*, Wagner provided the first clear articulation of this discord in his earlier *Lohengrin*, the opera centered on the theme of the forbidden question, that is, on the paradox of self-destructive female curiosity. A nameless hero saves Elsa von Brabant and marries her, but enjoins her not to ask him who he is or what his name is—as soon as she does so, he will be obliged to leave her. Unable to resist temptation, Elsa asks him the fateful question; so Lohengrin tells her that he is a knight of the Grail, the son of Parsifal from the castle of Montsalvat, and then departs on a swan, while the unfortunate Elsa falls dead. Although both in *Lohengrin* and in *Parsifal* the hero is split between the Grail *qua* pregenital "partial object" and the love of a woman, the two operas differ with regard to a crucial feature: in *Lohengrin*, the hero continues to yearn for a happy sexual relationship (when, at the opera's end, he bids his farewell to Elsa, he is full of romantic mourning for the lost opportunity of at least one happy year of marital life with her), whereas in *Parsifal,* the hero unambiguously and with no remorse rejects the woman (Kundry) as his sexual partner.[41]

In what, then, on a closer look, consists the discord that corrupts the relationship between Elsa and Lohengrin? It may appear that *Lohengrin* is just another variation on the old theme of a prince who, in order to make sure that his future bride will love him for himself, not because of his symbolic title, first wants to arouse her love dressed up as a servant or a messenger. However, the enigma of *Lohengrin* resides elsewhere: why can he exert his *power* only insofar as his name remains *unknown,* that is, only insofar as he is not inscribed in the "big Other" of the intersubjective public space, so that he has to withdraw the moment his symbolic identity is publicly revealed? What we are dealing with is thus the opposition between Master-Signifier and *a,* the "incastratable" object that can exert its efficiency only *qua* concealed: the misunderstanding between Elsa and Lohengrin resides in the fact that Elsa perceives Lohengrin as the traditional figure of symbolic authority, whereas he functions as a spectral apparition that cannot sustain its disclosure in the public symbolic medium.

And, back to *A Heart in Winter,* is Stephan also not an object that cannot bear its symbolic revelation? Is his subjective position, like that of Parsifal, not also marked by a radical *indifference,* namely indifference toward the *desire of the Other?* Stephan is a subject who is simply not "gnawed" by the desire of the Other, by the enigma of "*Che vuoi?*" of what the Other wants from me—and since (Lacan *dixit*) desire as such is the desire of the Other, one is compelled to draw the inevitable conclusion that Stephan strictly speaking is not a desiring subject, that he simply does not dwell in the dimension of desire. Therein resides the uncanny "cold" of his character, its "flatness," the absence of any enigmatic depth. On that account, Stephan is incapable not only of love but even of common friendship, which always involves a minimum of empathy: he is able, without any hesitation, to deliver a lethal injection to his elder friend-teacher, a kind of paternal surrogate, thereby putting an end to the meaningless agony of his mortal illness. Is not this indifference toward the Other's desire strictly equivalent to what Lacan designates as "subjective destitution"?

We can see, now, in what, precisely, resides the difference between *A Short Film on Love* and *A Heart in Winter*. In both films, we encounter a man's "I want nothing," which puts an obstacle in the way of sexual intercourse, that is, both Tomek and Stephan turn down the woman's proposal, but this rejection has a totally different meaning in each case. In *Love*, we are dealing with "I want nothing" of the *desire* that aims at the *objet a* in the other: the true meaning of this "I want nothing" is "I want you absolutely, in the very kernel of your being, in the void that constitutes the elusive vortex of your subjectivity, and I am not ready to exchange it for any substitute in the guise of some positive (sexual) service." With regard to Kierkegaard, this means that Kieslowski remains within the religious: at a level more fundamental than the Catholic communion of souls in the longer version of the film, Tomek's attitude is religious, his "I want nothing" is a desperate attempt to counteract the "debasement in the sphere of love" by way of elevating the woman to the dignity of a Thing. Sautet's Stephan, in contrast, confronts us with something incomparably more uncanny: what we have here is a man who "wants nothing" because he simply lacks nothing: he is not "gnawed" by the enigma of the Other's desire, he is fundamentally indifferent toward *objet a*, the object-cause of desire, his subjectivity is not organized around a traumatic excess of the surplus enjoyment. Why not? There is only one answer possible: *because he himself occupies the place of this object*. In short, the opposition between Tomek and Stephan is the opposition between $\$$ and *a*, between the pure subject of desire and the "saint," somebody who has undergone "subjective destitution" and thereby turned into the pure being of a drive beyond desire.

Notes

All English translations have been done by the author, with the exception of those cited in the notes.

1 A detail to be noted is that, in both cases, this motif announces an act of a homologous nature: an element is torn out from its "natural" place where it was resting — the gold from the bottom of Rhine, the sword from the tree trunk.
2 See Claude Lévi-Strauss, "A Note on the Tetralogy," in *The View from Afar*, trans. Claire Jacobson (Chicago: U of Chicago P, 1985), 235–39.
3 See also, in the present volume, Mladen Dolar's "At First Sight." It should be a surprise only to those who cling to the standard textbook image of Hegel's "panlogi-

cism" that an exemplary case of a homologous Hegelian reversal is found in the work of Jeremy Bentham. In accordance with his utilitarian economy, Bentham always tends to replace the "thing itself" with its (less costly) appearance, provided that the effect is the same—what counts is only the effect. So, in the case of punishment, the only thing that effectively counts is the deterrent, inhibitory effect that the spectacle of punishment achieves in potential future criminals—wouldn't it then be far more economical to replace real punishment with its appearance, with a pure staging? Bentham nonetheless opts for real punishment; yet his argument in favor of it is far more refined than one would expect from him and possesses a properly Hegelian allure: what ultimately counts is only appearance, i.e., how things appear, the effect of their appearance, and it is for that very reason that "real" punishment is to be preferred to a faked staging—reality is in a sense *the best, the most effective, appearance of itself*.

4   The closest Hollywood got to the properly *ethical* notion of repetition was in the series of so-called "comedies of remarriage" from the late thirties and early forties: their point is that it is only the second marriage among the same partners that brings forth an authentic, mature intersubjective link (see Stanley Cavell's *In Pursuit of Happiness*, Cambridge: Harvard UP, 1981). Incidentally, the interest of Mike Nichols's *Heartburn* (with Meryl Streep and Jack Nicholson) is that it provides, as it were, the negative of the comedies of remarriage: it is literally a "comedy of re-divorce," i.e., the first divorce of the couple remains within the confines of a narcissistic love-game, it is only with the second divorce that the symbolic bond that united the partners is effectively dissolved.

5   A homologous self-sacrificing gesture of dirtying one's image in the eyes of the beloved in order to save him for morality is found in Michael Curtiz's *Angels with Dirty Faces* (1938) in which James Cagney plays a charismatic Brooklyn gangster admired by a group of slum boys. When he is finally caught and sentenced to the electric chair, he is, of course, not afraid to die and intends to turn his execution into a display of his heroic defiance of death. However, on the eve of the execution, a priest who is aware of the redeeming qualities beneath Cagney's tough act, visits him in his cell and begs him to pretend next morning that he is dying in fear—in this way, he will render a last service to society, i.e., instead of remaining an idol in the eyes of the kids, he will serve them as an example of how crime doesn't pay and will thus promote their reintegration into society. On his way to the electric chair, Cagney casts a quick glance toward the journalists who witness the execution, and, when he is sure of being observed, he starts to feign panic, to cry and shout that he doesn't want to die . . . . Next day, when the boys read in a newspaper the report of Cagney's cowardly death, their world falls apart, they are deeply shattered and depressed: they have lost their hero, their ideal ego, the point of identification—and are thereby saved for the morality. Henry Staten (in a private communication) pointed out that this scene stages perfectly Nietzsche's notion of the "decadent," "nihilistic" character of common morality, which is founded on the renunciation of assertive life energy. Here we have the Lacanian distinction between morals and ethics: Cagney's final act is moral, yet definitely unethical. Incidentally, notwithstanding the superficial analogy, Cagney's act is wholly

incommensurable with the profoundly *ethical* gesture of Barbara Stanwyck at the end of *Stella Dallas,* where she also puts on the image of a vulgar debauchee in order to enable her daughter to drop her and enter high-society married life without remorse.

6   This paradox can also be explained against the background of the dialectical short-circuit between possibility and actuality: the moment the conquest (of a woman by her seducer) becomes effectively possible, he has to withdraw, i.e., the possibility as such already counts as success. Therein resides a common feature of the psychic economy: often, deep satisfaction is provided by the mere awareness that we *could have* done something that we desired (slept with a passionately desired sexual partner, taken revenge on a longtime enemy, etc.)—as if the realization of this possibility would somehow spoil the purity of our success. . . . And is not the extreme example of this logic a possibility that counts as actuality, i.e., which, as a possibility, exerts actual effects, the Cold War paradox of the "mad" logic of nuclear armament: the possession and further development of nuclear arms were perceived as the supreme guarantee that they would never be used: since each side knows that the other also possesses the means to annihilate, both sides are aware that any use of nuclear arms will inevitably lead to mutual self-destruction. In short, the greater the threat of the catastrophe, the greater the certainty that this threat will not be actualized. . . . Far from bearing witness to a kind of Cold War "perversion" of our rationality, this "madness" simply renders palpable a feature constitutive of the symbolic order as such.

7   From the Nietzschean-Deleuzian perspective, this inherent impossibility, this hindrance that prevents us from consummating the process of seduction, of course, bears witness to the "nihilistic" perversion of our life force: force loses its purely assertive character and becomes infected by negativity, by the split between what it *can* do, conceived in itself, and what it actually accomplishes within the complex network of relations with other forces—it changes into a pure capacity that can never fully actualize itself. . . . For Lacan, on the contrary, this very splitting between possibility and actuality, i.e., the fact that possibility as such already counts as effective, which is why its actualization is experienced as anticlimactic—in short, this structure of "symbolic castration"—provides the basic, constitutive feature of the symbolic order.

8   One is tempted to claim that the triad of *Tristan, Meistersinger,* and *Parsifal* repeats at a different level (in a higher "potency") the triad of *The Flying Dutchman, Tannhäuser,* and *Lohengrin.*

9   One is tempted to suggest that the same procedure can also throw a new, more appropriate light on Bertolt Brecht, this great anti-Wagnerian: the key to Brecht's *Jasager,* which also advocates the subject's radical self-sacrifice, is to read it together with its two later versions (*Neinsager, Jasager II*) as the three possible variations allowed by the same underlying matrix.

10 Friedrich Nietzsche, "The Case of Wagner," in *The Birth of Tragedy; and, The Case of Wagner,* trans. Walter Kaufmann (New York: Vintage, 1967), 166.

11 Ibid., 175.

12 Ibid., 176.

13 Richard Wagner, *The Ring of the Nibelung,* trans. Andrew Porter (New York: Norton, 1977), 24.
14 Ibid., 40.
15 Carl Dahlhaus, *Richard Wagner's Music Dramas,* trans. Mary Whittall (Cambridge: Cambridge UP, 1979), 97.
16 We rely here on Eric Santner, *My Own Private Germany* (Princeton: Princeton UP, 1996).
17 Deryck Cooke, *I Saw the World End* (Oxford: Oxford UP, 1979), 17.
18 Ibid., 18.
19 F. W. J. Schelling, *Sämtliche Werke,* vol. 7, 472.
20 See Dahlhaus, *Richard Wagner's Musical Dramas,* 5–6.
21 Philippe Lacoue-Labarthe, *Musica Ficta,* trans. Felicia McCarren (Stanford: Stanford UP, 1994), 11.
22 Ibid., 12.
23 We rely here on Michel Chion, *La Musique au cinema* (Paris: Fayard, 1995), and Claudia Gorbman, *Unheard Melodies: Narrative Film Music* (Bloomington: BFI and Indiana UP, 1987).
24 Chion, *La Musique,* 105.
25 Dahlhaus, *Richard Wagner's Musical Dramas,* 135.
26 Nietzsche, "The Case of Wagner," 172–73.
27 See Jacques Lacan, *The Ethics of Psychoanalysis,* trans. Dennis Porter (New York: Routledge, 1992), 210–14.
28 William O. Cord, *An Introduction to Richard Wagner's "Der Ring des Nibelingen"* (Athens: Ohio UP, 1983), 125.
29 As to this notion of the forced choice that forms the base of our social allegiance, see also chapter 5 of Slavoj Žižek, *The Sublime Object of Ideology* (London: Verso, 1989).
30 Of course, the problem is, what if the other to whom the offer to be rejected is made actually accepts it? What if, in Brecht's *Jasager,* the boy had said "No" and refused to be thrown into the valley? What if, upon being beaten in the competition, I accept my friend's offer to get the promotion instead of him? A situation like this is properly catastrophic: it causes the disintegration of the semblance (of freedom) that pertains to social order—however, since, at this level, things in a way are what they seem to be, this disintegration of the semblance equals the disintegration of the social substance itself, the dissolution of the social link. Former Communist societies present an extreme case of such a forced free choice: in them, the subjects were incessantly bombarded with the request to express freely their attitude toward power, yet everybody was well aware that this freedom was strictly limited to the freedom to say "yes" to the Communist regime itself. For that very reason, Communist societies were extremely sensitive to the status of semblance: the ruling party wanted at any cost whatsoever to maintain undisturbed the appearance (of broad popular support of the regime).
31 Cooke, *I Saw the World End,* 16–17.
32 Robert Donington, *Wagner's "Ring" and Its Symbols* (London: Faber and Faber, 1990), 265.

33 We can see, now, in what consists the crucial difference between the *Ring* and *Parsifal:* in the *Ring,* knowledge is not yet accessible to "the pure fool" Siegfried—he has to die so that Brünnhilde, the woman, can become knowing ("dass wissend wird ein Weib"), whereas in *Parsifal,* the hero himself, the pure fool, becomes knowing ("des reinsten Wissens Macht, dem zagen Toren gab"). Syberberg was thus fully justified, in his film version of *Parsifal,* to turn Parsifal into a woman after his conversion: the moment he gains access to knowledge, Parsifal effectively occupies the "feminine" position of Brünnhilde.

34 At the opposite end, Wagner composed *Parsifal,* this hymn to the radical rejection of the sexual drive, in order to be able to pursue his affair with Judith Gautier, the real-life model of Kundry.

35 The prototype of this Jungian approach is Wieland Wagner's "psychological diagram" of *Parsifal.*

36 At the very end of his *Parsifal,* Syberberg raised this resubjectivization to the second power by first locating the entire action in the gigantic Wagner's head and then by locating Wagner himself in Kundry, who covers up with her hair the Bayreuth theater.

37 For a Lacanian reading of *A Short Film on Love,* see Roland Chemana, "La Passion selon Tomek," in *Éléments lacaniens pour une psychanalyse au quotidien* (Paris: Le Discours psychanalytique, 1994), 363–66. Incidentally, the two versions of *A Short Film on Love* offer an exemplary case of how, by way of merely rearranging or leaving out part of the material, one can radically change its entire scope, or, as Lacan put it, interpretation is in its most fundamental dimension an act of scansion, of establishing the proper syntax, not an act of bringing to light the "repressed" meaning. Perhaps an even more illuminating example is provided by the finale of Moussorgsky's *Boris Godunov:* according to the composer's original idea, the death of Tsar Boris is the penultimate scene, so that the opera concludes with the scene of the crowd hailing the new Tsar Dimitry and the saintly beggar-fool predicting hard times for Russia; Rimsky-Korsakov, however, who put the opera into its final shape, was worried about the weak dramatic impact of the original finale and changed the order of the last two scenes, so that the version we all know ends, as befits tragedy, with the death of its hero. It is clear that, beneath the purely theatrical question of "dramatic impact," there lurks the far more fundamental question of interpretation: Rimsky-Korsakov reinscribes *Boris* into the traditional hero-centered framework, whereas the original version "decenters" it and asserts the acephal "crowd" as the opera's true hero. A simple decision about the order of scenes thus involves an interpretive act of far-reaching consequences: it is really a decision about inserting (or not) the opera into the traditional hero narrative.

38 There is a homology worthy of notice between this reversal of the metaphor of love and the final reversal in Delmer Daves's psychological western from the late fifties, *3.10 to Yuma.* The film tells the story of a poor farmer (Van Heflin) who, for two hundred dollars that he needs badly in order to save his cattle from drought, accepts the job of escorting a bandit with a high price on his head (Glenn Ford) from the hotel where he is held to the train that will take him to prison in Yuma. What we have, of

course, is a classic story of an ethical ordeal; throughout the film, it seems that the person submitted to the ordeal is the farmer himself, exposed as he is to temptations in the style of the (undeservedly) more famous *High Noon:* all those who promised him help abandon him when they discover that the hotel is surrounded by the gang sworn to save their boss; the imprisoned bandit himself alternately threatens the farmer and tries to bribe him, etc. The last scene, however, in retrospect totally changes our perception of the film: close by the train, which is already leaving the station, the bandit and the farmer find themselves face-to-face with the entire gang waiting for the right moment to shoot the farmer and thus free their boss. At this tense moment, when the situation seems hopeless for the farmer, the bandit suddenly turns to him and tells him "Trust me! Let's jump together on the wagon!" In short, the one effectively under an ordeal was the bandit himself, the apparent agent of temptation: at the end, he is overcome by the farmer's integrity and sacrifices his own freedom for him.

39 The notion of *A Short Film on Love* as an inverted slasher was suggested to me by Paul Villemen. Incidentally, the basic matrix of slasher films is contained in the paradox of the *objet petit a* elaborated by Lacan in the last chapter of his *Seminar* XI: "I love you, but, because inexplicably I love in you something more than you—the *objet petit a*—I mutilate you" (Jacques Lacan, *The Four Fundamental Concepts of Psycho-Analysis,* trans. Alan Sheridan [Harmondsworth: Penguin, 1979], 268).

40 What our reading of the film did not take into account is, of course, the fact that the woman (Camille) is an *object of exchange* between the two men: is it not that the two man fight their own battle through her, the one betraying his partnership with the other by entering into a relationship with her, the other taking his revenge for this betrayal by seducing her in his turn? For that reason, he can reject her the moment his seduction succeeds and she offers herself to him—she has no inherent "use value" for Stephan, the only point of seducing her was to deliver a message to his (male) partner. Such a reading, which introduces the motif of latent homosexuality and male bonding, adequate as it is at its own level, nonetheless fails to provide a satisfactory account of Stephan's gesture of rejection.

41 In *The Flying Dutchman,* too, the hero is divided between a damned-sacred object (his ship) and the woman whose sacrifice can bring about his redemption. However, in contrast to Lohengrin, the angelic hero, the Dutchman is a damned sinner; the vocal expression of this opposition is, of course, that between tenor and baritone.

Notes on Contributors

Elisabeth Bronfen, Professor of English and American Studies at the University of Zurich, Switzerland, is the author of *Over Her Dead Body: Death, Femininity, and the Aesthetic*.

Mladen Dolar is Professor of Social Philosophy at the University of Ljubljana, Slovenia. He has published numerous books, including *"Wenn Musik der Liebe Nahrung ist . . .": Mozart und die Philosophie der Oper*.

Fredric Jameson is Distinguished Professor of Comparative Literature at Duke University. His numerous books include *The Political Unconscious* and *Postmodernism; or, The Cultural Logic of Late Capitalism*.

Renata Salecl, Researcher at the Institute for Criminology, University of Ljubljana, Slovenia, is the author of *The Spoils of Freedom: Psychoanalysis and Feminism after the Fall of Socialism*.

Slavoj Žižek is Senior Researcher at the Institute for Social Sciences, University of Ljubljana, Slovenia. His many books include *Tarrying with the Negative: Kant, Hegel, and the Critique of Ideology* and *The Indivisible Remainder: An Essay on Schelling and Related Matters*.

Alenka Zupančič, Researcher at the Institute for Philosophy, Slovene Academy of Sciences, Ljubljana, is the author of *Ethik des Realen: Kant und Lacan*.

Index

Adultery, 214-215
Almodóvar, Pedro: *Tie Me Up, Tie Me Down*, 193
Althusser, Louis, 180, 190
Anderson, Michael: *If*, 100
Anti-Semitism, 108-110, 217
Anxiety, 139
Asceticism: in early Christianity, 171
Augustine, Saint: on music, 20-22; as a political intellectual, 174-175; Western subjectivity and, 158, 174-178

Beauty: of the feminine corpse, 72-73
Berger, John, 71
Berkeley, George: theory of vision, 39-41
Blindness, 33-49
Bounty: mutiny on HMS *Bounty*, 98-100
Brecht, Bertolt, 231
Brown, Peter, 156, 157, 160, 163

Campion, Jane: *The Piano*, 193
Castration: symbolic, 75, 107-110, 217, 226
Catholic Church: music and, 21-23
Chion, Michel, 92
Choice: forced, 129, 232
Christianity: parallels between early Christianity and contemporary extreme Left, 169; sects in early Christianity, 165-167; sexuality and, 157-178

Class struggle, 113, 239
Condillac, Etienne: on blindness and vision, 42-44
Contingency: in love, 129-131, 134
Cynicism, 100-101

Dahlhaus, Carl, 224
Derrida, Jacques, 11-13, 19, 94, 112, 216; versus Lacan, 16
Descartes, René, 116; on vision and blindness, 32-35, 47
Desire, 184-186; versus demand, 188; as the desire of the Other, 195; versus drive, 243
Diderot, Denis de, 46
Double, 136-137
Drive, 69-70, 244; death, 140, 228-233

Enlightenment, 100, 117, 143; and blindness, 32

Fantasy, 47-48, 101; desire of the Other and, 117; phantasmatic specter, 111-113; "traversing the fantasy," 117-118
Father, 75, 80, 83-85; *jouissance* of the, 27; paternal symbolic authority, 108-109
Flaubert, Gustave, 132, 223; *Madame Bovary*, 213-4
Foucault, Michel, 66, 158-162
Freud, Sigmund, 59-60, 69, 81-82, 137-

Freud, Sigmund (*continued*)
 138, 145–147, 155, 160, 179, 183, 198, 235, 237

Gaze, 13, 60, 73–81, 88, 90–95; gazing and killing, 62–63; love and, 132–137; sexualization of the, 62; woman and, 64
Gossec, François-Joseph, 23–24
Guilt, 155

Hate speech, 105–106
Hegel, Georg Wilhelm Friedrich, 92
Heidegger, Martin, 102, 155
Hildegard of Bingen, 22–23
Hitchcock, Alfred, 90
Hoffmann, E. T. A.: "The Sandman," 144
Hysteria, 185–186: modern art and, 215; symptoms in, 199; Wagner and, 224–227

Ideology, 112–115; sacrifice and, 235
Ishiguro, Kazuo: *The Remains of the Day*, 181–186

Jakobson, Roman, 8
James, Henry: "Lord Beaupre," 145
Jameson, Fredric, 235
Jouissance, 2, 139–140; in ideology, 118; music and, 17–23; of the father, 27

Kafka, Franz: *The Trial*, 95–97
Kant, Immanuel, 50–56, 91; "paralogism of personality" in, 52; transcendental illusion in, 52–56
Kierkegaard, Søren: the triad of aesthetic, ethical, and religious, 210–212
Kieslowski, Krysztof: *A Short Film on Love*, 238–241, 244
Kubrick, Stanley: *Full Metal Jacket*, 101–102

Lacan, Jacques, 1–3, 9, 15, 25, 27, 85, 103, 130, 134, 139, 142, 182, 191, 198–200, 212, 217, 226, 229, 244; Descartes' *cogito* and, 116; on gaze as object, 33–34, 43–44, 90–91; on transference, 147–148
La Rochefoucauld, François, 191

Laurent, Eric, 201
Law: divine, 25–27; the split between public and obscene, 100–104
Lévi-Strauss, Claude, 113–115, 208
Locke, John: versus Descartes on vision, 36–38
Love, 129–135, 238–244; for the double, 140–141; falling in, 187; forced choice and, 129; gaze and, 132–135; institution and, 193–194; marriage and, 186; narcissism and, 196; as a symptom, 149; as transference, 146–148
Lynch, David, 222

Marx, Karl, 145, 216
Meriam, Chevalier de, 45–49
Metaphor: paternal, 86
Miller, Jacques-Alain, 10, 15
Millot, Catherine, 197–8
Mozart, Wolfgang Amadeus: *Così fan tutte*, 143, 210
Music, 94; as a threat to meaning, 16–24, 103–104

Narcissism, 13–14, 82, 137, 196
Nietzsche, Friedrich: on Wagner, 224–228; versus Freud, 228

Objet petit a, 3, 91, 105, 107, 111, 138, 187, 189, 244. *See also* Gaze; Voice
Obsessional neurosis, 182–184
Other: the big, 131, 141, 199; love and, 190–194, 205

Perversion, 70, 81
Phallus, 200; as signifier, 108–110
Plato: on music, 17–20; *Symposium*, 203
Poe, Edgar Allan: "William Wilson," 137
Poizat, Michel, 17
Powell, Michael: *Peeping Tom*, 59–88
Psychosis, 106: James Joyce and, 198

Rank, Otto, 137
Real, 87, 134; in Lacan, 16; versus reality, 113
Reik, Theodor, 25–26
Riefenstahl, Leni, 230

Rorty, Richard, 104
Rushdie, Salman: *Midnight's Children*, 134

Sacrifice, 234-235
Saussure, Ferdinand de, 8, 12
Sautet, Claude: *A Heart in Winter*, 241-244
Schelling, Wilhelm Joseph Friedrich, 219
Schopenhauer, Arthur, 94, 215, 229
Scopophilia, 59
Sexuality: Christianity and, 157-178; the political and, 3; psychology and, 175
Sexual relationship: in Wagner, 219; "there is no sexual relationship," 2, 199, 208-212
Shofar: as the voice of the dying father, 25-27
Signifier: as differential, 9
Silverman, Kaja, 14-15
Singer, Bryan: *The Usual Suspects*, 110-111
Soler, Colette, 202
Subject, 52, 56; subjective destitution, 243-244; totalitarian subject in Wagner, 219
Suicide, 87
Superego, 100; vocal status of, 103

Symbolic, 232-233; fiction, 104, 112-116

Transference. *See* Love

Uncanny, 136
Unconscious, 147-148; Cartesian subject and, 102-103

Violence: fantasy and, 103-104
Voice, 7-16, 90-95; *jouissance* and, 27-28; in psychoanalysis, 14-15; versus signifier, 8-9; superego and, 103

Wagner, Richard, 17, 133, 208-237; anti-Semitism and, 217; Hollywood and, 221-223; *Lohengrin*, 242-243; *Meistersinger of Nürnberg*, 209, 213; music drama and, 220-221; *Parsifal*, 97, 212, 213-214, 225-227; *Ring des Nibelungen*, 111, 215-219, 233; *Tristan und Isolde*, 212, 213, 229, 237
Welles, Orson: *The Trial*, 95-97
Wharton, Edith: *The Age of Innocence*, 186-190, 233; "The Muse's Tragedy," 194-205
Woman, 197; feminine corpse, 71

Library of Congress Cataloging-in-Publication Data
Gaze and voice as love objects / Renata Salecl and Slavoj Žižek, editors.
p. cm. — (SIC ; 1)
Contents: The object voice / Mladen Dolar—Philosophers' blind man's buff [sic] / Alenka Zupančič—Killing gazes, killing in the gaze : on Michael Powell's Peeping Tom / Elisabeth Bronfen—"I hear you with my eyes," or, The invisible master / Slavoj Žižek—At first sight / Mladen Dolar—On the sexual production of Western subjectivity, or, Saint Augustine as a social democrat / Fredric Jameson—I can't love you unless I give you up / Renata Salecl—"There is no sexual relationship" / Slavoj Žižek.
Includes index.
ISBN 0-8223-1806-7 (cloth : alk. paper).—ISBN 0-8223-1813-X (pbk. : alk. paper)
1. Criticism. 2. Psychoanalysis and literature. 3. Gaze in literature.
4. Voice in literature. I. Salecl, Renata, 1962- . II. Žižek, Slavoj.
III. Series: SIC (Durham, N.C.) ; 1.
PN98.P75G39 1996
801'.95—dc20   96-19285 CIP